BUSINESS

IS

SIMPLE

BUSINESS
IS
SIMPLE

FROM A FAMILY COTTAGE BUSINESS

TO WORLD PROCESSING & MARKETS

TERRENCE CONWAY

PYP **Publish** Your Purpose

For permission requests, write to the publisher, addressed "Attention: Permissions Coordinator," at the address below.

Publish Your Purpose
141 Weston Street, #155
Hartford, CT, 06141

PYP **Publish** Your Purpose

The opinions expressed by the Author are not necessarily those held by Publish Your Purpose.

Ordering Information: Quantity sales and special discounts are available on quantity purchases by corporations, associations, and others. For details, contact the author tc@terryconway-bis.com.

Edited by: August Li, David Aretha, Lily Capstick
Cover design by: Maureen Johnson
Typeset by: Medlar Publishing Solutions Pvt Ltd., India

ISBN: 979-8-88797-227-5 (hardcover)
ISBN: 979-8-88797-220-6 (paperback)
ISBN: 979-8-88797-222-0 (ebook)

Library of Congress Control Number: 2025924446

First edition, March 2026.

Publish Your Purpose is a hybrid publisher of nonfiction books. Our mission is to elevate the voices often excluded from traditional publishing. We intentionally seek out authors and storytellers with diverse backgrounds, life experiences, and unique perspectives to publish books that will make an impact in the world. Do you have a book idea you would like us to consider publishing? Please visit PublishYourPurpose.com for more information.

I first saw Susan O'Connell at a St. Patrick's Day party, sliding down the long banister in a mansion once owned by a Pittsburgh tycoon that housed graduate students. She was gorgeous, full of life, sober, and (as I soon learned) on her way to graduating summa cum laude. Who was that tall redhead?

With Susan O'Connell at Carnegie's Mudge House, where we met in 1961

Throughout much of our years of friendship and sixty-two years of marriage, Susan put aside her teaching career to become an admired mother who skillfully guided our five children and later was a joyful role model for our twelve grandchildren. Along the way, she earned her Masters degree and tutored hundreds of adults and children with dyslexia, taught aerobics dance, and directed tennis programs at the local Y.

All the while, I was able to keep a sharp focus on the business, including those four- to six-week trips to Asia, and still enjoy a wonderful family.

We cherish the adventure vacations she planned and led for us, and we take pride in the admiration and thanks Susan continues to receive from those with dyslexia she patiently tutored.

TABLE OF CONTENTS

INTRODUCTION

This isn't just a business book; it's a blueprint forged in the fire of real-world risk and relentless transformation. It's the candid story of a four-decade journey—my journey—from the security of a successful corporate career to the adrenaline-fueled chaos of building a thriving international business from a humble seafood company on Maryland's eastern shore.

At thirty-one, I was the first CFO for Perdue Farms. Ten years later, at forty-one and a father of five, I took a daring leap of faith: I left corporate stability for the dream of ownership, taking on the task of transforming 130-year-old Handy Seafood into a global brand.

CHAOS TO STRUCTURE

What greeted me as the new owner was not a well-oiled machine, but chaos. Resources were scarce, decisions were based on limited experience, and crucial business functions needed to be built from scratch. For years, I had the constant, familiar feeling of being "always in the weeds."

Does that sound like your business? Whether you're a manufacturer, hospital, farmer, physician, or an entrepreneur, the initial struggle for a clear decision-making structure is universal. My desire for longevity—to build a business that could be passed down—required extra thought and care.

BUSINESS IS SIMPLE

To navigate that chaos, I fell back on my evolving, time-tested structure I call "Business Is Simple." It strips away complexity and focuses on just three core, interconnected focal points that drive all success. It's the lead-er's simple to-do list:

1. Continuously develop superior products.
2. Process at a competitive advantage.
3. Develop leads for sales to close.

This structure is layered onto unwavering Core Values, chief among them: *Trust is the cornerstone of everything, and free-flowing collaboration is necessary for growth.* We manage the day-to-day by defining and checking on "All Abouts," or the bottom-line metrics for every operating segment, from generating leads in marketing to ensuring finance has the funds to grow and blend with overall Principles: *Take care of the customer, measure what counts, and build leaders.*

THE STORY OF TWO REINVENTIONS

This book is part memoir, part manual, tracking the incredible journey through two necessary makeovers.

The first, guided by the Business Is Simple structure, transformed Handy from a single-product, seasonal soft-shell crab processor with one telephone line into a coast-to-coast national company. We implemented major upgrades, built a modern processing facility funded through bank borrowings, and achieved a premium quality that met the standards of Japanese and European customers.

The second makeover was a matter of survival, forced by environ-mental changes that severely reduced our crab supply. With zero con-tacts and little more than a rumor, I booked a flight to Bangkok. This led to far-flung adventures in Thailand and India, where I navigated sleepless nights and cultural challenges to establish international soft crab pro-cessing and, later, two more product lines—crab cakes and pasteurized crabmeat—in additional Asian countries.

WHO SHOULD READ THIS BOOK?

This book is a guide for everyone who believes extraordinary results are possible:

- **Aspiring small business owners** ready to consider a whole new world of growth possibilities, including international expansion. This book is designed to land on your desktop.
- **Business managers** seeking practical guidelines for makeovers and startups.
- **Aspiring entrepreneurs** who need practical advice on navigating unexpected obstacles and turning chaos into structure.
- **Family businesses** contemplating longevity, with lessons on successfully passing ownership to future generations.
- **Graduating business students** looking for a fast start and real-world application of business principles.

And yes, it's a personal account for my twelve grandchildren—a legacy of who Grandpa Terry was, what he built, and the thinking that drove the transformation of Handy, from Crisfield to Asia.

I hope this book provides the structure for your great decisions and helps scale your own extraordinary business adventure.

ONE

FROM DINNER TABLE TO CARNEGIE TECH

Are business leaders born or made? That topic has been the subject of papers, including one I wrote as a student. As I examined the lives and legacies of charismatic leaders, I realized that they are blessed with communication talent and, perhaps even more importantly, a drive to succeed. No doubt, leaders also benefit from a great education, mentorships, and experiences.

Even during the early days of dreaming about eventual business ownership, I knew I'd need to be prepared with influencers, a solid educational background, valuable experiences, and an ample amount of luck. Fortunately, everything would materialize as I needed it.

Good fortune has been a constant companion in my life, and I've had more than my fair share. I was raised in a loving family and supported with excellent education opportunities. My parents were involved in our activities; they always had time for us.

My father was a remarkably successful trial lawyer, trying more than six hundred juried cases during a career spanning six decades in Kansas City. Along the way, he was elected lead partner in a firm specializing in litigation. He continued practicing until he was eighty-two.

When I was growing up, my dad often recounted stories of his latest cases over dinner, taking me along the lawyerly path he traveled, sifting facts to discover the most relevant truth and win justice for his clients.

"The jury was with me" was an ending that always made me smile, as I would see Dad's quiet satisfaction with another case closed.

TRUST AS A GUIDING PRINCIPLE

This was one of the ways I first came to appreciate the value of building trust in any relationship. Win a client's trust with a straightforward view of how he would approach their case. Win a jury's trust with a straight-forward narrative of facts and knowledge of the law to build the case, plus "make them laugh at least twice" during a trial.

To honor my father's legacy, the Kansas City Metropolitan Bar Association created an annual Thomas J. Conway Award to recognize young trial lawyers who display courage and compassion as fierce advocates for clients, talent in presenting constructive evidence, collegiality toward opposing lawyers, respect for the courts and the rule of law, "and a lifelong spirit of youth and a song in their heart." Did those peers know Dad loved to sing around the house, especially impromptu love songs to my mother?

Trust was also a guiding principle in how my parents taught me and my younger brother, Brian, and sister, Diana. We learned responsibility for making our own choices and enjoying (or, at times, regretting) the consequences of those choices. "Just make us proud" was our parents' standard.

I loved scouting, rising to Eagle Scout with twenty-one badges, and then kept going until I topped out with fifty-one on my sash. I was too small through high school to compete in sports like baseball, basketball, and football, but scouting gave me leadership opportunities and respect for the mottos "Be trustworthy" and "Be prepared." Those virtues have served me well.

Trustworthiness reflects an all-encompassing behavior and track record of doing what you say you will do and doing the right thing. Deliver on your promises and commitments. Being prepared means having researched and organized plans to meet some objective and also anticipating the unexpected, adjusting to change, and delivering results regardless of the obstacles. A reputation for keeping my word and the ability to plan, organize, and execute were early foundations for traits and skills I would need to run my own company. (Our Handy brand tagline, "Trusted since 1894," is carried on every product we sell.)

Younger scouts, of course, depend on older, more experienced scouts with the knowledge and teaching skills about specific tasks such as preparing for an overnight hike. This is how overarching scouting values of lifetime obligations to parents, country, community—and each other— are passed down. Teaching skills, or coaching skills if you prefer, are essential for leaders.

MEN FOR OTHERS

My high school years studying under the Jesuits built on these values. Almost every class at Rockhurst High School was taught by a Jesuit, at least three-quarters of all classes at this college prep school with four hundred students. (Today, there are only one or two Jesuits on the faculty of a typical Jesuit Catholic high school.)

The school's motto: Men for Others. My Jesuit teachers were hard-nosed, committed. They infused their curriculum and teachings with the value of respect for one another and all humanity.

They expected their students to be committed too.

Going to school is work. Working the brain, but also physical. Stay focused, organized. You have to do the work. If you're not willing to do the work, I don't want to spend much time with you. Your education will be wasted.

Latin translation gave me the most trouble for two years: Here's the alphabet. Here's how you diagram sentences. Now translate Homer. I kept going back to fundamentals but couldn't quite put a sentence together. I was struggling.

"Well, this is work," my Jesuit instructor said. "You've got to work your brain to put these pieces together, and then come up with a sentence and then a paragraph. You've really got to work your head."

Eventually, he straightened me out. He and my other teachers always had time for individual guidance.

Competing on the speech team was a Rockhurst highlight, an early success that quieted my fears about public speaking, which most people as adults have a hard time shaking. A talented crew, we won a trip to the state finals. Assigned "humorous declaration" as my category type, I imagined and acted out a lively conversation between Tom Sawyer and Huckleberry Finn, winning third place in the Missouri competition and again later in the regionals in Oklahoma.

That experience bolstered my confidence for assembling and presenting compelling concepts—skills that I would put to work routinely in my undergraduate and graduate studies, then onto my years in consulting, heading corporate finance at Perdue Farms, and especially in tending my ambitions for my own business's growth.

Leaders in any field have to be adept at marshaling facts to create a compelling course of action. What is the current situation? Where do we want to go? How are we going to get there?

"OKAY, BRING YOUR GROUP."

That classic education at Rockhurst was my springboard to a great university. I wanted to continue my Catholic education, so my Jesuit advisers encouraged me to apply to the University of Notre Dame. Notre Dame, best known in the late 1950s for perennial national football prowess, was earning a reputation for academic excellence.

Notre Dame's organizational strategy in those years, framed by Rev. Theodore M. Hesburgh at the dawn of his thirty-five years as president, was not to expand enrollment but to improve the quality of its students and faculty, and to set a measurable goal for student success at a remarkably high graduation rate of 97 percent.[1] As an

---

[1] In recent years the graduation rate for Notre Dame's first-time, full-time students was 96 percent, according to the U.S. Education Department's College Scorecard.

alumnus watching the university's continuing progress over the past six decades, I made mental notes and applied the lessons at my business: *quality precedes growth; setting goals and achieving buy-in is a key for business success*. President Eisenhower spoke at graduation while he was still in office.

One of my dad's poker friends, a partner in the local office of the big accounting firm Arthur Andersen & Company, made a case to me for pursuing a professional accounting career that I found energizing. "You work with CEOs and other senior executives on high-level problems and projects in a variety of industries. You have to really understand what's going on in the business. It's a great way to prepare for running a business yourself."

Man, I thought, *this has got to be a great experience.*

I picked accounting as my major, loading up with several quantitative courses in what was then, and is still today, one of the best undergraduate schools for business. Notre Dame typically is ranked among the top five.

A course taught by a marketing professor with quantitative leanings who became a totemic legend in that field, Jerome McCarthy, gave me important concepts that I have applied in every one of my roles in business.

When I was a student, McCarthy was teaching what he called the Four Ps of marketing: product, price, promotion, and place (distribution). His coauthored book delving into each, *Basic Marketing: A Managerial Approach*, was published my senior year and is now a classic in its nineteenth edition.

That year I also was president of the management club. The news, filled with articles about massive labor–big business clashes, made us curious about how big companies actually managed these issues. Is it as confrontational as it seems?

As I wrote the letter I thought to myself, *Why not go to the most famous business leader of the time? Why not?* I selected Henry Ford II, grandson of Henry Ford and chairman of Ford Motor Company. I wrote, "We're a group of management students interested in how labor relations actually work."

This business leader's company ranked No. 7 in the Fortune 500 that year with revenues of $6.5 billion, competing aggressively with General Motors, the kingpin of the US auto industry and topping the Fortune 500 with more than twice Ford's annual revenues. Amazingly, Mr. Ford replied within a week, inviting us for a briefing by his labor management team at company headquarters in Dearborn, Michigan. "Okay, bring your group," he said.

Sitting in oversized leather chairs in the vast, imposing boardroom, fifteen of us were taken behind the scenes on how Ford Motor intended to approach its upcoming bargaining sessions. At the time, Ford's net profits amounted to nearly $550 million. The company had more than a quarter million employees, a large majority of whom were factory workers—and United Auto Workers (UAW) members. (A quarter century before, not far from where we were sitting, Ford security guards violently attacked UAW leaders seeking to organize Ford workers for the first time; four years later, the UAW succeeded.)

The Ford team explained how they intended to share information with economists and negotiators from the UAW. They made it clear that the union had no desire to interfere with Ford's strategies for managing the business and competing with General Motors and Chrysler Corporation, the smallest of the Big Three. Both sides wanted an agreement that would be the best for everybody. I was impressed

It was an important lesson. There are two sides to every story. Both needed a win. Negotiating is not necessarily combative. It can be productive for both sides.

ANIMATED, IN ENDLESSLY CREATIVE WAYS

I expected to move directly from Notre Dame into one of the big accounting firms after graduation, but I changed my mind after reading an enthusiastic Ford Foundation analysis of top graduate business programs: Harvard for its famous case-study method; Carnegie Tech for its emphasis on broad-based economics and analytics to solve problems and discover opportunities.

"You should go to Carnegie Tech. It's more quantitative, better preparation for running a modern business," Professor McCarthy advised.[2]

"We're all about research," the assistant dean of Admissions told me before I applied.[3] "You get on both sides of an issue, you research it, and you discuss it. Five years from now, anything we teach you will be obsolete. You'll need to dig into new subjects, see both sides, and present your conclusions."

I liked that approach. It seemed logical as well as animated in endlessly creative ways, applicable to almost any problem that might arise. Championing quantitative rigor was innovative for business education in that era. Since then, top schools have incorporated more of these disciplines in their curricula as advanced computing tools have become more ubiquitous and powerful.

Carnegie Tech's presumption was that all fifty students in an entering class would have completed undergraduate studies in engineering or science with extremely strong credentials. As an accounting major, I was an outlier.

"You're going to have to work a lot harder than your classmates," the dean cautioned me in a bracing letter that came in the mail after I was accepted into the two-year master's program. My entering class for the fall of 1960 posted a mean score of 97 percent on the standard Graduate Management Admissions Test (GMAT), meaning that the upper half scored higher than 97 percent. (I was in the lower half.) Nearly everyone had degrees in engineering and science.

All right, I thought, I'm willing to try it. If McCarthy thinks this is the best graduate business school in the country, that's where I want to be.

---

[2] Carnegie Tech merged in 1967 with the Mellon Institute to become Carnegie Mellon University.

[3] My admissions counselor, Dr. William R. Dill, later became president of Babson College in Boston.

The first year was tough. The students were motivated and serious. We might take three hours off on a Saturday night to walk a mile into neighboring Shadyside and have a beer or two, but then we hit the books for another hour. The second year was a little better. I had time for occasional handball matches.

Half of my professors taught from their own authored textbooks, and every class required research papers. Three of my instructors had won Nobel Prizes for Economics, and another seven, including faculty and former students, have since achieved this honor, including one of my classmates, Oliver Williamson.[4] These professors were demanding. Papers they assigned were invariably tied to models and theories in their own fields of research.

To be frank, while I learned from and contributed to that research, the practical aspects of managing a business were rarely discussed in class.

What really mattered were increasingly superior products, processed at a competitive advantage, and generating leads for sales to close. It took me another decade before I grasped these three essentials on my own. That is one of the reasons I'm writing this book! If I had known these and other basics and how to execute them as a consultant and finance executive before I bought my first company, Handy, I would have been a more effective leader much sooner.

However, what I learned over those two years added great value to my business career, especially the emphasis on using analytical tools to solve problems and find opportunities. I also learned to be prepared for challenges and adversity, to keep focus on a firm's economic engine (and its inevitable changes), and to keep up with evolving technology to prosper. Perhaps most importantly, those years instilled in me the need to continuously develop superior products for a competitive advantage.

---

[4] Williamson won in 2009 for his concept of "transaction cost economics," a theory on the costs and benefits of how firms design their organizations to be efficient and effective in market activities.

Of those fifty students in my entering Class of '62, thirty-five made it to graduation day and a diploma reading Master of Science in Industrial Administration. I was grateful to be one of them.

I also learned that every success story is the story of a team; no one ever gets there alone. I was fortunate enough to form one of the most important partnerships in my life and career when I met Susan O'Connell at a St. Patrick's Day party held in the home of a former Pittsburgh tycoon that had been converted to graduate student housing. We hit it off right away, and before long, we were talking about the future.

For nine months we discussed life after graduation, and then we became engaged. Susan had a clear picture of her career—a large family followed by a master's degree in special education and a position as a professional teacher—that was important for me to understand. All would come to pass.

We both looked forward to the joys of a large family. Susan found positions while the five children were at school—tennis director at the YMCA and aerobic dance teacher.

After her master's degree, Susan changed lives during a twenty-year career as a private tutor, patiently teaching learning-disabled children and adults how to read. We encounter her former students often. They beam with gratitude.

We married two years after our first meeting, in 1963. We picked up my father's new Volkswagen convertible at the factory in Germany and drove five thousand miles throughout Europe on a six-week, low-budget honeymoon with no reservations. We stopped in Marseilles to visit a classmate from Carnegie Mellon—Glen Jones—who was deep into an interesting project to globally brand his company's products.

On this trip I first became acquainted with European history, geography, and culture. The visit would later become useful as Handy expanded internationally.

It was the first of our adventures into the unknown. After sixty-two years and countless blessings, Susan has been not only an outstanding mother and wonderful wife, but an integral part of Team Conway.

My dad knew from all those evenings we shared at the dinner table that I had a fascination with business. During my college years, he gave me this advice: "Focus on working for great leaders, seek out a variety of challenging experiences, and you can enjoy the financial and personal freedoms that can come with owning your own enterprise."

Now it was time to find great people and seek out those challenges.

T W O

S T E M W I N D I N G   W I T H
E N T R E P R E N E U R S

1 9 6 2 – 6 7

In the early 1960s, as American companies became larger, more complex, and more international, the major accounting firms, then known as the Big Eight, took advantage by broadening their offerings beyond audits and financial accounting to management advisory and tax services.

One of the firms, Touche Ross, hired me for its small Pittsburgh office and told me to start immediately after I completed six months of Army basic training in Fort Knox, Kentucky. I was excited driving to Pittsburgh, looking forward to working with the outstanding senior manager who had interviewed me. I can really learn a lot from this guy.

But when I arrived in the office the first day, I was told he no longer worked there. My presumed mentor had been "let go." I was so unnerved that day, I locked myself out of my Morris Minor car . . . *twice* (successfully releasing the flimsy lock with a coat hanger). I was assigned that week to work on audits and management consulting projects for two years; after, I would move directly into consulting projects.

The partner stressed to me that "we are in the trust business." Audits were our product, and to deliver a superior product, our people had to be impeccably trustworthy. This concept reverberated through my years with Touche Ross and beyond.

To my surprise, this turned into an ideal situation for me to learn the basic, real-world operations of varied businesses in a short period—fifteen different medium-sized companies, in manufacturing, construction, distribution, and retail industries.

After starting on those conventional client audits, making sure tallies for assets and liabilities were reasonably accurate and the numbers added up, I realized I had to develop my own clients to get into assignments I preferred, so I began scoping and executing projects to make operations more effective and to save clients' money.

I had to put a lot of time into raising my profile in the community. I taught managerial accounting in a Carnegie Mellon night class. I took a leadership role in the Catholic community's charitable Holy Name Society. I made presentations to the Rotary Club on leasing versus buying and to bankers at the Mellon National Bank conference on advanced management accounting. This worked, and gradually I succeeded in attracting new clients. It was my first experience with business development. Many more were coming.

My role with potential new clients was to dig into cost analysis and budgeting or forecasting (basic elements of management accounting), then draft proposals for me to help top management better understand the key metrics of their economic engines, critical factors such as revenue streams and how they positioned themselves differently and more attractively from competitors. You can see in the following two examples how those experiences helped shape some of my convictions about entrepreneurial leadership.

"I NEED HELP . . ."

The core business at Pure Carbon was manufacturing carbon graphite seals and brushes that acted as a natural lubricant in engines and motors and selling them across the country. A young new CEO, thirty-two years old with an engineering background, had just been hired by the parent company when he reached me by phone.

"I need help," he told me with a sense of urgency on a first call from the small company's office in St. Mary's, Pennsylvania, a quiet town

120 miles northeast of Pittsburgh. "I don't have any numbers, and I need a reliable job order cost and profitability system immediately. I have no way to know which jobs are meeting my profit goals and whether my estimating process is working." In other words, to prepare bids, he needed reliable cost estimates by department, accurate costs as the order was processed, and the final number—did the final profit number meet expectations?

The project was a challenge. It required a detailed understanding of each phase of the production process for hundreds of different products. The company sold highly engineered specialty products that had to be manufactured to meet specifications. Every job was different. It wasn't high-volume, repetitive processing, so accurate costs varied with each customer order: materials, labor, and machinery-rate time.

They had attempted to track the profitability of each order, but the numbers did not tie to the general ledger and cash, the CEO told me. Not having accurate numbers can make life difficult for CEOs because missing profit projections erodes their credibility.

The CEO was delighted with my results and soon encouraged me to identify other pieces of the business where I might contribute. Next, I prepared ongoing operating and capital budgets.

One major capital project proposed scrapping manually operated machinery and replacing it with the more precise, computer-automated machine tools that were just coming into the market. When I presented my analysis of likely benefits to the parent company's CEO, justifying all the costs, he approved the purchase.

Once we had costs more closely buttoned down for the job order project, we developed a system to set sales targets for sales representatives around the country. Instead of guessing based on prior years' experience, as the company had previously done, I came up with the idea of identifying potential customers with codes that the government used to classify industries based on the primary products or services they offered.

Known as Standard Industrial Classification (SIC), these codes gave us clearer insight into actual demand by region for different manufacturers of engine and motor parts using carbon graphite seals. We assembled good data. The CEO now had a reasonable, fact-based target for each of his sales representatives out in the field. It was a very satisfying project to work on.

For two years I spent more than half my working hours in Pure Carbon's office in St. Mary's, pulling together and crunching the numbers, reviewing them with the CEO, making recommendations, and often working with his small staff to put approved plans into action. I was on the Touche Ross payroll, of course, but in effect, at age twenty-four, I was Pure Carbon's acting CFO.

I would drive three and a half hours each way from Pittsburgh in my old Morris Minor, a bulbous little British two-door sedan with a tiny 36-horsepower engine and no heater. In the winter, I needed blankets and a heavy coat to ward off the cold. I had bought the Morris Minor for a song when I was at Carnegie Tech after it had been damaged in a hurricane during passage across the Atlantic. When the vehicle's top speed was the minimum for an interstate highway—forty-five miles per hour—I had to let it go. In St. Mary's, I slept nights in an eight-dollar budget motel. Hardly glamorous, but overall it was a fantastic learning experience fresh from graduate school.

Creating a new job order cost system tied to the general ledger was one of the most satisfying projects I had there. Pure Carbon really tightened the ship. That young CEO became highly prized by the parent company. My professors at Carnegie Tech had it right: The more accurately you can quantify a business problem, the better your solution will be.

This experience taught me the importance of reliable, accurate financial forecasts and their importance for lender as my financial career moved forward. Put another way, it showed me another aspect of inspiring trust in my business partners as my financial career moved forward.

THE INSPIRING GENIUS BEHIND GENERAL NUTRITION

One day, a businessman selling discount vitamins and health foods on racks and shelves in five little stores in downtown Pittsburgh appeared in our office without an appointment. Major drugstore chains were refusing to stock any of the discount vitamins or health supplements that he and his brother were also selling to consumers through mail order.

"I have no choice but to become integrated and own my own stores," David Shakarian said, lighting a cigar as he described his problem to me.[5] "I have some experience with real estate in Florida, but not merchandising. I don't know what the stores should look like, how to merchandise the products, or how to finance an expansion. I understand your firm has several large retail clients. Can you help me with this?"

We had the talent. After a walkthrough in his little stores while taking notes, I drafted a summary for a scope of consulting work: The stores carry quality products but they are not clearly displayed on racks and shelves, and customers need to know before they come in what they are looking for and how to find it.

A retail marketing services expert joined our team from the Touche Ross[6] national office in Detroit and took the lead . . . with me as his sidekick to record even the smallest details we needed for stores to better present and communicate quality vitamins and other products at bargain prices.

"It's got to look like a discount place," the marketing services expert told me. "It's got to be clean and well-organized with the right kind of merchandising displays (known as merchandising barrels). It's got to look like everything is a good bargain, but not cheap."

I analyzed how well different products were selling and what the profit margins were, a critical factor for how we developed the new interior design for the five stores. The new design was the beta test for a rollout Shakarian was eager to begin.

---

[5] *The New York Times* reported in his obituary that Shakarian smoked twenty cigars a day at the time, quitting after suffering a heart attack several years after I had worked with him.

[6] Touche Ross merged with Deloitte, Haskins & Sells in 1989, becoming Deloitte & Touche. Its formal name now is Deloitte Touche Tohmatsu Limited, but it is commonly known as Deloitte. Ranked by annual revenue, it is the world's largest private professional services firm.

This was how the remarkable rollout and growth of General Nutrition Corporation started. The senior accountant I worked with during my time on the audit staff soon became CFO, then CEO, of General Nutrition. GNC stores later added a wide range of nutritional supplements, beauty and weight loss products, and more, and grew to more than 8,000 locations, including more than 6,000 in the United States.[7]

That burst of sustained growth is a testament to David Shakarian, an amazing businessman who made a big impression on me. Inheriting control of two small stores from his Armenian immigrant parents selling yogurt, buttermilk, and Bulgarian cultured milk, and anticipating accurately the surge of consumer interest in fitness and healthy living, he shifted the focus to discount vitamin and health food. When I met him ten years later, his refusing to have his vision for growth blocked when major drugstore and supermarket chains turned a cold shoulder to carrying his products was inspiring. I was determined to help him succeed. He was a tenacious owner I'll never forget.[8] It was important to note that ownership is necessary for growth.

DISAPPOINTMENT, THEN WALL STREET UPLIFT

Getting promoted to the national office in Detroit and onto project teams of seven partners advising big clients sounded appealing and would help burnish my resume. The client projects were substantial, such as introducing new cost-control or billing systems, but, with one exception, my tasks were limited to much smaller parts of the big picture than I had played in Pittsburgh. There I was responsible for my own projects from

---

[7] Like many retailers, GNC suffered a significant sales slump during the first years of the COVID-19 pandemic. It continued operations, but after a bankruptcy reorganization, GNC was acquired by a Chinese pharmaceutical company, Harbin Pharmaceutical Group Holding Company.

[8] Shakarian remained CEO and chairman at GNC into 1984, the year he died at age 70. *Forbes* magazine put his wealth the previous year at more than $500 million.

beginning to end—defining the scope, ensuring high quality, sending out and collecting bills, and making clients happy. I enjoyed that. But in Detroit, I didn't enjoy the work.

The Detroit years were especially difficult for my wife, Susan, raising three young boys mostly by herself with no family and no friends nearby because I was away often on client projects. My first day in the office, with multiple unopened cardboard boxes crowded into our new home, I was told, "Pack your bags. You're going to spend the next four months on a project in Clinton, Iowa." Things like this were a shock to the system.

The exception was my very first assignment. I was picked to lead a team with two other associates to introduce a job-order cost system similar to what I had developed at Pure Carbon for a large Champion Papers plant in Clinton, Iowa. Enormous paper rolls would be cut into various products such as milk cartons based on current orders. Our project, including training plant staff, became the model for all Champion manufacturing locations to replicate.

Otherwise, most assignments were boring. They were less challenging, less rewarding; just big-time consulting with little carry-forward value for me personally. In some cases, the lead partners never explained how my tasks fit into the bigger plan. They never told me what I would be doing or introduced me in advance to the client. Just "show up tomorrow. You'll figure it out." It was very frustrating.

After two years of this, I was thinking, well, accounting and exposure to different businesses has been great, but if I want to be a CFO by my early thirties, to lead corporate finance in a fast-growing company, I've got to go to Wall Street to create more opportunities. (I had passed the four-part CPA exam on my first try when I was in Pittsburgh.) A CFO has to be proficient in accounting and cost controls, skills honed and applied in my Touche Ross experience. That is half of what a CFO does. The other half is financing operations and acquisitions, and I didn't have that experience yet.

THREE

ON WALL STREET

1968–1970

I spotted a front-page article in *The Wall Street Journal* that sparked an idea for filing the gap in my resume. Laird & Company, a Wall Street firm on Park Avenue owned by the DuPont family, had a unit that specialized in helping savvy entrepreneurs acquire companies in a specific business that had caught my eye.

A different unit at Laird, one that acquired controlling stakes in struggling companies and ran them, responded quickly to a letter I sent, inviting me to New York City for interviews. Known as Laird Industries, it was one subsidiary of a big organization. Laird & Company had five hundred people engaged in oil and gas and real estate investments, securities research and brokerage, and coaching and financing entrepreneurs (corporate development). This diverse yet focused model would later become common in twenty-first-century private equity.

DOGS THAT WOULDN'T HUNT

Laird Industries invested in companies it envisioned improving with better management to achieve higher market share and profits. "We've been involved with some dogs that didn't turn out very well and we've got to turn them around," one of my recruiters said.

I hoped to work with Laird's corporate development team supporting entrepreneurs, but I was happy to accept an offer to move with Susan
and our three boys to the New York area and start in the "dogs" group.[9] It
was led by six high-powered people, including a pedigreed former management consultant, but, as I saw firsthand to my dismay, none demonstrated the instincts or talent to dig into and master details of these
businesses and their markets, as we'd done at GNC. Without the aspect
of ownership and not knowing the business, they were unable to grasp
how to help them recover and grow.

The Laird CEO was convinced smart people with strong academic
backgrounds were capable of managing any business. That was just
crazy. The concept was doomed to fail, and it did. Entrepreneurs have to
be there full-time to know and operate their companies. I worked onsite
at three companies and was not able to move them ahead.

In one case, a writing instrument company was losing too much
money at an old plant in Selbyville, Tennessee, because the equipment
was old and the products were obsolete. That became obvious to me
during the three months I spent, once again as an acting CFO, laying
plans to shift production to Mexico and putting in a profitability and
cost system for job orders—similar to what I had done for Pure Carbon.
Meanwhile, the Laird Industries executive in New York, my boss, looked
past new product opportunities I'd identified and was not able to develop
competitive products or new markets. That was one failure. He did not
know the business.

In another, a children's clothing company with headquarters in
New York City's garment district had high-quality products sold at major
department stores but descended into bankruptcy after bad decisions by
prior management. I was assigned first to close a huge, outdated plant in
upstate New York, then to move production and introduce new accounting controls at a modern plant in North Carolina. Again, my ideas for

---

[9] "Dogs" is business lexicon for struggling companies, in contrast to "stars," which are
thriving companies.

new profit opportunities remained in the shadows. No one at Laird understood the garment business or how to close deals, and this effort failed as well.

PRIVATE EQUITY FORERUNNER FROM THE '60S

Back in New York less than a year after joining Laird, I asked the CEO for a transfer to the corporate development group, taking an administrative role with its operating committee. The group consisted of thirty professionals working on transactions with entrepreneurs. "I've got some skills in that area, and I'm a CPA," I said. He didn't say yes; he didn't say no. "Why don't you hang around and we'll see if it works out?"

That week, I took a seat in a meeting of the group's four top managers, uninvited but welcomed (as it turned out). I just showed up. This is where I wanted to be, on the fifteenth floor of the west building at 280 Park Avenue. I soon was having more fun, along with a very enlightening experience.

The team in corporate development was energetic, highly motivated, with good educations. They were financiers, most coming from wealthy families that owned significant businesses or investments. But their discussions seemed a little chaotic. The operating committee was unorganized, rudderless, with no financial reporting or strategic direction to knit things together . . . unexpected for high-powered leaders of a business unit whose main calling card was selling business planning services for entrepreneurs and investors.

Those meetings turned into an advanced Wall Street seminar for me at the board level: how business financiers think and what they expect from effective CEOs. I listened, asked questions, made comments, and wrote reports on each entrepreneur we met, what the acquisitions were, and the status. We met with potential investors. I learned about different financing instruments and their particular advantages, such as preferred stock, subordinated debt, and convertible securities. I was right at the top level in that operating committee. I was beginning to understand long-term investor preferences for ease of ownership transfer and keeping estate taxes under control.

Laird's business was to recruit entrepreneurs interested in an ownership stake. They were thoroughly vetted. Their track records demonstrated command and management success in a given industry. Now they wanted a situation with an equity stake to build personal wealth.

In contrast to Laird Industries, this group demanded that entrepreneurs know their business and be active in managing it. As we vetted candidate entrepreneurs, we covered the basics. Does this plan make sense? Does this client have the passion, commitment, and experience to make this work? Can this industry be expanded? Would acquisitions be logical, either separately or as part of a rollup strategy, to achieve market leadership as rapidly as possible?

Laird's role was to join the entrepreneur to locate a business to purchase, finance the acquisition, assist with additional acquisitions, and eventually go public.

The Laird model was immensely successful; twenty-nine of the thirty companies they acquired returned profits to investors.

It bothered me that Laird gave the entrepreneurs only 10 percent of the business they would run. I was about to turn thirty and was still serious about one day owning my own business. I noted to myself, was 10 percent worth giving up control?

Watching this Wall Street ritual up close was sobering. This is nuts. All that work of risk-taking, changing careers, to own just 10 percent? I wondered too, *How am I ever going to own my own business?* I lacked the funds and collateral to borrow at the time—and wouldn't for another ten years. My goal then became to own a controlling interest, at least 65 percent, in whatever business I committed to.

Having outside investors seemed like torture to me. They would all have different agendas. They had the votes to sell a company out from under you after all the effort you put into building it. *I can't see how this is a good motivator*, I was thinking. But I kept going with Laird.

I joined the board of three of these companies, representing investors who participated in the financing.

In one case, I was able to identify a good candidate to join the board of a company in Kansas City that made flat-belt conveyor systems like the ones you see in airports moving passenger luggage from aircraft to baggage claim. The company needed an engineering expert. I introduced them to the head of engineering at a rapidly growing manufacturer of vending machines—Vendo Corporation, a hot stock at the time. He was another of my dad's poker-playing friends, and he stayed on the conveyor company's board for ten years.

JUMPSTARTS IN AMERICA: SUBARU, YOPLAIT

Four Japanese businessmen in New Jersey came to us with ambitions to scope out a network of car dealerships for Subaru of America. They had recruited an American executive who had helped Volkswagen of America build a successful network of early dealerships in the United States and wanted to replicate that business model for Subaru.

They needed Laird's expertise to draft a comprehensive plan to persuade Subaru's parent company, Fuji Heavy Industries, to make the investment. I volunteered to write it. How would Subaru work with dealers on compensation and quality? How large of an advertising budget was needed to bring customers into the showrooms and drive sales? How were they going to pull this off?

The pitch worked. Fuji Heavy Industries agreed to the plan, and Subaru's first dealership in the United States opened in 1968.[10]

A group of French dairies came to us looking to sell franchises of their popular Yoplait brand in the United States. I had never sampled any before then but found it delightful . . . nice texture, smooth, and tasty. Dispatched to their factory outside Paris to learn more about the business, I thought the management team was solid, manufacturing process disciplined, and early sales growth in Europe promising. The dairies had

---

[10] In 2022, Subaru counted more than six hundred dealers throughout the country and ranked ninth with more than a half million total car sales, ahead of Tesla, Mercedes-Benz, BMW, and, yes, Volkswagen of America.

first marketed Yoplait in 1964. I noted in my report that Yoplait was looking for investors from the dairy industry. The company planned to start
in the United States with five franchises, each priced at $1 million.

SPINOFF BECOMES SHUTDOWN

At that time, Laird Inc.'s top executives were planning to spin off corporate development as a separate private equity firm within the DuPont
family holdings, a firm to be registered with the Securities and Exchange
Commission (SEC) and qualified to raise funds for investors in its portfolio of businesses. That sounded promising and exciting. I envisioned
myself as an active contributor to even bigger projects, with higher
compensation.

One of my colleagues, a good friend, had begun drafting a prospec-
tus for the private equity group investment, but he had never written a
business plan and was stuck. I picked it up after he left for a three-week
vacation, and by the time he returned, I had written a full sixty-page draft
explaining the subsidiary's range of services, its strategy, potential risks,
finances, and track record.

That document was approved, with the offering printed on the cover
at $5 million. A limited number of copies were printed, and distribution
for private placement investors was underway. Then the wheels fell off.

The DuPont family decided to shutter Laird—its entire operations.
I never learned the reasons for this, and I didn't follow the next chapters
of Yoplait's aspirations, which had to be recalibrated after Laird folded.[11]

A senior family member went from office to office, explaining to each
of us that we would be laid off with three weeks' pay. He was empathetic
and handled this well, but I was really upset walking that evening into our

---

[11] General Mills later bought the franchises and began operating them in 1977. Yoplait was
the leading brand in General Mills' yogurt business, which had reported $2.1 billion in sales
in the United States and Canada for its 2020 fiscal year. In the spring of 2024, Yoplait's market
share had fallen behind Chobani and Dannon. According to Reuters, General Mills had hired
JPMorgan Chase to help find a buyer for the business, which it valued at more than $2 billion.

four-bedroom home in the Riverside section of Greenwich, Connecticut, a forty-five-minute commuter train ride from Grand Central Terminal. Along with that mortgage, we now had *four* small boys under the age of six. But Susan was wonderful when I gave her the bad news. She wasn't worried. "I'm sure you'll find something else soon," she told me.

The phone rang the next day, and by the end of a week I had seven new opportunities to explore.

My three years with Laird were fascinating and doubly rewarding. Whether I continued on a CFO-CEO career path or found a way to own and build my own business, working with talented professionals on high-stakes client situations gave me the Wall Street *bona fides* I was seeking.

FOUR

A DRAMATIC SHIFT OF FORTUNE

I was thirty-one when I walked into the New York offices of the hottest recruiting firm for financial executives. I felt confident, recovering from the jolt of Laird's dissolution, prepared for bigger challenges.

My credentials signaled a solid career ahead in corporate finance, perhaps rising to CFO with a large industrial company in another decade—then even on to chief executive.

I arrived on time at Russell Reynolds Associates, but my excitement and anticipation deflated for a moment. A partner explained the office had no record of my appointment and no information about me, but he added politely, "Tell me about your career."

I had no way of knowing at the time, but as I recounted highlights from my experience at Touche Ross and Laird and my aspirations (I was most interested in investment banking opportunities), my future was about to change course—dramatically.

This improbable turn would give me deep experience and insights over the next decade that would become indispensable, stepping stones enabling me to realize my dream: to own and build my own business.

Where did this magical shift of fortune take place? In the poultry business.

THE MAN FROM SALISBURY

As we chatted, the recruiter was assessing whether I might be a match for a visiting CEO client. The client was unhappy after nine months and more than sixty candidates assessed and rejected. He was still looking for someone to run his finance department and, as a member of senior management, contribute to the company's growth and profitability. "Do you have time to chat with him?" the recruiter asked me. *Of course. Why not?*

The man was tall, fit, and energetic and wore tailored clothes. I didn't recognize him or his name, Frank Perdue, but as we chatted, I relaxed and began enjoying myself.

"I'm in the business of growing and processing chickens," he began. "We are the best in our industry, but it takes hard work to keep ahead of our competitors."

DETERMINED TO BE THE LOW-COST LEADER

At that time, in 1970, Perdue Farms Inc. had just become a fully integrated poultry business, expanding into chicken-meat processing and sales when Perdue purchased a former Swift processing plant and reopened in 1968. (Frank Perdue's father, Arthur, started the business in 1920, selling table eggs from its chickens and later live chickens on the open market, at auctions.) Processing chickens under the Perdue brand was the final step in achieving Frank's plans to become a fully integrated company. The expansion more than tripled employment, to 450. With annual sales of $63 million and doubling every five years, Perdue now was one of the largest of seven farm-processing poultry operations in eastern Maryland.

At age fifty, Frank seemed sincere, ambitious, savvy, and in command of his business. He emphasized these guiding principles:

- Hire winners. Listen to them.
- Creativity happens when leaders are free to explore.
- Pride motivates as much as or more than money.

- Thoroughness is next to godliness.
- Winning is about being the best at everything—no exceptions.

This might be a good match, I thought. We did not discuss why he was searching now for a CFO or what that senior executive's priorities would be, but maybe I would find out soon.

After an hour we agreed to meet again in Salisbury. I met his management team, walked around his operations, and got a feel for the slightly slower-paced rural family life of Salisbury. After my brief sojourn there, while driving home to Connecticut, I warmed to the idea that opportunity might be knocking for Perdue Farms—and for me. While life in Salisbury itself was calmer than the big city, senior executives inside Perdue were bustling.

The nation's appetite for beef was slowly giving way to a heart-healthier, lower-priced alternative, chicken, a trend that would accelerate and extend for decades. The average amount of chicken eaten per person in the US in 1970 was less than thirty pounds; by 2022 this would more than triple to a hundred pounds. Average consumption of beef per person would fall from eight-five pounds in 1970 to fifty-seven pounds in 2022.

I wasn't aware of any industry growing as fast as poultry. Moreover, Perdue appeared to have the best operations—a very unusual situation—with more opportunities ahead. In its own industry, Perdue was raising chickens at slightly lower costs than competitors and selling them at a slight premium. Frank was determined to be the industry's low-cost leader—and more.

"Our product is higher quality, but I don't really know how to merchandise it," he told me that day. "That's what I'm going to do next: go to New York and talk to every ad agency I can find."

He was about to begin advertising on television in New York City, then Philadelphia and Boston. Frank knew that big-time advertising for a commodity product such as chicken works if consumers believe one brand of chicken is noticeably superior. The advertising budget would have to be large enough to "get the boat across the ocean." (By the early 1980s, it was $6 million a year.) He knew the risks. Wading in halfway on a major campaign would be a waste of money.

Here was a company that appeared to have those three elements for business success: increasingly superior products, processed at competitive advantage, and, if the new marketing push succeeded, and with sufficient funds and the best quality, had the resources to sell very profitably. My visit to Salisbury reinforced those thoughts. An impressive leadership team, with everyone pulling in the same direction. I was convinced. *This company is going to grow.*

A FIVE-YEAR COMMITMENT: A SEAT AT THE TABLE

Frank Perdue had a knack for hiring top professionals, a task he conducted personally. His leadership team included PhDs in poultry nutrition and genetics and two veterinarians. Their roles were to keep chickens healthy during the eight-week growing period and do this at a lower cost than competitors. "I want to be the best in our industry in everything we do," he said. (This, I confided to my friends back at Laird, was the best educated team I'd ever worked with . . . on a chicken farm!)

Frank's operations were, in fact, more efficient when compared with data from publicly traded poultry companies. When he expanded operations (before I arrived) from raising chickens to processing them, he was passionate about learning the tiniest details about processing, and then he made sure Perdue did them better than anybody else. He had mastered raising healthy animals on Perdue's contract farms.

I had never seen a CEO do this the way Frank did. And I liked it. When Handy expanded overseas for the first time years later, I knew I had to be there at all the plants when the staff began processing soft crabs, making crab cakes, and so on. I had watched Frank make sure the processes were right, the quality control was in place, and the numbers were right, and I made this mental note: You are as you start. If you accept anything less than your highest standard in any new business activity, it becomes impossible to upgrade. The foundation you build influences everything to follow. Set quality outcomes high from the beginning. Remember, you are as you start.

Most importantly, Frank spent hours, days at a time, in conversations with merchandisers and customers in grocery stores, gleaning the smallest insights from anyone he talked to keep ahead of competitors. He would talk to merchandise managers, to store managers, and to every consumer in the grocery store aisles. "Do you see any better chickens? How are they different from ours?"

I had never met any CEO so disciplined about staying in tune with his markets and listening directly to customers. His intense focus here probably became ingrained years earlier when he traveled constantly along the eastern seaboard, learning everything from other poultry growers to improve quality and command a slightly higher price at auction for his live chickens. Over time, I had no doubt that as a business leader, this connection with customers was Frank's greatest strength, the wellspring of Perdue Farms' competitive edge. I made a note that face-to-face selling was the only way to move a company forward.

Would this career move be worth the risks?

One thing Frank Perdue didn't have was a finance department. He knew little and cared less about accounting, finance, or profit-and-loss statements. Clerks ran the payroll and paid the bills. There were no accounting professionals, no treasury function to manage borrowings with lenders and customers.

Instead, he kept his eye on key performance indicators reported by operations managers, jotting the numbers on a yellow pad—the percent of eggs hatching into live chickens, the amount of feed required to raise a live chicken, the number of chickens processed per man-hour, the unused portion of bank credit lines, and so on. One of his trusted friends in the business, a chicken breeder, had persuaded Frank for years that these yellow pad numbers, twenty altogether, contained all he needed to run any large and growing business. Finance staff? A waste of money.

Obviously, he had reconsidered. "I'm looking for a CFO. Never had one before," he said during our first meeting. "I think it's time if we keep growing."

By then he had weighed the profiles of or met personally with those sixty-three different candidates. I presumed some weren't interested in a leap away from the corporate finance career to a family agri-business, working in an old, converted feed mill surrounded by corn and soybean fields, and perhaps most of all the uninviting challenge of taking the finance reins under a CEO unable to offer any guidance.

Reflecting on all this, I turned down Frank's offer. But five weeks later, I changed my mind after a Laird partner's casual invitation to join him had not gained much traction. I gave Frank a commitment that I would stay for at least five years. Here was an opportunity at age thirty-one to have a seat at the table of senior management and report directly to a CEO who was posting top profit margins in a fast-growth industry, a situation that might take me another ten or fifteen years to match in a big industrial company.

In Salisbury with Susan (four boys not shown), 1971

Consumer demand and sales were growing, operations were efficient, and pricing in grocery stores carried a slight premium—the hallmarks of my three essentials for business success. Moreover, I would be able to build my own staff, forge my own project agenda, and approach each day knowing I would not have any old-timers objecting.

Even so, I couldn't ignore reality. I would be leading a startup . . . with no guidance and possibly not even support from the CEO. If I stubbed my toe, I would be in trouble, isolated in Salisbury, far removed from the vibrancy and opportunities of a metropolitan area. With four young boys at home, the oldest in first grade, the job carried huge risks for me, risks that loomed even larger during my first day with Perdue—December 8, 1970.

A staggering realization: How am I going to finance this cyclical company?

YOU'RE THE CFO. YOU DECIDE.

During my first weekly management committee meeting at seven o'clock that Monday morning, I learned in the first half hour that operating profit was negative:35 percent. This negative margin was larger than any I had ever seen with clients I advised. *What?! Will we run out of cash?*

My new colleagues were surprisingly calm about this loss position and possible cash shortage. As I would soon learn, chicken pricing typically runs in four-year cycles. At the moment, prices were low. No one was alarmed because in their experience, margins always recovered. "If we're negative –35 percent, our competitors are probably at negative 40 or 45 percent," someone said.

An old hand with these pricing cycles, Frank welcomed the low ebbs as an opportunity to take market share from rivals by adding more processing capacity, setting the stage for more sales volume and increasing sales as prices recovered. I learned at this meeting that construction on a new $5 million processing plant to triple production capacity was underway, but, according to the head of operations, costs were 40 percent higher than anticipated. Spending was going to increase by $2 million, to $7 million, to complete construction. This was the first time Perdue Farms had constructed a plant from the ground up, so I was not that surprised by the projected overruns.

Did we have long-term financing for this plant? "No, no. That's your job." I tensed immediately. Things were getting more complicated by the minute. While the company's operating expenses exceeded revenues—a red flag for lenders, I would have to persuade our banks to advance us another $2 million at a time when the company was losing money and money generally was tight in a weak economy. A nightmare.

How in the world, I wondered, *am I going to finance this growing yet cyclical company with its escalating expenses and cash needs over the next several years and keep the Perdue family in control?* When revenues to support sales growth flag during down cycles, more borrowing from banks is needed to offset the sales shortfall and keep operations funded. I would be the one responsible for getting those bank loans.

When the meeting ended, given all we had just heard, I asked Frank what he thought my priorities should be. He just looked at me, as if to say, "You're the CFO. You decide." (It was only later that I began to believe it was his bankers who pushed Frank to hire a CFO, a step he had resisted.) Then he departed Salisbury to meet with ad agencies in New York City. I wouldn't see him for nine weeks.

I was on my own, but I knew what my priorities should be. There was only one thing to do: Take one step at a time and go in the right direction.

That same day, I had my first conversation with the controller who led the financial group, my financial group.

"What is your plan for the department?" I asked.

"The banks keep asking us for monthly statements, but it takes me more than three months to generate the numbers," he said. "I finish one quarter and must start over again." With no trained accountants in the office, I shouldn't have been surprised by this. But three months? In a small company, that work should require two weeks or less.

He went on to say that the costs in the monthly reports were not accurate. They did not tie to the checkbook, so banks didn't have much confidence in our reports. "At year-end there is usually a million-dollar gap between the numbers I prepare each week and what our outside auditors report."

I saw this as a fixable problem. "I'll talk to Frank and see what he says," I replied. At Touche Ross, I had seen companies keep two sets of books, typically companies that were small and fast-growing. This takes time but can be sorted out. I estimated that for a complex organization like Perdue with seventy cost centers, the transition might take three years.

But I soon learned that my staff recorded financial data on ledgers, by hand; they had access to an IBM 360-20 computer, but it was used only by the nutrition manager to help him optimize feed costs. There was no accounting or treasury staff. This was going to be a world-class challenge, a startup situation from scratch. I hoped I'd have the time and Frank would be patient and supportive. But again, I knew what had to be done. Produce monthly financial statements adding up to the year-end and audited statements that lenders now required.

Banks need accurate, dependable forecasts to guide lending decisions and give them confidence that borrowers will repay their loans. As Perdue Farms grew, bankers would be expecting monthly statements to gauge the company's financial health and funding. Well, on this day one, I didn't have any dependable forecasts. If I failed to secure both short-term and long-term funding, Perdue's growth potential would have to be scaled back, and I would be held responsible.

A related, bigger reason that I didn't have accurate numbers was that, as I soon learned, operating managers did not have a good handle on actual costs. One million dollars in costs were not accounted for. The problem was that the company did not tie costs to cash. More on this shortly.

EMPTYHANDED (ALMOST) NEGOTIATING WITH BANKS

The company did have a $5 million, five-year term loan from its two primary banks, J.P. Morgan and Philadelphia National, for plant construction. "We need to add another 40 percent to the existing loan," I explained to our Philadelphia National lending officer during our first meeting in his Philadelphia office.

He was a bit testy. "How long have you been at Perdue?" he asked.

"About four weeks."

"Have you updated your projections? Do you have confidence in them?"

Pressing further, he asked whether additional cost overruns loomed and whether I, as a young, first-time CFO, was assertive enough to impose and enforce spending controls on older, long-tenured executives overseeing this project (or other projects to follow).

I wasn't rattled. The graph of the four-year cycle I prepared showed one high-profit year typically followed by a year of lower profits, then two moderately profitable years. Thus, I explained, we should be on the cusp of the two profitable years. I pointed out that Perdue also had a practice of locking in corn and soybean costs for chicken feed in the commodity futures market.

Accepting my homework, the banks approved the 40 percent increase. That decision likely had more to do with Frank's admirable payments record, and perhaps an impression that I would be up to the task, but they saw an opportunity to test me—the thirty-one-year-old rookie.

Within a year, rising profit margins outpaced my projections. Loan payments on the new plant were completed ahead of schedule.

PULLING FAT FROM THE FIRE, AN EARLY WIN

In his classic book *Leading Change*, Harvard business professor John P. Kotter says one reason transformation efforts fail is because leaders don't build support quickly through short-term wins. As he cautions, appropriately, "Real transformation takes time."

I was extremely fortunate in that regard. I had asked my predecessor in running the finance group, the controller now reporting to me, to do something he neglected to do. In our federal tax return, we consolidated all the profits and losses into one taxable number, but we had to provide the profits and losses separately for each subsidiary for the state of Maryland, with a separate tax-due amount for each.

I asked him to fill in those details for the Maryland filing, to make sure each subsidiary showed similar profit levels, a common and legal practice. But he didn't do it, instead combining results of the different subsidiaries into one overall total. The error cost us $20,000 in higher state taxes.

"We made a dumb mistake," I told Bill, our senior account manager at Price Waterhouse. "Is there anything we can do?"

He had an idea. "Let's see if we can refile the taxes with different transfer prices (reflecting the value of transactions between the wholly owned subsidiaries) so the subsidiaries all make roughly the same amount of money. That would sharply reduce the taxes."

We filed revised tax returns. I was surprised when the Maryland state controller accepted the new numbers; we received a $20,000 refund. The entire management team was astounded and delighted when I gave them the news. "Financial people can actually make money too!" Generating that $20,000 refund earned me new respect in those Monday morning meetings. A prized short-term win for me.

Four months into his team's work, Bill at Price Waterhouse pulled me aside. "When I review reports from operations, the profit in the balance sheet is $2.5 million. But when we audit the balance sheet for the same period, the profit is $1 million. Why the big difference?"

The explanation was simple. "Bill, we have two sets of books." Bill and I had seen this situation several times when small business grew rapidly. I replied, Handy's accounting department needs a complete overhaul to achieve one set of books where all transactions tie to cash. "It's a large project for all ninety cost centers. The project will require accounting talent and may take three years to build." Bill understood immediately and agreed.

One set of books with monthly reports is the basis of credible financial forecasts—a tool every CFO must have to borrow money and manage cash.

FIVE

"I'M AGAINST IT"

This was an uncomfortable time for Frank Perdue and his company's evolution. His father had hired him as employee No. 3 when Frank was nineteen. Now the family business he had grown up around and had helped lead for more than twenty years was transforming into a more complex, faster-growing enterprise.

Demands on him were expanding, often unfamiliar and challenging. Frank had to delegate more, either by design or default. He often did not know whom to trust, especially someone like me, whom he had not worked with for long. And I wasn't a farmer. I was seen as the Yankee from Wall Street. Brash too in Frank's eyes? Yes, probably so.

PARSING THE MATTER OF SHRINKAGE

One day, after I had been in the company for several months, I saw Frank getting into his car in the parking lot. I didn't know where he was going or how soon he would return, but I thought this might be a rare opportunity for a one-on-one conversation. He was about to drive off. "Can I ride with you?"

"Sure, hop in," he said. "What do you think of my new Mercedes?"

"Frank, our accounting system needs an overhaul," I began.

"What's wrong with it?" Frank replied, looking puzzled.

I replied "We're producing two sets of books. One set is for management reports that are reviewed weekly in the operating committee meeting. The other set is the quarterly financials from general ledger that our accounting department takes ninety days to generate for taxes and reports we send to our banks. The profit difference is over $1.5 million lower than the management reports," I explained. Frank asked, "How can this be? We've been borrowing money for years." I replied, "Yes, but the borrowings are growing very fast."

I explained, "Perdue's operations are integrated. As you know, corn is purchased from farmers, dried, held in storage tanks, mixed with other ingredients, processed into pellets, and loaded onto trucks for delivery to grow-out farms at a feed cost per pound. But does that cost include the normal shrinkage? It may only be 1 percent incurred from corn purchase to loading the feed truck, but it's a sizeable number when multiplied by the tons of feed produced each year. The point is that the cost of 1 percent shrinkage at the feed mill is invisible and needs to be managed. When passed up the line and combined with other shrinks, the final cost of a processed chicken is understated and the profit is overstated."

The second cause of overstating profits until the year-end audit is the total costs of operating each center do not tie to the checkbook. Unusual costs such as inventory shortages, customer credits, breakdowns, and nonrecurring costs are sometimes not recorded as part of each center's weekly cost. For accuracy, every expenditure in a cost center must tie to the checkbook, normal and nonrecurring. Management's job is to investigate unusual costs and make plans to fix the source.

Bill, the audit manager from Price Waterhouse, asked me, "Which set of books is accurate?" I replied, "Of course, audit the balance sheet in the general ledger. We'll begin working on one set of books that ties management reports and the general ledger together."

ONE SET OF BOOKS HAD TO BE DONE

I continued speaking to Frank in the car. "It probably will take three years to put a new accounting system in place for all ninety cost centers and recruit a staff to manage it. The project to tie costs to cash and record shrinks may not be a problem now, but as Perdue grows and we need to borrow more money, the lenders I know will need confidence that our monthly financials add up to the auditor's annual report."

Frank was visibly irritated, but not by these discrepancies I'd just explained. He didn't dispute anything in my analysis, but he didn't like my plan. "I'm against it," he said. "That sounds like more overhead. Things are working okay now." Frank completed his errand and we returned to the office parking lot.

I went ahead on my own and, without Frank's support, began overhauling the accounting system as I had envisioned. I was sticking my neck out guessing that Frank trusted me to do the right thing and leaving Frank free to second-guess my decision. Here was another situation where I was determined to do the right thing for Perdue and professionally, and if necessary, deal with any criticisms or retributions later. I was hoping that Frank would trust me to do the right thing.

It was not insubordination as I had observed. Frank basically allowed his management team to operate in their own area. I admired this. He selected outstanding people and challenged them but did not meddle.

At Touche Ross, I had often worked with clients to design and activate new cost-control systems, so I was well-prepared to identify reporting gaps and design fixes at Perdue Farms. If Frank wanted the best financial department in the industry, this had to be done.

The transition to the new accounting system was surprisingly smooth. Once operations leaders understood the value in tighter cost measurements, they adjusted quickly and were fully engaged within months. Coaching cost center managers to pay more attention to actual costs and shrinkage gave us what we were missing.

Knowing actual costs made it easier for senior executives to set pricing with the cost-plus method. This means just what the term suggests: Once you know your costs, you add a desired percentage in profit margin to set pricing. Now, our profitability would improve because we had a clearer understanding of actual costs.

Price Waterhouse no longer questioned our one set of books, and we didn't have the added expense or restated annual results. Those restatements had been a red flag for Perdue Farms' bankers, indicating that Perdue might not have adequate control of its operations.

Finally, and this was huge for me, assertive accountants providing accurate costs and visible shrinks for operators to manage makes money for the company. As their stature rose among middle and senior managers across the company, my staff took even greater pride in their contributions to the bottom line.

Three years after I committed to the overhaul, the accounting staff was able to track and report accurate weekly operating costs for the management team's Monday review. We were producing matching financial reports—monthly reports for banks and annually for auditors and the IRS—with even more benefits in simply being able to run the business more efficiently.

Bill, now a Price Waterhouse partner, signed the audit opinions fifteen days after we delivered figures to him for the year-end audit. A vast improvement over thirteen weeks.

Despite our occasional disagreements, I gained a growing appreciation for the insights that had helped Frank become a driven, successful business leader. I think he understood my zeal as our interactions, direct and indirect, accumulated over time. He was relentless in pursuing his principles:

- Be the low-cost producer. Acknowledge oversight by the technical team—flock health, nutrition, and genetics. Always invest in equipment to lower costs.
- Focus more and more on better quality for a competitive advantage, which was generating a one-quarter cent pricing premium for live chickens. A better chicken and the premium was a huge competitive advantage.
- Integrate every operation where possible to avoid yielding any profit margins to middlemen and to control quality in production from start to finish.

- Control quality at every step.
- Manage cash to expand operations during the low-profit period of the chicken cycle to enjoy high margins that historically follow.

BUILDING MY TEAM

One afternoon after my first month, I caught up with Frank on one of his quick-paced hallway walkabouts. "If growth continues at the current pace and revenues double in the next five years, I'll need more staff and time to develop them." He seemed preoccupied and didn't respond. I interpreted this as "go ahead."

I had two advantages in recruiting talented CPAs and MBAs. Maryland at the time was the only state that did not require auditing experience before sitting for the CPA exam. This was especially appealing to the older group coming out of the military. Most accounting majors would eagerly opt for entry-level corporate finance positions over the two or three years of drudgery and travel at auditing firms. In Maryland, new MBAs are eligible to add "CPA" to their resume just by passing the test.

I traveled extensively over the next seven years, meeting undergraduate seniors and second-year MBAs at top business schools along the East Coast: University of Virginia, University of North Carolina, North Carolina State, the University of Pennsylvania's Wharton School, and others. Search firms produced more promising candidates. I also discovered good talent in other departments at Perdue who were eager to take on more responsibility.

Frank typically would only get personally involved when recruiting his direct reports. "I need to know their weak spots, and if they're trustworthy," he believed. If the leadership team was effective, they would hire good managers. The company had no human resources department.

He did agree to meet my top candidates. I assured all of them that they would have time to study for their CPA exam prep courses. Fourteen of my new hires became CPAs, with thirteen passing the exam on their first attempt; eleven of these were MBAs.

My second recruiting advantage was that I was able to place my hires into positions with immediate responsibilities—a fast track for professional advancement. Five CPAs were immediately assigned as division controllers. My MBA recruits were assigned to banking, finance, credit, and data processing roles—and in new departments for credit and insurance.

I wanted candidates eager to advance their careers—self-starters. I would watch their progress and step in if necessary to prevent failures. I loaded more and more responsibility onto their plates at a pace that I felt each had the ability to handle.

We needed to catch up fast in those first years and then get ahead of Perdue's annual sales growth pace—at 22 percent during much of my tenure, doubling every four years. We were handling more than $77 million in my first year in credit and finance transactions with customers, primarily wholesalers and distributors to grocery chains and restaurants.

To help them develop further as a team, I led review updates on company growth, status of current projects, and plans for others at breakfast meetings each quarter. Turnover in this group was minimal.

Most of the division operating managers—in chicken processing, grain storage, chicken feed, and others—valued the finance team's work. I heard often, "Your people are doing a great job for me." Although Perdue Farms was a private company, one year we produced an annual report with fabulous photography and all the financial elements the Securities and Exchange Commission required for public companies. We in the finance department were delighted by the results, although the printed report was never distributed outside the company to lenders or family stockholders.

One day in my seventh year as CFO, I asked Bill how he would rate our finance team among dozens of clients in his Price Waterhouse Mid-Atlantic territory. "You are number one, definitely the best," he said. This was deeply gratifying, a top-of-the-heap ranking. I considered it my finest achievement to that point.

Another goal when I began building my team was to have strong candidates prepared to step in when I eventually decided to resign. There were two, as it happened, one from Wharton and one from New York University. Frank chose the one from NYU to succeed me, and four years later he promoted him to president and chief operating officer. I was delighted. (Tragically, my successor as CFO died while skiing after two years in that role. He was just forty-seven.)

FINANCING A FAST-GROWING CYCLICAL BUSINESS

Congress created The Farmers Home Administration Act 1946 to help the farming sector get back on its feet after World War II and, much later, encourage economic development in rural areas. Farming's share of total US gross domestic product had plunged by then to less than 10 percent. Twenty years before, the US still was primarily an agrarian economy.

One of our best funding sources for growth turned out to be something I had never heard about before coming to Perdue Farms: the cash method of accounting for income taxes that ignores increases in inventories and is available for family-owned farms. The benefit from lower tax outlays was higher cash flows available to fund growth—part of my toolkit for financing long-term assets such as flocks and feed.

Here's how the accounting worked: As Perdue's increasing cash outlays each year for grain to feed its expanding flocks of live chickens came close to matching rising revenues, taxes would be deferred and not due to the IRS until the farming operations declined or shut down.

And here's how the politics worked: As Perdue's cash spending for feed and flocks rose, the IRS wanted to eliminate our rights to apply the cash method. Our representative in Congress, in tandem with a tax attorney/lobbyist, organized meetings for me in the House cloak room on Capitol Hill to explain a cash-method exception for family farms to any lawmaker taking a break from floor debates. Our lobbyist worked directly with the IRS. When the IRS approved our exemption, I exhaled with relief.

I remained focused on this every year—keeping our House representative informed, meeting with anyone he and our lobbyist recommended, and keeping lines open with the IRS. Later, after I moved to Handy and Perdue Farms' annual revenues grew toward $1 billion, the IRS eliminated this tax-deferral provision for Perdue and other larger family farming operations. (It still is available generally for farms with annual revenues less than $26 million.)

We learned about another financing program the Department of Agriculture underwrote to support long-term financing of agribusinesses. One of its agencies, the Farmers Home Administration, guaranteed 10 percent of long-term financing for farming assets. That guarantee gave comfort to lenders, and I am sure it made it easier, at least in some cases, for us to secure long-term loans we needed to keep expanding chicken-processing facilities. The partial government loan guarantee was an extra cushion in the event a farm borrower fell into hard times and defaulted.

AVERTING AN ESTATE TAX CRISIS

During my first weeks at Perdue Farms, I discovered yet another festering issue with potential to become a full-blown crisis, one that could force Perdue into a fire sale. Estate taxes at the time were alarmingly high, outrageous for farmers when the value of the land was tallied. Closely-held business often had limited cash and financing options to pay estate taxes when the leader was no longer available. A sale was often the only option.

At Laird I became aware of heirs forced to sell the business to pay the estate taxes, a terrible and I think unjust outcome for any family after years of hard work toward wealth-building. A client at the time, the cosmetics giant Elizabeth Arden Company, was an extreme example.

The company's founder and lone owner, Elizabeth N. Graham, was by reputation one of the world's wealthiest women, presiding over an empire operating at one time in twenty-two countries. After her death in 1966, the IRS valued the company nine months later and calculated the estate taxes. Unfortunately, the company had not made plans to fund estate taxes, and the business floundered without her leadership under an executive she had appointed. Eli Lilly & Co. stepped in and purchased the company in 1971 for $38 million. When the proceeds were applied to the estate taxes, Elizabeth Graham's lone heir, a niece named Adelaide Bishop, received $1 million, a small portion of the sale. What a debacle.

I wasn't directly involved in financing the company, but I listened carefully to my colleagues discussing the sale.

Taxes on estate values above $10 million at the time were 77 percent. Congress later reduced the rate; it was set more recently at 40 percent on values of estates above $11.7 million. Funding the estate tax without prior planning remains a substantial burden for heirs left behind.

I noted that if I should be fortunate enough to own a business, estate planning must be an important part of protecting my family's accumulating value from estate taxes.

A DISTRESSING "WHAT IF?"

That Elizabeth Arden case made a big impression on me. In my first months at Perdue in 1971, the specter of a massive tax exposure in the event of Frank's unexpected passing loomed large. No one in the office talked about it (Frank never mentioned it). But I knew that as CFO I would have to raise enough funds within nine months to pay the estate taxes if Frank unexpectedly left the scene.

That funding would have been impossible to finance on our balance sheet, which was vulnerable to the vagaries of commodity pricing cycles and fluctuating earnings. At the moment, we were in an earnings down cycle. Unless I were able to design an alternative plan, the Perdue family might have no choice but to sell the business. Not on my watch. I had to figure out how to avoid that outcome.

Over the next ten months, I asked four estate-planning attorneys and tax professionals recommended by my Wall Street contacts for advice. Yet, the only path they advised, one after another, was for the Perdue family to gradually reduce their ownership stake, and potential tax liability, by giving away shares and taking a charitable contribution tax write-off.

In my view this made no sense. I wasn't going to go to Frank and recommend he give away stock ownership in Perdue Farms at the same time we were laying plans for aggressive growth in annual sales and profits—and value creation.

One day early in 1972, I broke the logjam when one of my new hires, a recent Wharton School graduate, suggested I contact a professor who taught a popular estate-planning course and whose clients included the Cargill and DuPont families. Charles McCaffrey lived two hours away in Wilmington, Delaware. When we soon met in Salisbury, he immediately suggested something totally different: exchanging a large portion of Frank's common stock for preferred stock with voting rights.

The value of the preferred stock would be fixed at the time of the exchange, thus freezing the value of Frank's total stake in the company in what was known as a "peg and freeze." Moreover, it would pay a dividend of 5 percent only once, not annually. The value would never change, regardless of how much earnings increased in future years, a perfectly legal interpretation under federal tax law at the time.

The next step would be to place the preferred shares in a so-called "hundred-year trust" and cover any potential shortfall in the value of the preferred shares and an estate tax liability with a life insurance policy. (In hundred-year trusts, estate taxes are not due until twenty years after the youngest living heirs have died; in Frank's case, he had small grandchildren, so the hundred-year label seemed accurate.) "I usually sell policies valued at millions of dollars to cover the difference," McCaffrey told me. Brokering these policies was how he earned his fees. He charged me nothing for the "peg and freeze" advice.

DELIVERANCE, BY SULLIVAN & CROMWELL

I had never heard of this transaction. It seemed credible, but I was unable to locate any estate lawyers with experience drafting the documents, which were quite complicated. By luck, through one of my neighbors in Riverside, Connecticut, I learned about a fantastic lawyer who was familiar with the process at one of the country's largest and most distinguished law firms, Sullivan & Cromwell.

Here's how that happened. Susan and I had installed climbing bars, swings, and other jungle-gym elements in our home's large basement for our four active little boys, then seven to two years old. A friend of mine from Laird, fascinated by the scene, told his sister, who had young kids too, "You have to see this." She came soon with her husband, a junior associate at Sullivan & Cromwell.

I casually mentioned my stalled estate-planning project to him. He immediately gave me the name of a senior partner who was an expert in "peg and freeze" estate planning. "He's really good."

That partner was expecting my call when I reached him the next day. "Yes. We've done these before, and we'll set it up for you," he told me. "When we get the particulars, I'll give you a call, go over how it works."

Man, I thought, this is wonderful.

Within a week, I was in Sullivan & Cromwell's New York office. On the third day, working on the details for the draft legal papers, Frank called me.

"Where are you?"

"I'm in New York."

"What are you doing? You're supposed to be back here."

"I'm working on your estate planning, Frank."

"What?" He was outraged, for the moment, as I explained what I was doing and how much time I had spent in the past year without his knowing anything about it. (Here was another case where I was committed to doing what I considered the right thing and was willing to suffer the consequences if it came to that.) It's likely Frank had some concerns about his own estate taxes, with calamity stories such as Elizabeth Arden occasionally in the news, but he had never mentioned it to me.

"Get back here now."

"No, I'm not coming back until the lawyers here have the papers drafted."

His tone was markedly different when I walked into his office three days later. "Well, what'd you find out?" he said, curious and eager to hear.

"Well, Frank, I'm working with this fantastic law firm, Sullivan & Cromwell. They have a plan where you can freeze some or all the stock you own in the business and avoid paying estate taxes." I explained why estate taxes would become a real financing challenge for his family if he suddenly was not on the scene. "They would have to come up with the money," I concluded flatly.

He agreed to join me in New York a week later and go through the details with that brilliant Sullivan & Cromwell lawyer, Frederick Terry. At the meeting, Terry explained the law, the details, and the benefits of this transaction, and Frank didn't hesitate. "You know, this makes sense," he said. "I'll redo my will. Let's set it up, get it done."

The documents were complicated. It took the lawyers a month to finish them, but when they did, Frank flew immediately to New York and signed them. We had to file a required independent appraisal of the value of Frank's preferred stock with the IRS as part of all the Sullivan & Cromwell documents. By law, the IRS had two years to file a challenge and dispute the plan, but that didn't happen.

As Perdue Farms' CFO, I was greatly relieved that Frank moved quickly to approve and sign the documents. A potential disaster averted. I thought to myself, *Let's just take a few minutes to enjoy this.* I look back on this now as one of those situations in my career where seeking the best talent available to help tackle a challenge paid off handsomely. As we'll see, there would be more.

I don't know how much money these "peg and freeze" and "hundred-year trust" provisions saved for the family after Frank passed away in 2005, but I would guess it was a big number. Into the late 1990s, *Forbes* magazine regularly ranked Frank among the four hundred richest Americans.

Frank never said anything to me directly about how I had pursued and presented a solution to this problem. I did hear separately from two of his friends that he was delighted. Essentially, he had told them, "I don't know what he did, but Conway set it up. I'm not going to have to pay estate taxes."

I figured he must have been happy with the plan if he was talking about it with his friends. For my part, I was greatly relieved. If it wasn't for that Elizabeth Arden chatter in the weeks before I left Laird, I doubt that I would have put two and two together. Now, that specter of Perdue Farms becoming another Elizabeth Arden estate-tax disaster no longer lurked over my shoulder.

SEVEN

ONCE UPON A LOVELY HEADQUARTERS VISION

It was obvious from the time I arrived at Perdue that the company needed to begin plans to renovate the headquarters or build new space. Sales were accelerating at a double-digit pace annually on the back of Frank's push for best-in-industry quality at every stage of production, tireless research with consumers onsite in grocery stores, and TV advertising.

All management and administrative staff worked in a crowded, converted feed mill (a wooden vestige of the company's pre–World War II chicken farm era) that was carpeted and featured a pleasing décor. The feed mill, originally in the back of the building, where chicken feed was processed for years, had been moved a short distance away.

Office designers typically plan for a hundred square feet of space for each employee on site; we had only forty feet and were leasing space at other locations in Salisbury. Rooms were divided awkwardly, a haphazard arrangement that disrupted the routine workflow of paying our associates and sending invoices. There were safety issues as well. A small fire could spread quickly in the wooden floor. And with twelve entrances, the place was a challenge for security.

Frank knew we needed new offices, but with the chicken business in a low ebb at the time, he wanted to wait. Plus, I knew that anything Frank regarded as overhead, an expense not directly needed to produce and process chickens at a lower cost and generate revenue, would be a hard sell. In any case, the chicken business was likely to recover by the time construction would begin. Here was another task for the CFO to anticipate.

My strategy to counter Frank's reluctance to spend on nonproductive new assets, or overhead, was to pursue a famous architect and hope my target would agree to create an eye-catching design for a great location that Frank's friends would admire.

One of the most famous architects in America then—hailed by some observers as "America's foremost living architect"—was Louis Kahn. When I put in a direct call to his Philadelphia office, he picked up the phone and was gracious immediately—receptive and surprisingly easy to talk with for such a renowned figure.

"Mr. Khan, I'm down in Maryland. We have a growing company and need a design for a new office building we plan to build, not terribly fancy but functional and accommodating, for two hundred people . . . something that needs to be expandable with growth."

As I described the prospective site—an appealing eighty acres we owned that featured a small hill and gently sloping terrain bordering a main highway in Salisbury, with plenty of land for an office building and other structures—I sensed his enthusiasm rising.

"That sounds very interesting," he said. "I'll send a team down to Salisbury. Can you arrange for a local surveyor to meet them?"

TASTEFUL LOUIS KAHN DESIGNS, PUBLISHED

Three months later, we had the preliminary design. It was simple and tasteful, with the structure blending beautifully into the small hill, which was about five feet higher than street level. The surveyor had observed that the water table was only six feet below ground. To take advantage, the Kahn team added a wide trapezoid-shaped lake, as long as a football field, to reflect the entire headquarters building. Cars passing on the highway—US Route 50, which spans the country's midsection from California to Ocean City, Maryland—would have a limited view.

I explained to Kahn that we would need to wait until the chicken business looked more favorable before taking action to initiate construction, perhaps another six months. I gladly paid for the designs (a quite reasonable sum), then bided my time for another three months before calling to tell him again how delighted we were with the design. I was vague about Frank's non-involvement to that point, saying simply that our next step internally was to obtain approvals.

"I understand," he replied, adding, "I always publish my designs in an architectural magazine. Would that be all right?"

Having Louis Kahn designs for a Perdue Farms headquarters published in a professional magazine struck me as a solid endorsement and thus favorable, if limited, publicity. I said, "Yeah, go ahead" and didn't think more about it.

One night, about six months later, a friend who was one of the top architects in Salisbury walked over to Frank at a nice bar around half past eight o'clock. Frank had a habit of stopping there each evening for a nightcap after leaving the office. His friend said with genuine admiration, "I really like the design of your new office building!"

"What building?!" said Frank, baffled. He never wanted to be embarrassed in front of others about something he should know that was happening in his business.

"Your new headquarters. The Louis Kahn design is in the new issue of this architectural magazine I subscribe to."

"YOU SHOULD INCLUDE ME IN THESE THINGS."

Around eleven o'clock, my phone rang. It was Frank, wanting an explanation. Fast.

"Conway, what are you doing? You must know that there is nothing in our plans for a new office building."

I tried to gather my wits and remember how my father had handled judges. "Well, Frank, you know we need an office building. We're crowded—just forty square feet per person. I just wanted to get to work early and find a really good architect and have a design in place so when the time came, we would have a head start."

He couldn't argue with that—at least not the concept. I reflected on how my father had skillfully handled judges during his law practice.

"Well, okay. But you should include me in these things when you're doing it."

"You know how it is sometimes, Frank. I just have to assemble all the pieces before reviewing any plan with you."

"That's not right. You need to include me."

"Well, right. Okay. I'll do it next time."

Of course, I was just humoring Frank. I had learned from others in senior management by then that it was essential to have all the pieces of any project lined up—and be prepared to defend and promote my approach—before any discussion with Frank. This approach was a workaround, basically, to avoid his tendency, his itch, to meddle and procrastinate.

Meddling and procrastination were expressions of Frank's instincts when he might sense that someone was overlooking important details or not striving to exceed competitors' standards. Once he developed trust in us, he understood why we waited so long before getting him involved.

In this case, I knew I had to find a famous architect for the office building and a setting that would meet Frank's standard to be superior to his competitors.

A WIN FOR THE SHOREBIRDS

Louis Kahn died within a year, unfortunately, and his team's vision for a modern, appealing headquarters that blended artfully into the small hill was never implemented. Five years after I departed for Handy, Frank had a traditional three-story office building erected near the onetime wooden feed mill.

Those lovely eighty acres? Frank leased the property to the Baltimore Orioles' Class-A minor league team in Salisbury, the Delmarva Shorebirds, and became one of the investors when they were looking for a good location to build a new stadium. The stadium, named for Frank's father, Arthur W. Perdue, opened in 1996.

EIGHT

RISKING QUICK ACTION TO ACCELERATE GROWTH

A core part of Frank's vision for Perdue Farms' growth before I arrived was to build a reputation for superior quality by controlling key elements of its farm-to-customer poultry operations. Perdue plants would process Perdue-raised chickens. Perdue truckers would distribute processed chickens to supermarket warehouses and to poultry distributors for restaurants initially in the Mid-Atlantic region. As rapidly as possible, with Scali McCabe's marketing and advertising genius helping to stoke demand, Perdue sales and deliveries would expand along the East Coast as far as Boston.

I was convinced after a half dozen years with the company and watching this strategy play out superbly that buying competitors' existing plants would accelerate Perdue's growth pace much faster than building our own. Moreover, I knew from my analysis that chicken pricing typically moves in four-year cycles, from peak to trough.

When you enter a pricing trough, most publicly traded companies are willing to offload their poultry operations at fire-sale discounts; they don't want weaker earnings from that business to damage their stock price. If you can be a *buyer* of plants and related facilities during a downturn, that timing is hard to beat. Ralston Purina, for example, had shed its poultry operations during the last industry downturn in 1972. *The next time this comes up*, I thought after reading the news about Ralston Purina, *we ought to be prepared to make a move*.

Early in 1977, I suggested to Frank that we investigate buying exist-ing plants during the cyclical downturn we were in. Public companies were desperate to avoid a dip in earnings. We should be prepared to take advantage, adding capacity needed for growth, but he was not interested. "No, do not do that," he told me flatly. "I don't care how difficult new facilities are to finance. I want all new equipment, all new plants."

What about the mothballed processing plant in Salisbury he bought in 1968—the final step in fashioning Perdue into a vertically integrated organization? "That was then," he said.

"Well, okay," I replied. I was biding my time to do the right thing.

DOING THE RIGHT THING

A month later, with chicken profits at low ebb, I dialed up one of my Wall Street contacts in mergers and acquisitions now at Kidder Peabody & Company. "When the market price goes down for chickens, some of these publicly traded companies don't like those drains on earnings per share," I said. "They're usually more than willing to talk."

"Let me place a few calls and I'll get back to you," he said. Remarkably, in two hours, he was on my line again.

"Can you be in Chicago tomorrow morning?" he asked me. Executives at Esmark Inc., a holding company that had evolved from Swift & Company, the meat processor, might be receptive to an offer for its five Swift facilities: two feed mills, a hatchery, and two processing plants. One of those plants was forty miles from Salisbury.

"I'll be there," I said, clearing my calendar. I crafted terms for an opening bid during the flight.

The plan: Offer a non-negotiable, rock-bottom price equal to the depreciated book value of the five well-maintained properties: $5 million. The properties might have cost a collective $30 million to build originally. They would need new equipment to meet Frank's "be-the-best" stan-dards if we did take control.

In contrast, I estimated it would cost Perdue close to $35 million if we followed Frank's directive to build and equip only new, best-in-class properties. We had just added debt to our balance sheet to finance a new poultry complex in North Carolina. I doubted banks would be willing to provide much additional financing, but if we expanded quickly through a bargain-priced Swift acquisition, growth would be accelerated without a major investment.

In Chicago the next day, on one of the Sears Tower's upper floors, I framed the bare-bones offer to an Esmark senior executive sitting across from me. Was my initiative brave or foolish? I was about to find out. No one sells assets for only depreciated book value. Yet bank financing was difficult to arrange during the industry's down cycle, so I doubled down with another condition. "I'll pay for the chickens in the field (value: $2 million), but you've got to provide financing for all of this for five years at the prime rate."

"Okay, okay," he said. "You wait here a minute." I expected a counteroffer of $25 million. Then, if so, I would confer with Frank, and, if he agreed, raise our bid possibly as high as $20 million—*provided* I found bank financing for most of that. Winning those bank approvals, I knew, would be a challenge.

I shouldn't have worried. When the Esmark executive returned, he handed me a two-page purchase-and-sale agreement with terms exactly as I had offered.

"Here's the price. Here's the deal," he said. "And we'll do the financing for five years at prime. We'd like to close in ten days. Read it over, then sign on this line here: Terrence Conway, Vice President."

Totally amazed but resolute, I didn't hesitate.

WOULD I STILL HAVE A DEAL—OR EVEN A JOB?

Contract in hand, I caught a flight back to Salisbury that afternoon, rehearsing how I should best break the news and cover the details of my high-wire act in the morning with Frank. He knew nothing, had approved nothing.

As early morning light filled his office, I stuck my head inside. "Frank, I'd like to see you." After hearing the deal's basic outline, capped by my assertion, "I agreed to do it—I signed the purchase-and-sale agreement," the level of rage he directed at me was something I had never experienced.

"You did what?!" he shouted, fuming. "This is terrible. You shouldn't have done that. I told you I want only new buildings and equipment. You did not even tell me you were having this meeting!"

Yes, I had been insubordinate. Yes, Frank, as CEO, should have been making acquisitions, not me. But if I had shared any details with Frank and asked his opinion in advance, the outcome at best likely would have been indecision and procrastination until the opportunity had passed. I had to do the right thing and be willing to be fired if it came to that.

The culture within Perdue was still in transition—a multigenerational family farm operation aspiring toward a growth-oriented, market-leading professional enterprise. Frank was the transitional figure, a second generation of Perdue family patriarchs. As I said earlier, he was feeling his way, often unsure who to trust.

If Frank wanted to fire me now for doing the right thing in making a great acquisition, it was okay.

"I'm going to call Don Kelly," he said crossly. Within minutes Frank was connected to the Esmark CEO on the speakerphone. "This is Frank Perdue. Conway had no authority to do whatever he did. Totally wrong. I want out of the deal."

"Well, Frank," Kelly said evenly. "We had a competitor of yours call this morning. He offered us a lot more money than Conway." My hunch was that the competing offer was for at least $20 million, possibly $25 million, and a reasonable price range for those five facilities.

"Oh, really? That contract Conway signed . . . is that valid?"

"Yes, it is. You're committed at the moment, Frank, but if you want out, we'll take a look at your competitor's offer."

"Oh, okay. Thank you very much."

Frank ended the call and looked away. End of discussion. I walked back to my office and turned my attention to an unrelated project. I was immensely relieved; my gambit seemed to have worked.

TWO SPLENDID DELIVERIES

The closing was set ten days later in Chicago—the date Susan and I were expecting the birth of our fifth child. Would the baby be on time? I lined up a private jet in advance to ferry me back to Salisbury just in case the baby arrived on the doctor's predicted delivery date.

It was nearing midnight in Salisbury—11:00 p.m. Chicago time—when Susan called. "The baby is coming tonight," she said.

"We're almost finished here," I said. "I'm on the way." I signed the signature page, slid it under our attorney's hotel room door, called the air charter service, packed, took a taxi to O'Hare International Airport, and waited for the plane to arrive and file a flight plan.

Less than two hours after leaving Chicago and three hours after the birth of our only daughter, the private flight landed in Salisbury.

Susan was wide awake when I arrived in her hospital room before sunrise, our little angel wrapped in baby blankets, sleeping beside her. After an hour or so, I dropped by the house and, following Susan's instructions, wrapped the mailbox with a large pink bow, announcing to our neighbors the birth of our daughter.

Later that morning, Frank was surprised and puzzled to see me in my office. "How did you get here? I thought this was closing day. Did the deal fall apart? Did a competitor step in with a higher price?"

"All the papers were signed this morning in Chicago," I said. "Our attorney cleaned up the details. The deal is now final. Susan delivered after midnight."

Unsure how Frank would react, I needed to add one more detail. "If flights were unavailable, I lined up a private plane in advance to get back here fast."

Without skipping a beat, he said generously, "I'll pay for it."

A week later the chicken market turned around. Pricing and cash flow headed north, and the temporary new division formed with the Swift assets became profitable in nine months. Another favorable result: We were able to cover the entire $5 million acquisition price during those same nine months by processing those chickens Swift had in the field and selling them.

We renovated one of those two processing plants, the one near Salisbury, for a new and what would become one of Perdue Farms' most popular products in the years ahead—Oven Stuffer Roasters. The other operations—the second processing plant, feed mills, hatcheries, and related farming activities—were easily integrated into Perdue's existing organization.

He never mentioned this to me directly in the coming months, but I knew that Frank was coming around, that growth by acquisition was both feasible and economical. Indeed, more acquisition deals followed.

That five-year financing with Esmark? It was so favorable we retained it for the full term. Esmark was true to their word on this, never wavering.

WHEN FORTUNE SMILES: KNOCKING ON AN OPEN DOOR

The timing of my call to Kidder, Peabody turned out to be close to perfect. I learned later that Esmark's new CEO that year, Donald P. Kelly, was eager to jettison cyclical poultry assets that were currently in the money-losing cycle. The word might have been getting around Wall Street when I came knocking, at least to Kidder.

Kelly became renowned during the 1980s as a master of leveraged buyouts, or LBOs—friendly acquisitions and hostile takeovers alike that were financed by junk, or low-quality, bonds. He would mount the largest LBO to date in 1988, the $2.5 billion buyout of Beatrice Foods, and book hundreds of millions in profits later by selling Beatrice assets.

Various profiles in the business press during this period described Don Kelly as having a reputation for acting quickly. I certainly can vouch for that. Our deal in March 1977 was barely a blip for him, considering what was to come, but it stands as one of Kelly's first moves in reshaping Esmark over the next decade into one of Chicago's largest corporations.

NINE

THE UNFORESEEN RESTAURATEUR

With the finance department now solid and performing well, I was thinking more about what I might do next. I was itching for something new, something more challenging to keep moving forward professionally.

There appeared to be three pragmatic options:

- Remain at Perdue with good prospects for higher pay as the company continued to grow rapidly,
- Take another position on the CFO career track with a larger public company, or
- Change my financial role to running a new Perdue profit center for the first time.

The last one, my first choice, could go a long way toward propelling my career upward and answering a question that had concerned me since I was at Notre Dame: *Do I have what it takes to lead a company someday?*

Then, something unexpected. Frank confided that he was going to make me president of a new subsidiary, Perdue Foods Inc., with the goal of taking the company further into the food-service business. The project: design, open, and profitably operate a restaurant with a menu highlighting a variety of Perdue chicken dishes.

"This is a prodigious task. Hundreds of detailed decisions to make," he said. "We have no one in the company with any restaurant experience, no one with startup experience of any kind to provide guidance. I want you to lead it."

Frank had never voiced this, but opening a restaurant with his name on the door would be a significant reputational risk for the Perdue Farms brand and for Frank personally. Failure, I knew implicitly, was not an option. This was scary business for me: not only opening and managing a restaurant for the first time, but doing it in the formidably complex and competitive dining world of New York City. I had to take ownership, really work at it, to get everything perfected. Identify problems, then deal with each one . . . one at a time.

I stepped away from most of my CFO duties into an entirely new role: restaurateur.

A CAREER SHIFT FAR REMOVED FROM MY COMFORT ZONE

The twists of fortune come into play during anyone's work life, nudging or bending the trajectory in unexpected ways. This was one of those times. Several years later when I weighed the opportunity and challenges in buying Handy, I might have hesitated, or even dismissed the idea, if not for what I had learned and accomplished in creating the Perdue Chicken Restaurant business. Leading the charge gave me direct, immersive experience in food processing, a factor that soon would enable me to visualize the opportunity with Handy to broaden the market for those wonderful crab items in Crisfield.

One of my principles for any new business activity has always been "You are as you start," meaning: get everything in the best shape possible before you begin operating. You create a first impression that will stick in the minds of your team and customers. Done well, with detailed precision, this model is difficult for competitors to duplicate.

I was determined to avoid failure by positioning every essential element of the business as close to perfect as possible. Your key constituent groups may present obstacles from which you can never recover.

I anticipated that Frank, a perfectionist, would be pressing constantly for updates and the logic behind each move. (He did.) As he often said, "Thoroughness is next to godliness."

One of Frank's principles, of course, was that in order to be the best at anything you had to master the details, do all the little things. For a new chicken restaurant to be true to the Perdue brand, he acknowledged, this would take time.

He had the right instinct, thinking ahead with no prompting from me, to open the door for Carol Haltaman to join me at a time he sensed she was looking for new challenges. That opportunity to meet and work with her had repercussions for this venture and far beyond. "If you are interested, you ought to talk to Terry," he told Carol. "I think he's going to need some help." I was glad—and fortunate that she said yes.

WOW! What a gift! Carol had joined Perdue eight years earlier when there were just twenty employees. She understood Perdue's culture for perfection and the need to avoid any temptation to cut corners. She had the reputation as a self-starter, a strong person, and she knew how to cross the finish line. Carol totally endorsed Frank's focus on thoroughness. She had no hesitation about a new venture in New York City.

Frank and I agreed that the key factor for success would inevitably be making sure we delivered on the advertised Perdue brand promise: The great taste of Perdue's tender, farm-fresh chicken should enhance the flavor of each recipe and deliver good value for customers.

In my planning, I listed more than 150 of these elements. In the kitchen: "cut whole chickens to keep moisture and flavor intact just before cooking." In the dining area, add a mezzanine to increase capacity. Above the ceilings, separate HVAC equipment to prevent kitchen odors from annoying customers. In our supply chain, whole chickens would be delivered fresh on Perdue trucks.

It was as if I were writing a symphony for a major orchestra without knowing how to read music. I had to learn the nuances of every instrument, every musician, every chord, and every voice in the chorus, and then stand on the podium to conduct them with discipline, spark, and creativity.

To grow our audience, and be profitable, we had to make the best music possible: great food at great value for the money.

STELLAR RESTAURANT EXPERTS DELIGHTED TO HELP

The biggest challenge was creating a dining experience that would blend seamlessly with the folksy "Tough Man, Tender Chicken" persona that our advertising firm, Scali, McCabe, Sloves, had created for Frank and the Perdue Farms brand in the minds of the public. That was our objective in developing the concept. What kind of restaurant would Frank Perdue open?

It wouldn't be another fast-food fried chicken place. It wouldn't be fine dining with wait staff and fine wine. We would maintain absolute control over chickens served in a Perdue restaurant. All production systems in Frank's organization were integrated, meaning they were controlled entirely within the company: chicken eggs, raising chickens, processing chickens, and deliveries to customers on Perdue trucks. No competing restaurant would be able to match this ability to bring consistent quality at every step—from Perdue farms to customers' plates. In essence, it was a farm-to-table restaurant long before that concept became so popular in the industry.

We knew from surveys that prospective restaurant customers felt they knew, liked, and trusted Frank, a brilliant payoff that Scali, McCabe's chief copywriter, Ed McCabe, cultivated so effectively and humorously (tagline: "It takes a tough man to make a tender chicken"). Ed, a Scali, McCabe founder, by then was an advertising legend, at age thirty-four the youngest person ever elected to the One Club Hall of Fame.

His iconic Perdue TV campaigns had been running in our biggest market, the New York City megalopolis, since the early '70s, and later in other cities along the Atlantic coast in the company's main distribution territories, from Philadelphia to Boston.

Why the personal connection between Frank and consumers? When consumers served Perdue chickens at home, the chickens delivered on Frank's promise in the TV commercials. They were that good—tender, meatier, tastier, and fresher.

The challenge was that a restaurant concept to capitalize on this enviable reputation did not exist. By default, my job was to start from scratch and invent it.

I asked the question, "What kind of restaurant would Frank Perdue open that fits his image?" to the reigning experts in restaurant-location leases and construction in New York City, the Riese brothers, and in restaurant design, Joe Baum. They didn't have a clue. But I was amazed by their response. These were busy people, among the most prominent in their fields, yet they were eager to help.

At the time, the Riese Organization was the nation's largest privately held restaurant operator and franchisee, with 150 eateries in high-traffic locations, mainly in Manhattan such as Times Square and Grand Central Terminal.

Barney at Riese showed me how to engineer and build HVAC, plumbing, electricity, and other basic elements to quickly open a restaurant location. These are important design aspects that I did not have to figure out. He then opened doors for me with reputable contractors for building restaurants in New York City and a legal expert on twenty-year restaurant leases.

For location sites, Barney guided me away from Manhattan, where available leases on appealing corner locations would be difficult to find. We landed instead on the ground floor of a new eleven-story office building on busy Queens Boulevard near a shopping area in the middle- and upper-middle-income community of Rego Park, ten miles east of Manhattan.

I first met Joe Baum in the main dining room at the iconic restaurant he created on the 107th floor of one of the World Trade Center towers, Windows on the World. (In 2000, its last year before the 9/11 attacks, Windows on the World was the highest-grossing restaurant in

Perdue Chicken Restaurant on Queens Boulevard in New York City, 1980

the United States, at $37 million.) A delightful, down-to-earth fellow, Joe also designed two famed gastronome destinations in Manhattan, Four Seasons and the Rainbow Room. He was so intrigued by new possibilities that a Perdue restaurant might uncover that he volunteered to advise me on how to think about the problem and key decisions I would have to make.

Their insights were priceless. And they would not accept any payment. They just wanted to help.

What *would* be our concept? Who would be our closest competitors and how would we be different from—and better than—them? What location would give us the best chances for success—to make an enthusiastic first impression with customers and create demand for more locations? What menu items would we serve? How would we take advantage of the Perdue reputation for tasty, fresh, tender chicken?

At each step, until the day we opened for our first customers, I would be in a perpetual state of suspense, asking myself, *Will this work?*

"REMEMBER, IT'S ALL ABOUT THE FOOD."

We researched a variety of formats aimed at the middle- and upper-middle-income customers we had in mind. We quickly ruled out copying the model of fast-food chicken chains such as rapidly growing Kentucky Fried Chicken, later KFC (takeout food); buffet-style steakhouse chains such as Ponderosa and Sizzler (dark settings, poor value for the money, low-quality food); and more stately white-tablecloth settings with a wait staff (too pricey).

Our pilot restaurant would feature cafeteria lines for diners to choose items served by line staff. We opted for stainless steel flatware, clear glassware, and bone china plates (cheaper in the long run than paper, and more distinctive), and a mix of booths with brown vinyl upholstery and butcher-block tables for seating. Capacity would be ninety-five people. With no wait staff, customers would not expect to leave a tip, saving them up to 20 percent for each meal. Our clean-up team, which cleared and cleaned tables, would carry trays from the serving line to tables for anyone who looked like they might appreciate the help.

Curved stairs would give customers easy access to a relaxed dining area on a mezzanine. Lighting would be warmly glowing but not dim; in restaurants, an axiom for good lighting is to avoid shadows on customers' faces. We chose tile flooring for the takeout area and kitchen and carpeting everywhere else. Surfaces would be natural wood.

The design by architect John Van Fossen was clean, tasteful, and fun. He designed an excellent flow inside the restaurant. He liked small tables so diners were better able to hear each other. He created an inviting "come on in" exterior.

Both of us were novices, though, with no experience designing restaurants. We had to figure out how to choreograph each activity for kitchen workers and each anticipated activity for customers in dining areas. How would people actually move in and through these spaces? Were the aisles wide enough? We didn't want people falling into each other.

I was quite concerned about how the kitchen staff would operate efficiently. We wanted a smooth flow in the kitchen as well as dining areas.

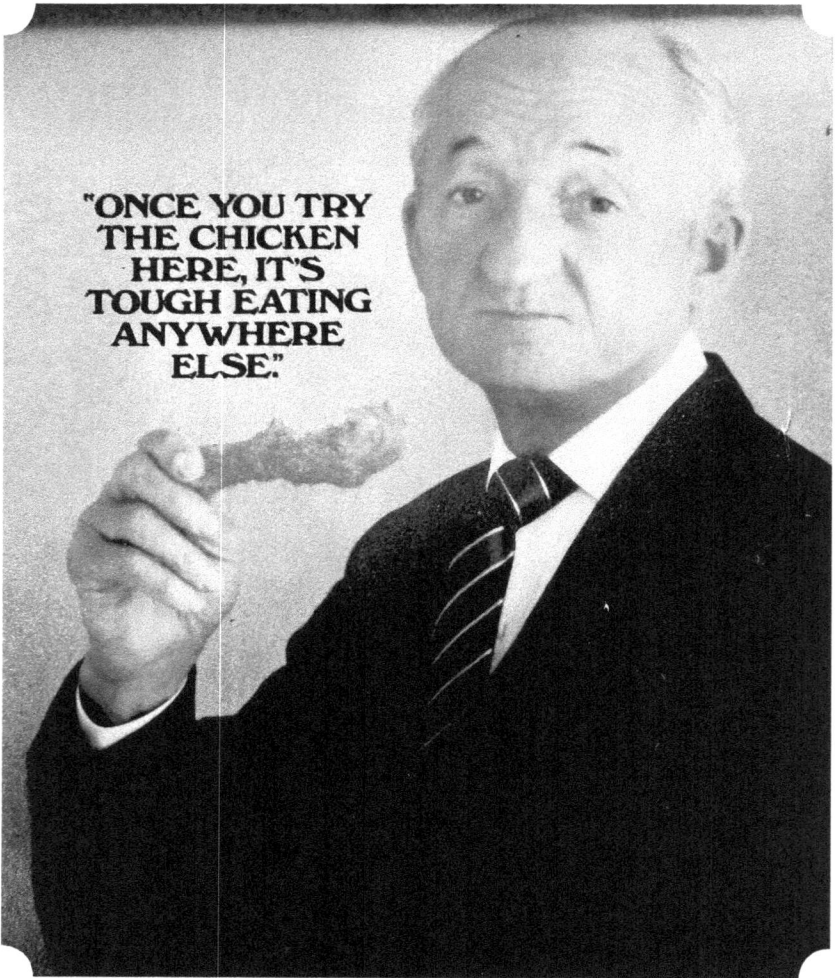

Advertisement for Perdue Chicken Restaurant

On a vacant second floor of an abandoned old industrial building in Salisbury, I methodically went about our work in an open space that roughly matched the area our restaurant would occupy in Queens.

I positioned pieces of plywood to correspond with the dimensions of each piece of equipment planned for the kitchen. I had difficulty visualizing it on paper. I needed to wander around so I could understand how it would work, then relay evolving designs to John in New York City.

Interior of Perdue Chicken Restaurant, 1980

We called it the plywood kitchen. John and I went through every idea. And we finally got it right.

Ed McCabe brought the fun, with several photographs of diners enjoying our food decorating the walls and an eye-catching, nearly two-story, floor-to-ceiling photograph of Frank smiling, about to bite into a drumstick.[12] "Remember," Ed often reminded me, "it's all about the food. That's what brings customers back."

In our analysis, we termed this plan "a 4-dollar restaurant," which was shorthand for the price of a single, top-priced menu meal with beverage. Chicken would be the star of the show.

Two pieces of fried or roasted chicken; a choice of rice pilaf, French fries, and steamed green beans; a biscuit or muffin with honey butter went for $3.29, plus a soft drink at sixty-five cents. (A $4 menu item in

---

[12] On opening day, Frank told me to replace that photo with something else, "I don't like the way I look," he said. He agreed to have Scali, McCabe take new photos (at some considerable expense), then picked one he liked better. It's another example of how Frank had to have everything just perfect. That new blown-up photo went into that same space on the two-story wall in the restaurant.

1980 would be the equivalent of $14.72 in today's inflated dollars.) Our tagline—"Perdue Farm to Perdue Table"—anticipated by two decades one of contemporary foodies' popular catch phrases.

Carol Haltaman and I were a team of two for six months up to opening. With me in charge of designing and executing the concept, meeting with advisers and suppliers in Manhattan or monitoring construction progress onsite in Queens, Carol created appealing menu recipes in Salisbury, judging them in part through group taste-panel reviews, and selected trusted suppliers of seasonings and vegetables.

After the opening, Carol worked weekdays, driving from Salisbury on Sundays and returning on Fridays; I commuted as well to be in the restaurant for the busy weekends and one or two adjacent days, driving home for two days midweek. A tag team of sorts, one or both of us were on location typically from 10:00 a.m., an hour before opening, until after dining room closing at 9:30 p.m. and takeout closing at 10:30 p.m.

We wanted every aspect of the restaurant to be true to the concept and be in synch with the menu. We often solicited comments and ideas from customers and kept a list of improvements for developing the next Perdue restaurant.

CAROL'S INGENIOUS RECIPE INNOVATIONS

Carol had experimented with a variety of recipes for a menu that would make sense for a family-style Perdue cafeteria. We wanted a mix of both traditional and contemporary items: simple, wonderful food made from scratch on site without a chef. In time, four menu items made fresh daily in the kitchen would set us apart: roasted chicken, healthier than fried chicken and ordered by a third of our customers; chicken salad with large pieces cut from fresh chicken breasts; hearty soups; and apple dumpling desserts.

Carol connected with two up-and-coming food experts, both friends of Frank. They were delighted to help, without pay, in part because Frank was such a celebrity. One was Barbara Kafka, a famed culinary author and teaching partner of James Beard, the dean of American cuisine, and later a food columnist for *Family Circle* and *Vogue*. Another was Rosalie Harrington, owner of an eponymous Italian restaurant in Marblehead, Massachusetts, and one of the early stars of the Food Network with her show *Eating Light with Rosalie*.

Kafka pitched in with a chicken soup recipe made from scratch featuring chicken, vegetables, herbs, and spices. The rich broth came from poaching Perdue's big Oven Stuffer chicken breasts for chicken salad.

Harrington eagerly demonstrated several recipes in her Marblehead restaurant and home kitchen for Carol. And it was Harrington who encouraged us to offer a rotating menu of special dishes on weekdays. These special dishes became extremely popular, items such as chicken and spinach crepes.

Aside from the specials, we limited entrée options to ten menu items, plus beverages and desserts, in part to keep kitchen operations simpler and to keep lines shorter and moving faster so diners could select their food quickly and, with two cashiers at the end of the cafeteria line, get to their seats faster. (Some cafeterias offered over forty items, with one cashier.)

Carol experimented with a variety of recipes, making large batches in a kitchen we rented after discovering it had been idled when a local restaurant closed on a rural road near Salisbury. She assembled a group of friends and friends of friends in the dining area for taste panels to sample most everything and comment.

We also attended several food shows to meet suppliers of specific ingredients we were experimenting with. For everything we would soon serve, each Perdue chicken item had to be unfailingly well-prepared, tasty, and popular. For example, after sampling breading for fried chicken, we picked one favored by the Roy Rogers fast-food chain.

To serve chicken as fresh and moist as possible, we separated a whole chicken into breasts, thighs, drumsticks, and wings to minimize drip loss before we battered and lightly breaded the chicken and put it in the fryer. To give wings more meat, we customized the cut to include a big chunk of breast meat so the value would be close to the other three parts.

Customers were willing to buy all four chicken parts; that meant fewer unsold parts for us.

MIMI SHERATON IN SALISBURY

Mimi Sheraton, the widely read *New York Times* restaurant critic, was intrigued when she heard Frank Perdue was about to extend the high-profile brand of Perdue chickens into the restaurant business. (More often, the path was reversed, with restaurateurs taking prized menu items such as soups and sauces and marketing them in grocery stores.)

At her initiative, and with Frank's eager welcome, Sheraton came to Salisbury for interviews and to sample menu items in Carol's test kitchen.

"There is bound to be a struggle when a company wants to run inexpensive restaurants and still retail a quality image," I said, explaining our strategy to her. "We don't want people to think this is a $3 or a $5 restaurant. We want it to be comfortable, but not too comfortable." Meaning chairs without arms and no place for hanging coats or placing packages.

In her *Times* article, "Perdue Chickens to Test Their Appeal in Restaurant Market,"[13] I added more about how our plans had evolved. "A $3 restaurant would have lots of plastic, paper plates, no carpet, very bright lighting that is probably fluorescent, and big glass windows that go from floor to ceiling so people feel secure eating there because they see others doing so. A $5 restaurant would have cloth napkins, much less glass, and something approaching table service—say a hostess serving second cups of coffee—and the lighting would be dimmer."

Chunky chicken salad, combining Hellman's mayonnaise with those large pieces from Oven Stuffer breasts, was one of the biggest hits. Mimi Sheraton gave it two thumbs up.

Shortly before we opened, she wrote, "Chicken salad, with large chunks of white breast meat from Perdue roasters, fresh celery and

---

[13] Mimi Sheraton, "Perdue Chickens to Test Their Appeal in Restaurant Market," *The New York Times*, Wednesday, September 17, 1980, C9.

Hellman's mayonnaise, would be good enough to draw at least one enthusiast from Manhattan to Queens, either for the version in the hard-to-handle but hearty pita bread or the one on a plate with salad and corn muffin, a far better bread choice than the inside soft white biscuit."

For our chicken menu items, we sought to exploit every competitive advantage and brand promise. As noted earlier, Perdue trucks delivered whole chickens to us straight from Perdue processing plants. Chicken for the salad was cut by hand exclusively from chicken breasts, no other chicken parts.

TAKING THE CRITIC'S REVIEW TO HEART

We took great advantage of Sheraton's published assessments of what was not working for menu options she sampled on her Salisbury visit, improving or scrapping items she disliked and proudly staying with dishes she praised.

Sheraton indicated strongly in her review that we would succeed in our goal to deliver on the Perdue reputation for high-quality, tender, affordably priced chicken. "Freshly fried and roasted chicken were admirable both for quality and quantity given the modest price tags," she concluded.

Noting that "recipes are still being worked on," she asserted she was not impressed by those early recipes for soups, salad dressings, and pre-seasoned chicken pilaf rice. The chicken Italiano recipe, she gasped, was "the biggest disaster," and added that the strawberry shortcake would be improved if we offered it "with real whipped cream instead of topping."

We took these criticisms to heart, gladly making midcourse corrections soon after her article was published. For example, that chicken Italiano dish never appeared in Queens; real whip whipped cream on strawberry shortcake did. And more.

For desserts, we kept our options close to home, focusing on traditional recipes of Maryland's eastern shore. What is more American than apple dumplings?

A mixture of cinnamon, margarine, and other ingredients for the bottom of the pan (before the apples were baked) became the cinnamon sauce poured over the dumplings. Carol recalls, "On each apple, we put cinnamon and a little margarine into the cavities. The pie crust was put over and folded around the apples; then we brushed them with some butter and egg wash and ran them through the conveyor oven. Simple, simple."

THE OPENING

When we opened, our business partners in creating this new dining experience and customers were complimentary. "It's beautiful, just the kind of restaurant Frank Perdue would open." "It's a great match with the Perdue quality image." "It has a fast and efficient food delivery system and a health-oriented menu with enough variety to keep diners coming back."

Restaurant team: Terry, Carol Haltaman, Bruce Petkovic, 1980

We soon corrected aspects we'd overlooked at first: Fryers were changed from electricity to natural gas. We added a second trash container by the exit door, switched toilets to flush valves, and added a cup warmer to keep coffee hot.

Frank came to the restaurant regularly when he was in New York City on business, usually once a week, for lunch or dinner. He never said a word about anything he wanted changed or anything he liked, a silence we interpreted as a ringing endorsement.

The Mimi Sheraton review was gratifying for Carol and me personally. Within another decade, the origins of popular "fast casual" chains such as Panera Bread (1987) and Chipotle Mexican Grill (1993) would strike me as a significant validation of our design. Whether by intent or coincidence, both adopted some key elements we introduced on Queens Boulevard: Panera Bread, hot food, no waiters; Chipotle, hot food, cafeteria line. They now operate thousands of locations.

The Perdue Chicken Restaurant was profitable and on track to meet our financial projections after six months—food costs as a percentage of sales, staff, and sales volume. The concept was gaining traction, with big crowds on Fridays, Saturdays, and Sundays.

Within days after the opening, I began sketching plans for a smaller format—the same Queens Boulevard concept with most of the same food—and build the business.

FADEOUT

But any enthusiasm I hoped to sense from Frank for expanding to new locations, and me shifting back to an executive role after more than two years on the front lines of food service, was not evident. He seemed uncomfortable with any details that he was unable to personally evaluate and master.

When his friends in the restaurant business peppered him with questions such as, "Why do you use fresh strawberries and fresh whipped cream in your desserts—isn't that too expensive?" his limited knowledge was no match for his encyclopedic command of the chicken business.

If Frank Perdue was uncomfortable with being in the restaurant business, what might that portend for me?

CARRY FORWARD LESSONS FROM FRANK

Looking back, the Perdue experience was incredible—dedicated leadership, prospering in a highly competitive and growing commodity business, and rapid personal development. The experience reminded me of my father's advice years earlier: "Plan your career around working for great people and work experiences. You'll need to know how to solve business problems, how to work with people at all levels, how to manage risks, and how to compete with established enterprises."

Perdue was my first deep experience with an integrated business—from farming to processing to the final consumer. As CFO I was in the middle of over a thousand gnarly problems to help solve within Perdue's principles and Frank's guidance. Each was a learning experience, and cumulatively, they were a superb education on how to make an integrated business work.

Frank Perdue had a unique leadership style that I'd never seen before. First, he led his company to the next level with more passion and attention to detail than I have ever seen. Nothing was delegated, and no detail was overlooked.

Second, Frank was in the marketplace more often than any other CEO I'd ever seen. He'd visit with retail shoppers, merchandise managers, buyers, and the customers' leadership teams to find innovations and ways to stay ahead of competitors.

Third, Frank trusted his leadership team, gave us ample room to explore and make mistakes, and listened. We were self-motivated. I carried these lessons into my own business.

Frank's business principles were similar to most others, but the details were unique, especially Frank's leadership style as he began, redirected, and summarized projects that brought his principles to life. I eventually carried forward each of Perdue's principles to Handy, with the details adapted to a wild-caught seafood business. I benefited from Frank's wisdom.

"Make Perdue the most profitable company in our industry. There's no glory in being the biggest," Frank would say to keep all eyes on cost. And he would sometimes add, "Build our walls thicker and taller," which we interpreted as keep growing.

Frank was most passionate about being a low-cost producer. In a high-volume commodity business that was heavily competitive, every 1/10 of a cent per pound made a difference over millions of pounds. "Be prepared to defend every cost increase," Frank said almost daily. "And know both sides of every story."

"Be the best in our industry at everything you do" was Frank's daily challenge. The leadership team clearly understood the message: Be very thorough, know our competitors, and make Frank proud. Decision-making became clear: Don't quit until you've found the best alternative and be prepared to defend it.

Frank believed and often remarked that "thoroughness was next to godliness," and he took charge with his trademark thoroughness when an opportunity presented itself, whether it was selecting an advertising firm or a public relations consultant or hiring a member of his leadership team.

Like my father, Frank placed trust above all else. Perdue was all about trust and building trust throughout the company. "You start with trustworthy people," he would say. Frank also reminded us: Consumers are very smart. They'll find any shortcut or quality slippage. I know because I read the letters, usually at night, from consumers who write asking for payment on our money-back guarantee.

"I work on building relationships with our customers. They tell me what my competitors are doing better than me. That bothers me, and I react quickly, sometimes placing calls in the middle of the night when I'm working late."

Frank also liked to say, "Business is really simple—numbers and competitors tell you what to do. Measure everything. I want to know the moment something slips." He listened intently to consumers and took every opportunity to improve. The management team understood that product quality was a continuous process. "I need better quality. It gives me a competitive advantage," Frank would say, and, "I like premium prices."

Frank took risks. "I'll spend money on any innovation that saves money. I'll also do whatever it takes to improve quality. I'll hire talented leaders before they're necessary." But I never saw him take an ego-based risk. I carried that lesson with me into my own business.

He also invested in people. Frank personally recruited his management team and checked their references. "I need to know their weak spots, and if they're trustworthy," he would say. "If the leadership team is effective, they will hire good managers."

"Humility moves the finish line closer. Arrogance stops the race" was another of Frank's truisms.

"Free-flowing collaboration is all-important. We don't have or want organization charts—their boundaries are too restrictive; we need everyone's input" were messages Frank delivered frequently.

Another saying that no one on the leadership team ever understood was "talk is cheap."

EASY TO WORK FOR?

I've surprised people when I've said, "Frank was the easiest person I've ever worked for." He did not have that reputation. I understood Frank had to be the best at everything about his business. He would say that those outside his business must be as good at their profession as Perdue is in its. So I had to have the best financial department, the most impressive staff, and the most highly regarded banks, accountants, and attorneys. Decision-making was easy. Implementation was challenging at times.

Around town my friends and curiosity seekers would ask, "I hear Frank calls his people in the middle of the night. Did he ever call you?" "Yes," I would reply. "It was usually about nothing, like there's a light on in the attic," I would reply. "While I have you on the line, Frank, may I ask your opinion on my projects?"

One call was memorable. He had recently spoken to his longtime, most trusted friend, Henry Saglio. Henry was an accomplished poultry breeder who often preached that he could operate any business with just a yellow pad. Henry had no use for office people and could get Frank riled up with his comment to Frank "they're just overhead." So Frank's call that night was "cut the cables on all computers! They're a waste of money. No discussion. Just do it." I saw Frank the next morning in the hallway and mentioned that I'd need to hire twenty people for payroll and preparing invoices, and before that, I should get started on an office expansion. Frank just walked away. It was the last of the middle-of-the-night calls.

TEN

FIRST-TIME BUSINESS OWNER, AGE FORTY-ONE

Following my experience at Perdue, the next step in a classic career progression for a finance executive would be running a multibillion-dollar corporate finance department and being short-listed by recruiters for a Fortune 500 CEO position years later. I didn't have to wait long before I had an offer to do just that.

This recruiting package from a New York Stock Exchange-listed company in Chicago carried a well-timed increase in compensation—salary, benefits, and stock options. With five children, the first three of four sons in boarding school in Rhode Island and the younger son and a daughter still at home in eastern Maryland, and a mortgage, my wife Susan and I agreed: This was our best path forward.

I should have felt more enthusiastic or at least relieved after making the decision to accept the offer. Oddly, resignation was more like it. From my teenage years sitting at the kitchen table with my father and hearing him discuss the businesspeople he advocated for and the issues he championed, I had internalized a visceral admiration for business owners and a dream of one day owning and building my own company.

WHEN AM I GOING TO DO THIS?

That vision to be an entrepreneur might have wavered over the years, but it never faded. In those last months at Perdue, I kept asking myself,

Now I'm forty. If I am going to do this, when am I going to do it? I did look at opportunities to buy a business, but there was no time off to travel, and aside from one California agribusiness specializing in prunes, nothing really appealed.

Months after I accepted the Chicago offer, I was still commuting each week from our home in Salisbury as negotiations over relocation payments and other matters dragged on. Susan continued directing tennis programs at the local Y near where we lived, and one day she introduced me to a business broker she knew casually. He tried to interest me in a small company situated less than an hour's drive away that had been operating under family control since the 1890s.

Handy Seafood, with $2 million in annual sales, processed and shipped soft crabs, a seafood delicacy, to food distributors and restaurants as distant as Boston to the north and New Orleans to the south.

The owners wanted to retire. Handy had been on the market for more than two years without attracting serious offers. I didn't give it much thought. Then, over Labor Day weekend, I decided to visit the five-acre Handy site. The setting was idyllic, near the southern tip of Chesapeake Bay's east peninsula, the Delmarva Peninsula, with a panoramic view of the Big Annemessex River.

The plant itself wasn't much, a tired concrete-block building with an open workspace. Better than ramshackle but light years from the epitome of corporate polish and energy that I once enjoyed on Park Avenue. Built in 1912, an era when Crisfield was Maryland's second-largest city after Baltimore[14] and known more as an oyster producer than what it was now, the self-proclaimed "Blue Crab Capital of the World," the Handy site looked sleepy. Not much had changed over the years.

It was hot, with doors open, when I walked in. No air conditioning and only one toilet for eighty workers, including office staff. I saw only one

---

[14] Fueled by the expanding seafood industry, Crisfield's population rose to more than 25,000 in the twentieth century's first decade. The town had billed itself as "The Seafood Capital of the World" since the late 1800s.

telephone in the owners' cramped office. The lead partner, Stanley Sterling, told me that this one handset was all he needed for calls with customers. "I can only talk to one person at a time." He definitely was eager to retire.

I might have quickly discarded the notion of buying Handy that day, but as weeks passed, two ideas kept me thinking. One was a delightful family memory from a decade before. We Conways, all seven of us, discovered soft crab dining at a waterfront restaurant in this little town of 2,700 people. That festive outing happened not long after we moved from Connecticut's New York suburbs, less than an hour from Midtown Manhattan, to the more tranquil eastern Chesapeake region where Perdue Farms was based.

I'd never tasted such wonderful food! We ordered sandwiches, soft crabs sautéed and served between two slices of white bread. (I would have preferred a bun, but it didn't matter.) The sweet, delicate taste was captivating. Next came handmade pan-fried crab cakes with loads of pasteurized fresh white meat from a picking house a half block away and other ingredients—breadcrumbs, mustard, mayonnaise, and Old Bay red powder seasoning—from the local grocery store.

In an adjoining room, we saw what the manager described as a "crab feast:" a group of old friends loudly conversing as they picked meat with pairing knives and small wooden mallets from a pile of freshly steamed hard crabs. Their table was covered with old newspapers. I made a mental note: dining on crabmeat picked from steamed hard crabs must be a tradition deeply celebrated along the Chesapeake. What's not to like?

The second idea was triggered by something odd that Sterling mentioned as we walked around the property. "The brackish waters around Crisfield in Chesapeake Bay are the only known source in the world for these soft crabs," he asserted. *That doesn't make sense*, I thought.

WIDESPREAD BRACKISH WATERS

Yes, Chesapeake Bay is the largest estuary in the United States, yet brackish waters occur anywhere in the world where freshwater flows into salty seawaters. Chesapeake crabs hibernate during the cold winter months, and as the water warms up they molt, or shed their outer shells, as they grow. It is during the four to six hours after shedding the outer shell and before a new shell grows and begins to harden that soft crabs are harvested and marketed as the "best-tasting product from the sea."

Was I looking at a major untapped opportunity to expand its crab supply capacities, upgrade Crisfield's management and processing technology, and promote this market-leading brand more broadly around the world?

A little research quickly confirmed this. Crab species have variations, more than six thousand. I had a lot to learn about crab harvesting, but here are the highlights from my first visit to Handy.

Blue crabs are most common when waters are warm along the coastline of the western Atlantic Ocean, from Nova Scotia to South America, and have prospered for centuries as part of Chesapeake Bay marine life. The Bay's blue crab population at the time was more than eight hundred million, with nearly ninety million pounds harvested annually.

The average lifespan of males and females is three years. Females molt eighteen times as they grow. They produce a huge volume of eggs, two million, during their terminal molt. This lifecycle was being repeated in thousands of natural habitats.

The business of processing crabs, as Sterling explained that morning, had some similarities to the poultry business I'd been immersed in for ten years with Perdue Farms, such as plant operations and cleanliness, food safety, relationships with providers of live animals (caught wild in the case of crabs, not chickens raised on farms) and distributor-suppliers.

I began to think about international processing: Soft crabs need brackish water. No doubt there are other countries where fresh mountain water mixes with saltwater from the sea. And there must be markets for these delicious crab products that I had tasted in Crisfield. Was processing possible in other countries, and are there foreign markets?

BUILDING A BUSINESS MAKES
COMMUNITIES STRONGER

In time, I came to develop several strong beliefs about the huge impact you can make in your own life and your community's vitality when you own and build your own business.

You create income-generating jobs and a safe, collegial workplace for your associates that make them proud and happy.

You support and encourage their dreams to develop talents in a direction and pace that suits them.

You strengthen your community . . . expanding operations, paying taxes, and advocating for good government.

You build family wealth and traditions that can bind generations to a common cause no matter how widely their chosen careers may vary.

You never have a boring day. Challenges expected, unexpected, and confounding appear all the time. You can't overcome them all but a high percentage must be managed to favorable outcomes. Above all, you never stop meeting people from all walks of life and learning new things.

As I began a look at Handy, I recalled that success depended on understanding what appealed most to customers and innovating continuously to differentiate my product and service from competitors. The success formula that first came to mind toward the end of my studies at Notre Dame applies everywhere: *increasingly superior products, processed at a competitive advantage, and generate leads for sales to close.*

FIRST IMPRESSIONS, HISTORY, FINANCIALS

Sterling and his co-owner, John T. Handy Jr., didn't express much enthusiasm about my interest or background that first day.

The broker told me before my Labor Day weekend visit that they had just cut their asking price in half. My immediate thought:

Why? What's going wrong here? Were they inattentive owners, letting the fundamentals of business deteriorate? I needn't have worried.

Sterling said the company had become focused solely on soft crabs long ago after a disease decimated oyster fisheries and Handy's other business (canning tomatoes) had failed. By 1917, Handy developed a way to keep crabs alive for two days while being shipped by truck to new markets in Philadelphia and New York. After World War II, the company improved its freezing process and began shipping to major cities across the country via truck and rail.

One of my strongest and most favorable impressions of Sterling and Handy Jr. was that as second-generation owners, they valued and took pride in this company, which their fathers had created.

The enterprise that they inherited from their parents remained the market leader by size and reputation. My contacts in food service said when I asked for candid assessments that trust and quality were Handy's hallmarks. "Handy is the go-to brand for soft crabs," several told me. What excited me most was their same enthusiasm for the food that had stayed with me since our family's first meal in Crisfield. "Soft crabs are a delicacy to be savored."

Sterling had assured me his company was trusted by all its key constituent groups: watermen who catch the crabs, a reliable cadre of eighty employees from the same extended families, distributor-customers, and final customers—food service operators who valued Handy's reputation for consistently reliable products.

Short-changing watermen on pay was common practice among Handy's six competitors, but it was ethically wrong and bad for business, he said. His reputation for trust in transactions with watermen meant he had access to more crabs than competitors. He also told me during our first conversation that he didn't pursue new customers because he was content working with current ones. With Handy's stable customer base, *he made money on every crab the company processed.* All this had me thinking: potential to add more customers; potential to buy, process, and sell more crabs profitably.

Sterling added that most competitors erred—again, ethically and as a business practice—by putting smaller crabs at the bottom of boxes marked as the largest-sized, or jumbo, crabs. He didn't. "A box of Handy jumbos is 100 percent jumbos. I don't throw little crabs at the bottom. Sometimes I lose out because my price is a little higher, maybe ten cents a dozen. But that's the way I run the business. I'm a trusted person. I want Handy to be trusted."

The company had no debt, which meant that if I became the new owner, I wouldn't be inheriting any bank loans. Annual sales were $2 million, stable but not growing. Sterling and Handy Jr. had not made and did not offer plans to expand the business. They had no vision for growth. This gave me pause. Yet the company appeared to be consistently profitable. Shareholder distributions—owners' take-home pay—in recent years was steady at $200,000.

That was impressive: a business with no debt netting 10 percent of sales for owners. In my case, that would be singular: "owner." Two hundred thousand was twice my annual income with Perdue. That would be enough to cover those hefty private school tuition and mortgage bills and would be comfortably sufficient for me to entice bankers to help fund working capital investments I knew would be necessary if I did buy the company.

In the plant, as I walked around, employees in hairnets and with rubber gloves responded pleasantly to my questions. The atmosphere was more than workmanlike. They rhapsodized about Handy's quality and the details of their craft. These folks were cheerful; I learned later that over half were related, going back one to three generations. Most lived in the area; some lived close enough to walk to and from work.

I AM GOING TO DO THIS.

I didn't hear much from the broker until that December. One day he called, saying Sterling and Handy Jr. were prepared to work out a deal for the sale.

Once again I analyzed the fundamental business case for why I should or should not do this.

Did Handy fit the acquisition criteria I'd developed for clients at Laird? Were there solid products with wide appeal, opportunities to grow the top line *and* the bottom line? Crab harvesting levels were in the lap of the weather gods, depending on Mother Nature. Market appeal was high but seasonal and narrow.

Was the competitive profile sound, with supporting supply-demand economics? The economics were acceptable, not great.

Was the management team talented and dedicated to a long-term vision for growth? No. Sterling and Handy Jr. would be retiring. But Sterling was willing to help me learn the business and advise me for at least a year.

I had asked myself over and over since that first site visit: Can I be a success in a seasonal, one-product company with its fortunes tied to unpredictable whims of nature, uncertain loyalties of watermen, continually shifting market dynamics and competitive forces, and occasional political obstacles?

I had never run a plant. I had never sold anything.

On the other hand, I could avoid outside investors and own 100 percent of the voting stock. As long as I stayed within a bank's boundaries, I would have an incredible amount of control. I could focus on the long term without anyone questioning my decisions. I might someday pass ownership to our five children when I chose to become less active.

There was no room for error. If I went ahead, I would be paying $500,000 for the business, funds accumulated from cashing in a decade's worth of my hard-earned Perdue stock options, and likely would need that much more from banks for working capital and to renovate the plant within a year or two.

But I knew that the timing for me was good—and maybe would never be better. I had these funds. I had the family commitment to do this. I had the experience and professional skills. I had ambition. I visualized the company growing and making money on every crab sold. *I am now forty-one*, I told myself. *I am going to do this.*

Just before the end of 1981, we signed the papers.

I knew I was taking a leap into a very different world. Improbable just a few months before, I was in business for myself! A dream that had begun twenty-seven years earlier at age fifteen.

ELEVEN

DANCES WITH WATERMEN

During my first summer as Handy's owner, I gradually realized that I was making a personal connection with a family way of life on the shores of the Chesapeake—the watermen's way of life. I hadn't expected this, a purpose that over time I came to appreciate as gratifying, even uplifting.

Handy was not a company that made shoes or boots or pliers or hammers. It played a vital role in preserving a mainstay of Maryland's eastern shore culture, providing a dependable source of income that watermen needed to continue a way of life that for some families extended several generations to the eighteenth century.

While Handy at the time was the largest soft crab processor and marketer in the area, we would make the business into much more of a commercial force, expanding and deepening Handy's partnership with the watermen.

Depending on weather, soft crab season most years runs from mid-April into October when crabs are active, moving with the tides and foraging on smaller marine life. During the winter, when crabs descend to warmer depths, most digging into the seabed seeking safety and warmth, most watermen shift to the far chillier but less demanding physical work of harvesting oysters.

WALKING THE DOCKS, BUILDING TRUST

It wasn't until that April that I made my first attempts to persuade water-men in the region around Crisfield and those anchored at one of three islands less than ten miles to the west—Tangier, Smith, and Deal—that I would continue Handy's reputation for fair dealings.

Watermen are always looking for more than one buyer. Walking around the docks and stores, I introduced myself: "Hi, I'm Terry from Handy." If I learned they had been a supplier for Handy the past sea-son, I thanked them, adding that I looked forward to another great year. If not, I asked, "Give us a try and see what you think." They were friendly. One invited me to his home for a piece of his wife's strawberry pie.

One day before my first season with Handy began, one of the most respected and experienced watermen, Eddie Brimer, came to see me. He was towering, nearly a foot taller than me at six feet, six inches, yet pleasant, level-headed, and respectful. He was a third-generation water-man, and some of his phrasings in an Old English inflection reminded me of Chaucer: "you know not."

He told me he was on a mission for his fellow watermen to deter-mine if "the Chicken Man," as they had taken to calling me, anticipated making any changes in Handy's dealings with them. I was the stranger, an unknown quantity, and the outsider with a history in the poultry busi-ness up the road at Perdue Farms but a blank slate to crabbers like Eddie.

"Tell you what's important to us: that we always have a place to sell our crabs." I knew immediately that I had to convey trust.

"That's our plan, Eddie. You'll see when the crabs start coming. We'll buy every crab you bring us. I know we'll be looking for more crabbers this year. We are financially stable. We appear to have more customers— and enough workers, with more applicants for jobs than last year. The plant is able to handle your catch. Stanley Sterling will still be on the premises, teaching me and to ensure that nothing has changed."

Months before, Stanley had told me two things about working effec-tively with watermen. First, you buy whatever they catch no matter what.

If a waterman arrives at your gate with two trucks loaded with thousands of crabs, you will buy. Second, watermen need to have confidence that you will pay them a fair price, week in and week out, compared to what the New York fish market pays for crabs shipped on consignment. Stanley further related that most seafood buyers in the area are unreliable and inconsistent. Some often shortchanged watermen by downgrading their crabs' classification. Those deceptions are costly. Watermen know that downgrading leads to disputes and lack of trust. There are five traditional sixes measured from end points of the crab's outer shell.[15] Each separated by only one-half an inch, the five sizes are known as Mediums (the smallest legal size), Hotels, Primes, Jumbos, and Whales.

As the new owner, I needed to look each of my soft crab suppliers and prospective suppliers in the eye. The watermen didn't want me to be their friend. In fact, they rarely initiated eye contact. As Stanley advised, they just wanted to be respected. Treated fairly. Paid on time.

The respect was there, yet we weren't surprised from time to time when some watermen tested us because, as I learned, not trusting buyers was part of a waterman's DNA, or certainly part of their experience with less-than-honorable buyers along the Chesapeake.

For me during that first year, the test discussion might go something like this:

"You know, I sent you forty boxes and you only paid me for thirty-nine."

"Well, I guess that might happen in the chaos of the summer. Our record-keeping is tight, but I'll tell you what. I will pay for that box based on what you had in the other boxes. If it happens again, we will sit down and talk about it."

Whether or not I had miscounted was not the point. This was an opportunity. That one unrehearsed response, perhaps once a month, went a long way in building trust. In this case, the waterman spread the word (that I would honor his request, this time) all along the shore that I was reasonable. Watermen talk to each other a lot on their radios.

---

[15] A once-common practice known as point-to-point measuring.

On the other hand, I knew to avoid the image of an easy mark. If watermen gave us crabs that became too hard after molting, I had nowhere to sell them and could not be expected to pay for them.

We always bought and paid for every crab watermen brought to our docks. And we defended their way of life. We did all that beautifully, in my opinion.

When state regulators blamed watermen for overfishing, which was not true, we fought back hard for them. When the town of Crisfield threatened to shut down dozens of them, and a Maryland governor backed a new boat-painting business that would endanger the livelihood of dozens more, we helped fight off these politically motivated schemes.

Within three years after I arrived as owner, we had doubled the ranks of watermen supplying us crabs in Crisfield to about eighty.[16] They came to us from as far away as seventy miles.

A DAY IN THE LIFE OF EDDIE DANIELS, WATERMAN

I knew little of the watermen's demanding daily routines until I read a classic book on Chesapeake Bay crab fishing that had won a Pulitzer Prize: *Beautiful Swimmers: Watermen, Crabs, and the Chesapeake Bay*, by anthropologist William W. Warner.

In the introduction, novelist John Barth, a celebrated National Book Award winner who featured scenes and characters set in Chesapeake Bay in his works, expressed what I would come to appreciate as an indispensable part of Handy's success. "But for the strong work ethic of Chesapeake watermen," he wrote, "this most delectable form of crab would have never come to market."

Another imposing waterman named Eddie, Eddie Daniels, at six feet, three inches tall and 260 pounds, still had the strength, stamina, and desire

---

[16] Total annual weight of blue crab "landings," or watermen's catch, has declined in Maryland and Virginia by nearly two-thirds since I bought Handy. Landings in 2022 amounted to 32 million pounds, down from 88 million in 1982.

at age sixty to work out on the water six long days each week. What follows describes what those long days then demanded of Eddie.

Up by 4:00 a.m. to sort and retrieve soft crabs from his shanty that had recently molted, he sorted them by point-to-point sizing before hauling them to Handy's dock a half block away. By daybreak he was out in his workboat, rain or shine, unless the radio forecast warned of winds above twenty miles an hour. He wanted to see at first light which kind of crabs—hard, "peeler," soft, and, occasionally, dead—and how many have been lured overnight into his small wire-mesh baskets, or "pots."

Years ago, watermen hoisted their pots, averaging ten pounds each, manually. This routine, repeated relentlessly for hours, required a strong upper body and lower back. Eddie couldn't count the number of pulled muscles he'd endured since he first went crabbing, steering a little skiff fifty years earlier when he was nine as his grandfather and father hauled up the pots.

"You try to work through it, work every day, because when your back is gone, you are gone," he said. "If you don't work every day, with more crabs in the pots, they'll chew each other and the death rate rises. You try to get them every day."

Bending over the sides of their low-slung skiffs or work boats, a waterman would lift between three hundred and nine hundred pots in the same day. (Pot count depended on each waterman's license limits.) That backbreaking work for most eased immeasurably after they installed faster and safer hydraulic winders before the millennium to raise the pots.

With the morning haul on board quickly, usually by 10:00 a.m., Eddie culled through everything for another two hours, sorting by size and examining back paddle fins to gauge how close each crab was to molting.

A thin white line on the paddle fin signals that the crab will shed its shell and become a soft crab within three or four days. A pink or red is a sign that molting is closer. I've never seen another crab species that gives a signal for natural molting. It's remarkably rare.

Paddle fin colors are difficult to see. Eddie waited for morning light before pulling and checking the overnight catch in his pots.

On a good day, Eddie harvested three hundred peeler crabs, usually from his favored habitat sites just east of Crisfield along Pocomoke Sound. He delivered them by early afternoon to a shanty that we reserved for him on our property, placing them by hand into twenty-eight molting tanks with circulating bay water known colloquially as "floats"— elongated, open plywood boxes four feet wide and eight feet long.

Crabs are cannibalistic by nature; if peelers with white and red fin markers are mixed in the same box, the whites will bite and kill the softer ones. This is why Eddie separated white-line crabs into one box and red-line crabs into another: to prevent hard crabs from eating defenseless molting soft crabs. Peeler crabs themselves have to be pulled from the bay before molting, or larger fish will devour them as soon as they turn soft.

Within moments after molting begins, crabs begin growing a new hard shell and become inedible if they are not fished out by hand and kept alive in 50-degree coolers.

Eddie inspected his Handy tanks for new molters and shells that had shed every afternoon, each night after dinner, and again in early morning before heading out on his boat. Crabs absorb calcium from water, which causes them to harden if you don't retrieve new molters quickly.

In months when the molting cycle quickened, Eddie's wife Debra added another check-in after midnight and again late mornings while he was still out on the water or taking a nap after lunch. Crabs in molting boxes have to be checked for molting at least every four to six hours.

"It takes a family" should be a waterman's refrain. I've known watermen whose wives, aunts, older children, and even close friends check each day for newly molting soft crabs at any hours when the watermen are either asleep or on their boats. Oblivious at first to these family bonds, I came to appreciate them as admirable, laudable, and even inspiring.

This is tedious, essential work. I was fascinated to become so closely linked with it and at times to help defend it. There were no off days for watermen and their family team in pulling freshly molted soft crabs from the shanty floats. Nature unfolds at its own pace.

After sorting soft crabs by size, watermen packed them into waxed cardboard trays for delivery to Handy's dock. We put them quickly into a large cooler at 50 degrees until the processing began.

Eddie, a preacher in his community church, observed the Sunday Sabbath—no crabbing on the waters for him on Sundays.

CELEBRATING WATERMEN AND OUR PARTNERSHIP

After our first crabbing season, we began hosting an annual dinner for watermen every winter in Crisfield's American Legion hall to celebrate our work together over the past season: Fried chicken. Roast beef. And a shucker for fresh oysters. For dessert, another local specialty, the nine-layer Smith Island cake. This was our way of thanking them for their hard work.

Spouses came as well to our delight; after all, they managed the floats while the waterman was in his boat. It was a happy occasion. "I'm delighted to share this feast, with all this food," I'd tell them. Then, pointing to a graph showing how many crabs Handy had purchased compared to prior seasons, I'd add with a smile, "But now you've got to listen to me for two minutes."

We gave individual awards to our three top harvesters in Crisfield and from the three local islands, Tangier, Deal, and Smith. People appreciate it when their contributions are recognized, and these watermen were proud to come up to receive their awards.

We still do this every year.

TWELVE

EXHAUSTING IMPERATIVES TO COMPETE

I must have looked a bit stunned to the Handy employees who greeted me in our plant after the first crabs of the 1982 season arrived on May 15.

Staring at this box of delicate live animals, I was lost in thought. Scared even. Nothing in my career so far had prepared me to face the living animals squirming, not my work at Perdue, certainly not my time on Wall Street. Had I bitten off more than I could chew? My workers here in the plant, not to mention the watermen, were counting on me to grade by size and pay a fair price, and I'm sure the anxiety was written all over my face. *I'm the owner now—these people are expecting leadership and guidance, and I have nothing to offer.*

I knew I had to follow Eddie Brimer's advice. "Treat all watermen exactly the same. No favorites or special consideration. And always pay a fair price every day for a waterman's total catch."

Four of the most experienced employees quickly put me at ease, telling me not to worry. They would get the processing underway just as they had done as the crabbing season ended the previous fall. What a relief.

A week before, I had emphasized in my first remarks to rally them as a group that my highest priority was to continue Handy's reputation as the most trusted company in the soft crab industry, the brass ring of excellence that some long-timers I was addressing had helped burnish personally for more than three decades.

Aiming to assure and motivate them with my vision for the business, I underscored that we had real opportunities to grow in several ways.

I was convinced from my prior experience that the best way for anyone to build a business for long-term, steady growth is with consistent, trustworthy products aimed at the repeat buyer. For Handy, I said, this would be our true north and our core foundation.

We would add new products, widen our geographic reach, and outpace competitors in developing new lower-cost methods through our production and distribution. Our basic principles would be:

- Continuously develop superior products that consumers find tasty, affordable, and safe,
- Process those products at a competitive advantage, and
- Generate leads for sales to close.

These three principles were simple—and essential to operate any business. Something that I had figured out during college but never had the opportunity to implement.

Privately, during those long first days in the plant, I kept thinking: *I hope this company makes enough money for me to improve these hot, cramped facilities.*

It was clear the previous owners had invested enough to keep operations going, make the business work, put out a high-quality product, and not try to pull the wool over anybody's eyes. Those last two characteristics were unusual in the seafood industry, and why Handy's reputation for quality was strong. This company had been in business since 1894, longer than any of its competitors.

GROWTH AS DESTINY

My ambition that first day was to go further, to introduce a variety of crab foods to people who had never enjoyed the sweet taste before, beyond the Mid-Atlantic region to the Gulf and West coasts, to Japan, Europe, and more countries. I was convinced Stanley Sterling was not exaggerating when he said he made a profit on every crab he processed and sold. As a business, growth should be, and would be, our destiny.

To achieve this vision, I had to fix two glaring production problems—inconsistent sizing of crabs and high levels of spoilage caused by poor freezing methods. I had to figure out how to solve those two problems with better technology and equipment. That wouldn't happen for another two years.

In these first months, I spent much of the day outside my small office, walking around the plant, being visible, learning names, and making

Soft crab plant in Crisfield, Maryland, 1982

mental notes about quick fixes I should make—opportunities that management gurus emphasize as picking low-hanging fruit.

Some watermen lived miles away from Crisfield, so they relied on carrier boats to deliver their crab catch to the town dock, a convenient location for us. The dock was only half a mile from the plant where we placed crabs in a chilled room and waited for processing. Meanwhile, crabbers living in the Crisfield area brought their catch directly to our buying dock alongside the plant grounds.

UPENDING TRADITION IN SIZING CRABS

There was the matter of sizing, assigning each crab a specific grade that determined how much watermen were paid for crabs. And at times how much we were paid by customers. (If a larger crab, a Jumbo, was categorized incorrectly as a Prime, we received less money on that sale.) It was a tedious, inaccurate process that at times caused spirited arguments between watermen and crab buyers in the Chesapeake.

The five grades were defined by point-to-point width across the body's outer shell. This was the watermen's and buyers' traditional measuring method, but it required a steady eye and often was imprecise. Some crabs had small bodies and long points, while others had large bodies with short points. Larger bodies had more meat, but that didn't matter in assessing prices to the watermen and packing crabs for shipment. It was points-to-points.

This seemed illogical. Shouldn't the amount of meat, and thus overall weight, be the focus for payment, not the point-to-point span?

As I watched the Handy workers sort crabs each day, I couldn't figure this out. The mix of short and long spans varied each week during crab season. Our team hand-counted, measured, and separated them into the five grades, each with different prices for buyers. Frankly, the sizes all looked pretty much the same to me.

There must be a better way to deliver soft crabs with more consistent size to the restaurant diner's plate. If we had a better way to size and weigh crabs, we could offer watermen a fairer, more accurate way to be paid for their catch, eliminate or at least minimize arguments about the value of their catch, and stop losing money ourselves when our crabs were labeled smaller than they actually were.

A stranger had an answer. Sitting next to him in Chicago that first summer, I described the sizing problem and hand-sorting tedium in casual conversation as we rode on a hotel shuttle bus to an exhibition of packaging equipment. Luckily, he knew about an electronic sizing machine that had the potential to continuously weigh each crab on a fast-moving conveyor, sort the crabs into five grades, and count them for each waterman at the same time.

My new compatriot took me to a vendor where I watched a demonstration: small wooden blocks on a conveyor masquerading as crabs. Handy's crabs, I was assured by the vendor, would be sized and ready for packing at the end of each continuous run. I was elated and ordered the machine that day. Later in Crisfield, after minor adjustments, the grader easily handled whatever volume of live soft crabs we processed.

Our watermen were skeptical at first. Suspicious. Soon a revolt was brewing. They expected that anything other than point-to-point grading would result in lower paychecks from Handy. It wasn't long before they came around, though, because grading by weight was consistently accurate. It didn't hurt our cause when I advised the watermen that the grading equipment would enable us to expedite their paychecks.

HOMESPUN SOLUTION FOR FAST FREEZING

Soft crabs lose their sweet taste after being cleaned and packaged if they are not frozen quickly. Peeler crabs molt into soft crabs seven days a week, but markets for live soft crabs are open only three and a half days a week. We use refrigerated trucks to ship them live as far as Boston. Crabs we couldn't sell live had to be frozen quickly. The freezing process had to be fast to preserve a fresh taste. Ours was not. I thought it was horrible.

The staff would wrap crabs they had processed in cellophane and put them in small cartons before driving them a mile to Handy's blast freezer building, a brief ride that in the hot summer warmed the crabs. Then the process really bogged down. It was another twenty hours before freezing would reach the middle layer of the crabs.

The same crab could have a varying taste, turning from sweet to sour where the fat turned slightly rancid, and might even become so spoiled that kitchen staff in restaurants we supplied would have to throw them out. I knew at some point poor outcomes such as these would impair our ability to further build Handy's reputation as a trusted brand. We were absorbing too many crab losses. They had to be reduced as soon as possible.

As I searched for answers, an old-timer whom I met during a routine day of crab buying along Virginia's eastern shore gave me a simple, brilliant solution. In his home, this friendly waterman showed me how he and his wife placed crabs for freezing from a daily catch onto individually wrapped cookie sheets, and then stacked the sheets on racks in a home chest freezer.

These crabs froze *within two hours*, yielding a plump shape and firmer texture that preserved the sweet taste. The technique was called Individually Quick Frozen (IQF). After tasting samples, I knew this soft crab was superior to what we were producing. I was so excited. Shortening our freeze times to thirty-eight minutes from more than twenty hours was a game-changer. We had to adopt and promote this IQF method as soon as possible. It was a lucky coincidence.

You've got to have that drive to compete, the conviction that you are not going to let anybody get ahead of you. Back in Crisfield, I told my team, "If we do this on a big scale, we are going to really outshine our competitors."

Most competitors eventually copied our IQF innovation.

To this day we are always aware that some competitor may be doing something a little better than us in some aspect, such as taste, texture, or a level of spice. When we spot something, we ask: Should we react? Can we do this a little better?

BE THE COMPLAINER

We had to contend with more than those two immediate challenges. In my walk-arounds, I noted that the production pace varied. We lacked continuous flow, which I knew from my consulting years was a sign of inefficient operations.

A team in the sizing-grading room might get ahead, causing a backup of crabs that would sit for a half hour or more in the hot air before moving into the cleaning, processing, and freezing departments. Anytime I saw crabs sitting around like this, I would get into it with the crews. We needed to keep crab-processing steps in balance almost hourly to keep product moving.

"Look, you can't park crabs in a hot building for thirty minutes or more waiting for somebody to begin work on the next process. Why isn't this moving?"

"Well, we've always done it this way." Or, "We have fewer crabs today so we slowed down to let the other department catch up."

"Things are a little different now. We have competition. We've got to do better. These crabs are losing moisture, deteriorating, losing their quality. We've got to keep this stuff moving."

As with the slow-freezing problem, I wasn't aware of any customer complaints about freshness, but I knew we had to take action to prevent them. I was the complainer. On some days balancing the workflow was a nightmare because the amount of live crabs coming in and how they would be sold (live or frozen) varied so much.

My solution those first two years was staying alert to shift some people from the "faster" department so that the "slower" department was able to catch up. Here was yet another reason to spend as little time in my office as possible. As operations became more efficient, I spent more time engaged in face-to-face conversations with customers.

PAY ATTENTION TO LITTLE THINGS

To prepare live crabs for shipments, Handy's crews carefully hand-packs each crab into trays lined with nesting material to restrict movement during shipping. To prevent osmosis, we keep the crabs moist during shipping by covering them with a piece of waterproof parchment paper dipped in fresh bay water from where they are harvested. It was something I learned during high school physics class. Customers told us that more than 85 percent of the crabs in Handy shipments arrived alive, much more than 60 percent typical of our competitors.

Like a lot of things in business or any endeavor, attention to the little things adds up to success. Why our competitors never copied these essential steps in preparing and shipping such a high-profit item I'll never know. It continues to puzzle me.

We packed and shipped them all over the country nearly every day. Our profit margins on live crabs were especially high, more so than frozen crabs. Robust demand at high-end restaurants enabled those customers of ours to charge premium menu prices.

The live crab business helped further build our reputation for quality among food distributors and high-end restaurants. Sized right. Not too hard. Not too soft. We had Handy soft crabs on lunch menus at Los Angeles' premium restaurants less than a day after those crabs were harvested in the Chesapeake. The sweet taste is highly prized. Chefs were delighted to sauté fresh Handy soft crabs and serve them to patrons. This is gourmet dining.

We soon found more good markets, shipping to large cities across the US. Then to Japan and Europe.

ELUDING A MUTINY

I need to underscore here that our plant workers were incredibly solid, reliable people. It seemed like the majority of our workers were from families whose members had worked at Handy for one, two, or three generations. It was a mixed group ethnically and included college kids who were living at home for the summer.

I noticed immediately that Saturday in 1981 when I first walked through the plant as a prospective buyer that the teams were cheerful, talking among themselves as they worked. As owner, I appreciated even more how genuinely eager they were to be part of this team, ranging anywhere from sixty to eighty people, putting out the best seafood quality in our area.

They knew what to do and went right to work. At the end of the day, they left the plant spotless, each person cleaning up his or her area without saying a word. They were proud to work at Handy—and that made *me* proud too.

That third year, the plant operated forty-two consecutive days, from 7:00 a.m. to 11:00 p.m. and sometimes later as we raced to keep up with the watermen's summer crab deluge. We catered lunch and dinners for our people and served doughnuts in the mornings to help them refuel, but the long hours took their toll.

Our associates could have said, "This is too much work; I'm looking for another job," or just stopped coming to work, but they hung in.

Our four sons—Todd, Daniel, Brendan, and Patrick—with Harrison Lake, 1983

So did my four sons, then aged twenty to fourteen. I roused them before three o'clock each morning to begin with me the long day ahead.

One of those days I squared off with the reality that you cannot please all workers all of the time.

New methods and technologies—any major change, generally—can be too much for some. One day after our renovation was finished, the lead floor manager, disgruntled with this new equipment ferrying crabs to workers that had been hand-carried before, stomped away, shouting at me, "I'm bringing everybody with me until we get rid of that conveyor!"

She had recruited the most wonderful workers over the years. We relied on her to help keep production humming. I gulped. What would I do?

Within minutes, a young woman in the packing department approached me, saying calmly, "Don't worry, I can keep the plant working." No one followed the lead floor manager out the door. This young woman—competent, respected, and unwaveringly loyal—stayed with us more than thirty years, rising to plant manager before retiring at age fifty-eight.

RECRUITING CAROL

It's dismaying to think how I could have kept my growth plans on track if I had not realized by the middle of my second year at Handy in 1983 that I was becoming stretched too thin to hit the high standards and goals I set for myself.

I needed to bring in someone with skills, experience, and judgment to assist with operations due to Handy's quickening business success.

The twentieth-century poet-playwright W. H. Auden coined the phrase "there are no priorities among essentials" in listing the core values for a fulfilling life: honesty, integrity, compassion, respect, love, responsibility, and faith. It is a powerful list and I agree with all—personally preferring "trust" over "honesty" and "integrity" because trust implies both—but now, in this context as a small business owner, I was feeling trapped by "no priorities among essentials" of my own making.

There was a deluge of priorities: keeping commitments to customers; campaigning for new ones; balancing crab supply and production; managing relations with watermen, employees, and bankers; mastering our finances; planning the plant renovation; monitoring competitors with the pressure to innovate faster; parrying with local and state government officials.

All these leadership imperatives had to be managed well, simultaneously. All were critical for me to move this business forward. There weren't enough hours in the week.

Less than two years in and I was exhausted.

Who could help me? Carol Haltaman? I had worked with Carol at Perdue Farms during my decade in senior management there. She had grown up on the eastern shore and attended a two-year business college in Wilmington, Delaware, before joining Perdue (five years ahead of me) when the poultry company employed fewer than a hundred employees.

She was smart, savvy, hardworking, and gracious.

At Perdue Farms, she and I applied some of the best practices Frank Perdue championed to build a small family-owned business for long-term success. She knew the Perdue standards for thoroughness and quality that I was pushing to implement in Handy.

My timing was inspired. Carol had become restless, bored by her work, and anxious for a new adventure. She wanted to stay on the shore close to her family. I was delighted and greatly relieved when she agreed to accept the new position I created for her as Handy's vice president for sales.

In another five years, after she had learned and excelled at most every facet of our business and I had promoted her to executive vice president, she would take charge. She would become president for a dozen years under a new owner beginning in the late 1980s when my energies turned more to consulting, investments, and Ironman triathlon competitions.

THIRTEEN

FRESH IDEAS, DODGED CRISES

Selling becomes much easier when a seafood buyer for a grocery chain, a chef at a white-table restaurant, or another customer wants to see you because he or she knows you have good products favored by *their* customers. For marketing in general, the key point is generating leads. Effective salespeople follow up on leads, listen closely to what customers say they need, ask good questions, and know how to close deals.

I had little wisdom to offer about how to improve Handy's packaging and promotion practices in these first months, but I knew they were badly outdated, another challenge I had to wrestle with that first year. The logo type font appeared as if it had not been changed since before World War II.

It was not long, however, thanks to a talented graphics designer we found nearby, before Handy had the best graphics and packaging in the industry, and a sales surge to prove it.

If we had considered only graphic artists with experience in the food industry when we first started, we might have missed out on a valuable relationship that continued more than thirty years with our designer, Robin English. We kept giving Robin more work until she became almost full-time with us.

Good people know good people. They really do. Here was a perfect example. An excellent architect in Salisbury I had collaborated with on a big project at Perdue Farms told me about a talented young graphic artist nearby. "Oh, there's a really great person in Salisbury."

Robin's designs were clean, modern, tasteful—and, in my view, on par with prominent high-quality food companies. Innovative as well. She teamed with famed food photographer Michael Pohuski in Baltimore to produce award-winning images and graphics. One of our best promotions was a large wall poster displaying actual sizes of different grades of soft crabs, from Mediums to Whales. We gave this freely to our business customers.

The posters were a way to reinforce our message that correct sizing is what you would get from Handy, at a time when Handy competitors would mix in small sizes in boxes labeled for larger grades. We saw it as a statement of trust and confidence in our products.

Soon our sales team was spotting the posters on the walls of every seafood buyer we supplied—wholesalers, restaurants, other large buyers of soft crab. We were stepping out, defining with specific dimensions the quality of what customers would expect in soft crab labeling and packaging, filling a void to set an industry standard.

To bolster sales generation even more, we bought a series of ads in the trade magazine *Seafood Business*, each an eighth of a page, vertical, with the distinctive Handy crab logo Robin created in 1982. The editor often included stories about us.

All this made an impact because the publication circulated among twenty thousand seafood distributors and retailers. People who might have heard of Handy soft crabs now knew how to contact us. Later, after we discovered how efficient seafood shows are, Robin designed an attractive booth without clutter . . . easy to understand. Her husband, a sign maker, made the signs.

JUGGLING PRODUCTION FLOWS

By the summer of 1985 all these innovations had established an even higher standard for Handy soft crab and our brand reputation.

With those three initial bottlenecks to growth now resolved—sizing, freezing, and promotion—I knew Handy was poised to grow beyond our sales territory along the Atlantic coast into New England.

Watermen continued harvesting more and more crabs, bringing larger portions of their catch our way. They knew I was committed to buying everything they had, a pact I was determined to keep. Sales were strong as well, but I knew the soaring production levels in our plant soon would be far beyond what we required to fill customer orders along the Atlantic coast. Our crab purchases were 75 percent higher than only four years before, averaging 130,000 a day during peak periods and sometimes as high as 300,000 a day that year—the all-time peak of Chesapeake crab purchases for Handy.

Maintaining a steady balance between production and demand is a challenge for any manufacturing business. When your business is working with a wild-caught species, the balance of incoming supplies and orders will always be uneven.

Managing this imbalance has to be a priority. It was for me, the second of those three ongoing imperatives for success: superior products, processed at a competitive advantage, and sold profitably. Generally, manufacturing companies need to generate enough sales to keep production capacity above 90 percent to be profitable.

COULD I DO THIS? A SALES BAPTISM IN COLD CALLS

After our first season in 1982, with our plant utilization and output pushing the envelope, my most urgent concern was: *How am I going to generate more sales demand?* I had never sold a product directly. *Where will I find new customers? Do I go outside our Mid-Atlantic territory? How do you actually sell a soft crab?*

Some executives insist on reviewing market research before answering that question, but not me. I had to move. Payments at 8% interest would pile up. Most research is outdated by the time you see it. Then, too, my style was to act and rely on my experience and judgment, not risk faltering into analysis paralysis. As the US Military Academy teaches future Army officers, *action creates opportunities.*

That's when I drove the refrigerated pickup truck and began cold-calling with face-to-face selling for six weeks. It was my only practical option, really. I drove to major cities along the Gulf Coast as far as Texas and cold-called on seafood wholesalers without an appointment. Then a second trip—another six weeks on the road—to the Midwest, Chicago, Denver, and more. To find the wholesalers, I would look up high-end fresh seafood restaurants listed in the Yellow Pages, call and ask for the chef's recommendation for a quality seafood wholesaler in the area.

"Hi, I am from Handy Crab Company. We are a soft crab processor."

"Oh yeah, we heard of you."

"We are looking for one or two reputable seafood distributors in Shreveport. Can you recommend any?"

And then I would go knock on the wholesaler's door unannounced. When the right moment arrived, I'd promise as Handy's owner to have a first shipment delivered within two weeks.

For the most part, wholesalers were glad to see me. I pulled sample cartons from the refrigerated truck, described the consistent quality, and explained how Handy's soft crabs were superior to competitors.

Most wholesalers would say, "We'll think about it," and when I followed up with a letter and a call, most agreed to take a first shipment. Some purchased an order for a full pallet load.

I had no choice other than to pursue cold-calling. You probably couldn't do that in these modern times, and I was rolling the dice even then, but I scored forty sales meetings in all without appointments on those three trips. Only one wholesaler, in Dallas, turned me away. Six months later, that fellow called me—"Can you send us some samples?"—and soon became a significant buyer.

Chefs paid distributors maybe $3 for each crab, then listed them on their menus anywhere from $10 to $15 and served the whole crab sautéed. Soft crabs are a seafood delicacy. As our distributors have told me over the years, "The best taste that comes from the sea."

With even more crabs flowing in from watermen the next season, I repeated my sales-prospecting trips. Again, they were a success. I became convinced over time that these prospective customers welcomed me without an appointment because I addressed basic pain points they had when buying seafood. I had a proven, quality product available directly from me, the processor, without the fees and administrative hassles involved in dealing with brokers or middlemen. As the owner, I closed the deals on the spot and began deliveries within two weeks or earlier.

I had been apprehensive before heading out to Norfolk, Virginia, my first stop on the first trip. Remember, I had never sold any product. These cold-calling excursions proved transformative for me and Handy. We became a national company—and smarter too.

My steady concentration on customers over each of these six-week spans gave me fresh insights that I would apply to sharpen operations. My notebook was crowded with soft crab serving suggestions, new recipes, ideas for packaging, and my pledges that Handy would move quickly in responding to specific customer requests.

FINANCING GROWTH

Handy was growing, and growth was expected to continue. Our bank suggested a $500,000 low-interest economic development bond to modernize a large, vacant building on the property that would have space for automated equipment to sort crabs by size and to IQF freeze. When the state-of-the-art plant opened in 1984, the sparkling new plant and both innovations led to high-volume customers in Japan and Europe.

I was amazed as the renovation progressed, watching one man handle each phase of construction across the entire plant by himself. He was remarkably good. All the plumbing, air conditioning, setting the equipment, wiring. We wanted to hire him after he finished, but he was content to drive trucks for the postal service.

In the first season with the new grading equipment, as soft crab sales soared to a new annual record, the renovated plant processed these record volumes easily with plant capacity now four times greater than before. That marvelous grading and weighing machine worked fine after some initial adjustments. Sales volume continued rising so fast in subsequent years that we added a second, a third, and then a fourth grading machine. This further opened a valuable competitive advantage in low-cost efficiency. As best we can determine, it's an advantage we have never lost.

Our bank recommended increasing the line of credit to $500,000, which would provide financing for additional inventory and receivables.

Within months, I was staggered when a junior associate at the bank called to say they were pulling Handy's credit line despite the fact that we had met all covenants in the three-year agreement and our reports had been timely and accurate.

He gave me no reason. Banks can terminate credit lines legally with no advance warning. I suspected the junior associate might have been nervous about our financial commitments to watermen, with crab catches rising fast, and that we might not have enough revenue to cover costs from the surge in production.

"I'm going to appeal this to the bank officers," I told the junior staffer.

"Go ahead," he retorted.

I had gotten to know three of his superiors in the bank's Baltimore office but none returned my calls that day. What now? Ask a competitor, the Maryland National Bank in Salisbury. I had good relationships with that bank's officers in prior years when I was chief financial officer at Perdue Farms. Maryland National (acquired later by Bank of America) quickly agreed to pick up our line of credit. Crisis averted. All payments were made on time.

I was pleased that Handy had the strength to finance its growth with bank financing with reasonable interest rates.

FROM BUYER'S SUGGESTION TO BESTSELLER

The idea for what has become one of our most popular products came from a buyer visiting Crisfield from one of our good customers, the

Washington Fish Exchange, a fish distributor supplying white tablecloth restaurants in the Washington, DC, area.

Annette wanted to buy cleaned and processed soft crabs chilled to a temperature just above freezing, individually wrapped, and ready-to-cook, similar to fresh fish. It would be labor-saving for the restaurant's kitchen or the retail staff without the complicated process of keeping the crabs alive at 50 degrees.

We worked up test samples and discovered there were advantages for us too. Shelf life for fresh, chilled, cleaned, and processed crabs would increase two days for live crabs to six days fresh, chilled.

We promoted these as Handy's Chilled Dressed soft crabs. Distributors and restaurants embraced them immediately, opening a new market that has continued growing for nearly two decades. In the mid-2010s, the chilled dressed product was about 40 percent of soft crab sales, with frozen and live about 35 percent. By the mid-2020s, with the Chesapeake crab catch declining markedly and shipments of live crabs too small and costly to truck to the Baltimore airport and ship to far-flung customers, most Handy soft crab products were chilled dressed. Customers preferred them.

TOP 3 PERCENT IN THE WORLD

I respect and admire plant inspectors. We voluntarily invited inspections by the US Commerce Department and welcomed required state inspections as well. The purpose of these government inspections is to maintain public confidence in the food supply. That said, we considered specialist companies hired by large retail customers such as grocery chains and food service companies such as Sysco to be the gold standard for inspections.

The most prominent because of its integrity, rigor, and authoritative reviews is an international group that inspects food plants all over the world, the British Retail Consortium. BRC, as it is known, is as tough as nails . . . incorruptible. We began paying them in 2015 to inspect Handy plants each year, as high-quality food companies do every year.

High marks from the BRC are coveted in this business. We know when they are coming and get everyone in the plant involved, coaching our teams to be sure to answer all the questions honestly. The BRC's passing scores range from as low as D and as high as AA. Our Crisfield plant has been rated AA each year since 2021, with an added "plus" to AA+ in 2023 because that inspection was unannounced. The AA ratings put Crisfield in the top 3 percent of all plants in the world that the BRC inspects, a testament to Handy quality standards that we underscore when introducing ourselves to prospective partners or government officials.

Inspectors help make us a cleaner, safer fishery. They point out things we might have overlooked. They follow up with reports and recommendations, ones we're usually eager to implement before they return the next year. We take pride in the high grades we receive from inspectors before they leave our property—and always celebrate with a big cake. Every time they come, they make us a better company and reinforce our commitment to deliver the best products available.

FOURTEEN

MR. TOMOTO COMES CALLING

The surge in soft crab supplies in the Chesapeake Bay continued into 1985, keeping up the pressure to find more customers. I never wanted to turn away a waterman who was counting on me to accept and pay for whatever his catch was. If I turned any away, many would lose trust, spread the word, seek other processors, and probably not return. Bad for business.

Well, then, with my crab supplies surging, where was I going to sell the crabs we were hustling to process? New markets we developed across the country on those cold-calling jaunts and seafood show promotions were solid and growing by the end of 1984, but not growing quickly enough.

Inventories of soft crabs were rising in our Crisfield freezer. The plant renovation had doubled our processing capacity. We needed more customers to raise the capacity utilization ratio above 40 percent. (Above *80 percent* is the threshold for profitable operations in seafood.) The bank financing our operations was asking probing questions.

What about Japan? How about Europe? International visitors at domestic seafood shows appeared fascinated by soft crabs and commented favorably on the taste. Could the Maryland trade offices help? Maybe Virginia's as well? For most of its history, Handy had processed crabs harvested form Maryland's shores on both sides of the Chesapeake Bay as well as Tangier Island in Virginia.

Both states had trade international offices with staff dedicated to helping local companies do more business in Japan. Maryland seemed a logical first call. Handy was based in the state, paying taxes for longer than any of our competitors, and operating for nearly a hundred years with a solid reputation. These attributes didn't matter, apparently. Maryland's Japan trade office turned me away. "We don't know you and we're working with one of your competitors," one officer told me. "Plus, we're busy with the Baltimore Orioles. They are about to play some exhibition games in Japan."

Virginia was more enthusiastic. "We'd be glad to help you. We have really good people in our Tokyo trade office, and there is a seafood food show in Tokyo soon," they told me. "We have an eight-foot booth reserved; we'll give you half of it." Virginia also made appointments with two of Japan's major seafood importers.

The day before the first appointment I treated myself at 4:00 a.m. to the sights and sounds of Tsukiji, the world's largest fish market, thinking I might draw some attention to soft crabs. Walking along the stalls, dodging fast-moving forklifts, I approached some proprietors to discuss soft crab along with a small sales brochure in Japanese. I did stir some oohs and ahs by pointing out that you could eat all of this crab. I left a business card, but no one followed up. That was okay. The immense variety of marine species in bustling Tsukiji is a dazzling memory for me.

The first appointment was on the tenth floor of a high-rise office tower. I arrived not a second early or late wearing a blue suit, white shirt, and simple tie for this formal business meeting. But I was a bit uneasy in my sneakers. I had failed to find a new pair of size 11½ dress shoes that morning to substitute for my pair in a still-unaccounted-for travel bag. Size 10 was the largest I could locate anywhere. We bowed and exchanged business cards. My hosts seemed amused by the story about my sneakers.

The meeting was welcoming and cordial. I listened to how Japanese importers discussed their business model. I was not impressed.

It was an inefficient distribution model, often with interlocking own-ers, quite typical of Japan's economic structure and a factor discouraging foreign competitors. After restaurants added more margin to cover their profit, price increases for Handy soft crabs through this multilayered distribution scheme would exceed an additional 50 percent, significantly limiting prospects for Handy sales in Japan. I wondered how many din-ers, even at high-end restaurants, would pay the price. After the extra expenses we would have to incur to supply customers in Japan, could shipments to Japan profitable?

The meeting ended cordially. We made our way up a flight of stairs to a small penthouse room. I quickly realized that this space appeared to be used only for important decisions. Urns filled with ashes of deceased ancestors, presumably founders of the family business, lined the walls where their spirits could observe their heirs' decision-making in action. Before we entered the room, I was reminded to remove my shoes. My heart rate suddenly spiked. I knew at that moment this would be a short meeting. It was. To my embarrassment as we walked into this hallowed space, and to my hosts' instant dismay, several of my toes were visible, poking through holes in the socks.

That is why I found myself the next day standing in a four-foot booth beside a small fryer at the Tokyo seafood show, cooking very small sam-ples of soft crab battered, dredged in flour, and fried in vegetable oil. I knew from supplying Japanese restaurants on America's West Coast that crabs were popular seafood, but it seemed that no one here had tasted a soft crab. When I looked up at one point, the queue before me was nine deep! I was fired up. Yet after manning my post for three days—cooking, cutting, and handing out small samples—nobody had stepped up to order. I caught a flight back home, mildly disappointed.

Three months later, I decided to participate in a food exhibition orga-nized by the US Department of Agriculture in, of all places, Kansas City, the city where I grew up. It was a good opportunity to visit my parents, but the event was lackluster, nothing going on, and I returned to Maryland a day early. Then one of my colleagues, still in Kansas City, told me someone from Japan, a Mr. Hideo Tomoto, had come to the event looking for me.

Raised by Baptist missionaries, perhaps orphaned after World War II, Mr. Tomoto owned and operated a successful Tokyo specialty foods importer, Ras Super, that featured more than a dozen high-end specialty foods from around the world. He had been one of those hundreds of people waiting in line and sampling my little soft crab nibbles at the Japan Seafood Expo.

And I had thought those three days in Tokyo were a bust. Maybe not.

Eager to speak with me in person, Mr. Tomoto traveled to Crisfield the next day. I introduced myself when he arrived at our plant and showed him around, describing each step of our process, underscoring the quality of everything we did.

There was no similar competitor with the capability to match our quality: electronic equipment for accurate weight and sizing and a freezer to IQF freeze newly cleaned crabs quickly and individually to preserve flavor and freshness. Plus, our plant was air-conditioned. I was confident that these unique features—and the immediate impression they conveyed: modern, clean, market-leading—would appeal to a Japanese importer.

Mr. Tomoto struck me as gregarious, forthright. He spoke excellent English. Within minutes after walking him through the plant, he said, "Okay, I want to buy." Then, to my great surprise, he added, "I prefer to pay in advance."

I suggested a price in response that was somewhat high, anticipating he would negotiate. But, as I learned, most Japanese business owners prefer to focus first on quality. "Okay," he said, agreeably, "let's start with one container. But I want an exclusive. If I develop the market in Japan, I want an exclusive."

"Great, happy to do it," I said immediately. Here was a man of trust. If anything in the transaction went amiss, we both knew, I would not lose money.

Suddenly, Mr. Tomoto had tossed me a glowing workaround for the daunting Japanese import model. He personally controlled a closed distribution system from the port directly to the restaurant consumer, delivered by motor scooter. I would not have to deal with a gaggle of distributors seeking higher margins and worry that restaurant prices for Handy crabs would go so high that demand would fizzle.

He and I could work together, to our mutual benefit, to establish prices. Our partnership would be a major cost advantage if any Handy competitors tried to follow my lead into Japan. They would have to contend with the high-cost, multilayered distribution networks that I would avoid.

Plus, Mr. Tomato's offer to pay in advance for the first shipping container, a smaller twenty-foot container holding 80,000 frozen crabs (in contrast to forty-foot containers with 160,000 crabs), was a big vote of confidence, reducing risks for me. We signed the exclusive agreement that day.

I was dancing on one foot. Breaking into the Japanese market was something no one in our industry had done as far as I knew, and I had the whole Japanese market to myself. The watermen saw that Handy was growing rapidly because shipments of chilled wax boxes into our Crisfield warehouses surged. (Watermen used the boxes for packing their molted soft crabs for delivery to our dock; after processing the crabs, we re-packed the boxes to keep the crabs moist during transport to Chicago, Los Angeles, or Tokyo.) I knew we could make money on every crab they brought to us.

The first year, Mr. Tomoto ordered three containers of soft crabs—amounting to more than 300,000 crabs, all harvested by Handy watermen from Chesapeake Bay. Two years later, in 1987, he ordered *nine* containers of Handy frozen crabs. By that point, Ras Super was my largest customer, contributing 40 percent of Handy's annual sales. Ras put us on the path to be known worldwide.

PRINCIPLES IN ACTION: FRESH CRABS FOR TOKYO LUNCH

One day Mr. Tomoto asked me, "Is it possible for these delicate soft crabs to stay alive all the way to Tokyo?"

"Let's try it," I said.

We had the live-crab shipping system in place, regularly sending containers of live crabs daily by air freight to California, Chicago, and Texas, but had never attempted trans-ocean flights with live crabs. Los Angeles was a six-hour flight; Tokyo would be fourteen hours. If all went well, we calculated, Mr. Tomoto would have fresh Handy soft crabs served to diners in Tokyo within thirty hours after watermen offloaded their catch onto our docks.

After selecting fresh crabs from the watermen's catch that appeared strong enough to survive two days, our practice was to pack the fresh crabs on three layers into waxed cardboard cases by midday and load the boxes into refrigerated trucks heading to the Baltimore/Washington International Airport two hours north of Crisfield.

For executing Mr. Tomato's idea, Japan Airlines proved the indispensable link. The airline arranged to place Handy crab boxes in a container cooled at 50 degrees in the cargo belly of the aircraft for the fourteen-hour flight to Japan. We estimated it would take six hours for a truck to get them to Japan Air's cargo warehouse from Crisfield and then for cargo handlers to load them onto an aircraft at New York's John F. Kennedy International Airport. If all this worked, we would have live Handy crabs, soft and ready for cooking, arrive in Japan about twenty-four hours after watermen brought them to our docks.

In Japan, Mr. Tomoto was prepared. He retrieved our crab boxes at Narita International Airport outside Tokyo, then ushered them quickly towards one of his best restaurant customers, arriving in time for chefs to sauté and serve this Handy delicacy to their lunch crowd. In a message to me hours later via Telex, a real-time communications circuit that predated personal computers, Mr. Tomoto was ebullient, beyond delighted.

"Ninety-seven percent of them are still alive!" he said. "How did you do it?"

He had known about our packing and shipping plans but not the final details with Japan Airlines to keep the dormant crabs alive and fresh after the long flight. "Only one difference," I wired back to him. "We worked with Japan Air to set up a temperature-controlled space during the entire flight."

After typing the message, I relaxed, savoring the moment. This was incredible, I thought. We had been satisfied when live-crab shipments by air to American cities arrived with more than half of the crabs still alive. That was our standard yield. For our competitors, it was often less than 40 percent. Now, after bearing down and tinkering here and there to improve little things, we had delighted our new customer in Tokyo.

We were delighted too. To be honest, I would have been happy if his Telex message had said *60 percent* of the crabs arrived alive. For a first shipment to Japan? That would have been good enough. Pushing the envelope, testing yourself in new challenges and exceeding your highest expectations, is one of the great pleasures of being in business for yourself.

We didn't ship any live crabs to him overnight again. He concluded the costs were too high, but doing this once was a remarkable achievement. We demonstrated to Mr. Tomoto that Handy routinely acted on our three principles: increasingly superior products, processed at a competitive advantage, and sold profitably.

A CLASSIC PARTNERSHIP

Japan's business culture appealed to me, perhaps because of Ras and Mr. Tomoto. People were very friendly, especially toward Americans. They kept their word. I observed that business conflicts in Japan usually were settled without lawsuits.

Ras flew an American flag outside their office on days we visited. They hosted us at an elegant performance by three generations of skilled Geisha ladies, each dressed beautifully in colorful kimonos and their abundant dark hair arranged by ornate, glistening combs. At banquets in Tokyo and Salisbury, the Ras sales team sang American songs, with "Yankee Doodle Dandy" a favorite. One year at the Boston Seafood Show, they feted twenty attending members of the Handy team.

Tokyo was clean. Mr. Tomoto's offices southwest of Tokyo were in a pleasant industrial park near the Pacific coastline in Atsugi. My journeys there were fascinating, fun. Overlooking the challenges of long-distance air travel (I always booked seats in coach) and driving in a city with road signs in Kanji characters and non-sequential street addresses, I found neighborhoods, business districts, and shopping meccas well organized.

I also made sure not to repeat my previous mistakes, and I learned more about Japan and its culture, like that given names were reserved for family, conflicts were settled amicably and with mutual respect, and businesspeople were trustworthy to keep their word. The opportunity to experience Japan and its wonderful people was an added bonus to a beneficial partnership.

IN SEARCH OF A CHINESE MR. TOMOTO

The sweetest-tasting crab is also the smallest, the Medium, at 1.3 ounces. The most convincing evidence for this was our most dependable customer for the thousands of Mediums we were processing each day, the restaurateur known as the originator of Creole cuisine, Warren LeRuth. His five-star restaurant in a New Orleans suburb drew diners from all over the world.

Our problem was that despite the growing popularity of soft crab delicacies among high-end restaurants, we did not have enough Warren LeRuths.

"I'm spending too much time trying to sell Mediums," Carol Haltaman, then our sales vice president, lamented during a daily staff meeting. "They may be the sweetest taste, but chefs say Mediums are too small for a sandwich or an appetizer, and it takes more than eight to fill up a dinner plate."

"Terry, why don't you look for an importer in China that can handle big volumes from us like Mr. Tomoto is doing in Japan? The federal government is encouraging more exports there. The Agriculture Department has space available at a seafood show soon in Dalian. You should go. The China market has possibilities."

I was only one of a half dozen American exhibitors a month later at the seafood show in Dalian. I had learned the night before, dining with a local representative in a US trade office, a thirty-eight-year-old Chinese national, that stoking interest in my Mediums samples might fail.

He had hosted me at a "special occasion" restaurant, which featured several aquarium-style tanks filled with different live species—fish, shellfish, crabs, and mussels. Diners chose their meal, chefs prepared it partially steamed, and diners picked the meat from their plates with chopsticks while the specimen was still gasping for air. The buzz in the restaurant suggested to me that the taste must be worth the menu price. My host's subtle message: "Chinese people love fresh seafood, and fresh means live."

Visitors at my expo booth the next three days were courteous, thanking me for samples I was frying from the stash of frozen Mediums at my side. No long lines, but I did trade business cards with four serious importers and explored terms for possible agreements, but I never heard from them.

I left Dalian, however, with an important insight. My quest for a Mr. Tomoto of Dalian, someone who would import shipping containers of frozen Mediums, promote and distribute them in huge volumes, probably was quixotic. Shipping frozen crab products to China would not succeed as it had in Japan. If "fresh" was a must for seafood in China, I wondered if that might be true elsewhere in Asia and other parts of the world as well. (It wasn't, except in the most expensive restaurants in other parts of China.)

One day I would return to China, especially Hong Kong, to test that theory with fresh crabmeat processing and sales. But that would not be for another twenty years. That abundance of Mediums that triggered my Dalian pursuits? Carol eventually did find customers for the small Mediums soft crabs in Texas.

FIFTEEN

A CURIOUS INTERLUDE

1988–2000

By the mid-1980s as we established the Handy name in these larger population areas, this novelty product, soft crab with an unusually sweet taste and soft texture, was becoming more popular in fine dining.

One question prospective entrepreneurs are always eager to have answered is: How did Handy grow from a one-telephone-line, single-product, seasonal, regional seafood company to expanding into international markets? Put another way, what was the secret to our growth?

There was no secret, and there was no one event that propelled our growth. Instead, Handy's success was a combination of free-flowing collaboration to produce the highest-quality products at the lowest production costs, along with taking measured risks and learning from past failures. I sought out talented people and invested in them. As a company, we adapted when necessary and kept our eyes constantly peeled for new opportunities to pursue. Throughout this growth, we maintained our core values of trust, teamwork, and never settling for less than excellence. As in all endeavors, luck played a part, but in the end, staying true to our principles paid off.

By now, some well-known food companies, including two listed on the New York Stock Exchange, had been circling, calling me and saying they might want to add Handy to their portfolio of businesses. Annual crab consumption in the United States was rising at double digits, and now, with our expansion into more major US cities and Japan and beginning into Europe, Handy's market share and brand equity were growing even faster.

I was convinced our best years were still ahead and had absolutely no interest in selling. It didn't take long for me to deflect the feelers.

"Okay, what are you paying these days?"

"Around three times earnings."

"If I kept this company three more years, and then gave it to The Little Sisters of the Poor, I would come out about the same, right?"

"Yeah, that's probably true."

"Thanks, but I think I'll pass."

Then, a chance meeting and the ways of Wall Street kicked into gear.

A JAPANESE OIL REFINER?

An investment banker I knew who followed Handy picked up a tip from a colleague that a Japanese oil refiner was looking for an American acquisition. The tip came from a journalist in a Manhattan bar who had just written an article about Taiyo Oil Company.

Within a week after checking our financials and watching an award-winning video we'd produced about Handy and its history, these bankers at Baltimore's Legg Mason put together the outlines of an acquisition offer that they proposed pitching to Taiyo management.

They followed my advice to name Carol Haltaman to lead the company as president and chief executive, with me transitioning to part-time consultant. Carol had excellent credentials. I had previously elevated her title, as Handy's lone executive vice president, and later, in 1999, she would become the first woman elected chair of the seafood industry's most prominent trade organization, the National Fisheries Institute.

The bankers knew and respected Carol and had no hesitation when I strongly advised inserting her into the agreement as the answer to what certainly would be a Taiyo question: Who is going to run the company?

"Japanese businessmen don't often negotiate," the bankers told me. "We need to know in advance if you would accept the financial terms."

The offer would be all-cash and equal to Handy's annual sales. Would I agree?

This was unexpected—a price higher than the big seafood companies had been talking about. Much higher. Taiyo would let us run the business as we wanted. No onsite presence. They just wanted to be owners.

After a day or two, still unsure whether this situation simply was too capricious to actually materialize, I said, cautiously, "Okay."

My investment banker friend called me two weeks later, saying a senior Taiyo Oil executive, Mr. Takazoto, was coming to New York City and wanted to meet me at a law firm. He reported to Taiyo's president, Shigeyoshi Aoki. "Are you available to come to New York tomorrow?"

I had reviewed acquisition offers as a consultant and private equity specialist. In nearly every case the first offer is not worth considering seriously, and then through negotiation you either find common ground for a deal or you don't. Flying to New York that morning, I still was skeptical about finding common ground.

Taiyo Oil was Japan's seventh-largest importer of crude oil. They operated their own refineries, converting crude into gasoline, lubricants, petrochemicals, and other products, and they owned a chain of gasoline stations. Why would they want to own Handy?

AN OFFER, RIGHT DOWN THE MIDDLE

Mr. Takazoto, a polished, athletic-looking man in his early sixties with a touch of gray hair, greeted Carol and me in the Midtown Manhattan office. He was engaging, friendly. After pleasantries and no discussion at all about Handy or Taiyo, he handed us a contract document. Now he was formal, to the point. "My company would like to make an offer," he said.

I had read dozens of legal contracts during my previous years in consulting and private equity. This one raised no red flags. None. *Oh my gosh. This is right down the middle*, I thought. *The terms, price, and payment were exactly as my banker had said.*

Carol and I requested some time to discuss privately what we had just seen. As I closed the door of an adjoining room, we both were thinking the same things: Do we trust Taiyo to respect and follow Carol's judgment as president? Would I regret stepping away as owner? Mr. Aoki would become chairman.

"Carol, what do you think?"

"I don't know, Terry, but this might be a good time to sell. You've heard all those other proposals. This is the best one you've had."

I quickly came to the same view. With five private school tuitions and a mortgage payment pressing the Conway finances at that time, maybe it was a good time to sell.

The contract was clean and fair. An all-cash price with carte blanche to continue operating Handy as we wanted: setting strategy, allocating capital, managing relationships with key partners.

MEETING MR. AOKI

Moments later, I signed the document. Ten days later, immediately after the closing, to my surprise Mr. Aoki was waiting when I was ushered into an adjacent room. "Welcome to Taiyo Oil," he said warmly, joyfully even, as he stood to shake my hand.

Why this scion of Taiyo's founder (in 1915) wanted to own Handy is a mystery we never unraveled. Our best guess, cobbled together from conversations over time, was that with Japan's soaring economy and equity values in the 1980s—the "Japan as Number 1" era—Mr. Aoki was looking to join the rush to own American trophy assets. (By 1990 Pebble Beach Golf Links in California had a Japanese owner, and Japanese investors were majority owners of the Rockefeller Center office complex in Manhattan.)

In soft crab seafood, Handy was the trophy asset. Our sales had more than doubled above $5 million since I became owner, with annual profit growth well above 20 percent. In Tokyo, the Handy name had gained prestige among upscale diners thanks to Mr. Tomoto and his ingenious promotion and distribution of our soft crabs.

We had seen with our thriving sales to Los Angeles restaurants that residents of Asian descent or people visiting from Asia were excited by the taste of soft crabs. Taiyo owned a Japanese restaurant named Aoki's in New York City near the United Nations Plaza. Maybe the chef had advised Mr. Aoki that his favorite soft crab delicacies came from Handy.[17]

LOSING MR. TOMOTO; STYMIED ON ASIA

I had heard that Japanese owners of other American seafood companies were intrusive and inflexible, but no one from Taiyo was planted in Crisfield, looking over our shoulders or second-guessing strategies. Taiyo was a fine owner. Very honorable people.

We just kept going, with Carol reporting our weekly activities such as production and sales, monthly financials, and business plans. She participated once a year in day-long senior management meetings in Tokyo.

She and I did attend a relaxing retreat once for Taiyo's entire management group on Guam. We mostly just sat quietly beneath palm trees for three days, surrounded by Japanese oil-industry executives. No presentations by anyone.

We were concerned at first about how our watermen might react when they learned Handy had been acquired by a Japanese company, but their response was positive. "It's okay with us as long as we're treated the same, you still buy our crabs—and they don't want to pay us in yen."

We did have disappointments. A year after the purchase, Taiyo forced us out of our wonderful relationship with Mr. Tomoto at Ras Super, arguing that Taiyo wanted exclusive rights to promote and sell Handy products in Japan.

Red flag. We were so concerned that Ras would shift orders to our competitors if they lost us as a supplier that I took the long flight to

---

[17] Not long after buying Handy, Taiyo experimented with a fast-food takeout concept that sold our soft crabs, hot dogs, French fries, and other American-style menu items. They named the takeout place Handy Dandy and located it just down the street from a McDonald's, but the concept never worked.

Tokyo just to plead our case with the executive committee, including Mr. Aoki, for keeping Ras. Ras Super was an important piece for Handy's future growth. Our largest customer! We met for two hours. Mr. Aoki was friendly, the first time I had seen him since the day of the acquisition deal. But no one budged.

"This was a shame," Carol remembers. "Mr. Tomoto knew how to sell Handy soft crabs, and Taiyo, as things developed, did not."

As we predicted, Ras did indeed source lower-quality crabs from Handy competitors in Crisfield. Ras proved such a fierce competitor that Taiyo eventually downshifted its plans for Handy in Japan.

Another setback came in the mid-'90s as Carol and I became increasingly concerned that Chesapeake Bay watermen might soon be unable to meet Handy's rising customer demand for soft crabs. The crab harvest in Chesapeake Bay fell more or less continuously through the decade by about 70 percent.[18]

Establishing new supplies from Asia was a practical option, a strategy some of our competitors were pursuing by importing soft crabs from Thailand and Vietnam. The quality was higher, with fewer missing legs and claws, more white meat, and a savory taste equal to the Chesapeake blue crab when cooked. Prices for farming and processing were lower too.

We needed that new supply, with crab cake sales taking off in the US and the soft crab business continuing to grow. We were making good contacts in Thailand and wanted to get moving. But the word from Mr. Aoki and his team was no. "We want you to stay focused on processing crabs from the United States."

We backed off. Carol and I believed that at some point, if the Chesapeake's declining crab harvest continued to worsen and impact Handy's financial health, they might change their minds. We quietly maintained those initial contacts in Thailand—a prescient move.

---

[18] The decline later was attributed to the population surge of a prized sport fish—the rockfish, or striped bass—which feasted on small crabs. I counted forty-two small crabs once in the belly of one rockfish. Conservation and sustainable management initiatives helped stabilize the smaller crab population in recent years.

A CRYPTIC NOTE, A BUYBACK

Just as our Taiyo relationship began twelve years before, we fielded another unexpected signal from Tokyo that triggered its ending. Carol had recently returned from attending Mr. Aoki's funeral when we received a cryptic note over our office fax machine. Addressed to another party, the vague note, with a tone intended to be confidential and discreet, indicated Taiyo might be interested in selling Handy back me.

Hmmm. This likely was no mistake, but rather a way for Taiyo's succession management after Mr. Aoki's passing to demurely invite a face-saving discussion about exiting the business. The Japanese way.

"I'm sure this is a mistake," I wrote back the next day. "I wanted you to know we received this fax in our office. We'd be glad to talk to you but please be aware that if we made an offer it wouldn't be at the same price we sold."

The response was swift and affirmative. "Okay. What number can you offer us?"

I gave them a desired price that indeed was lower than what they had paid, and then waited. I was optimistic, assuming that this exchange was playing out more or less exactly as the Taiyo executives envisioned. *If this comes through*, I thought while sending that fax, *we are going to get busy in Asia and grow the business even faster.*

They quickly accepted. No negotiations. Three months later, when the deal closed in June 2000, I again was in full control as Handy's lone owner.

BACK TO THE FUTURE

We did our best to make Taiyo proud of their investment. Despite losing Ras Super as our largest customer, sales held steady during those years at $8 million.

For me now, it was back to the future, an exciting, unexpected opening to again take the reins and prove that Handy's best days indeed were still ahead.

SIXTEEN

A TILAPIA FARM IN COSTA RICA

Yaacov was looking lost. Lean, athletic, maybe twenty-six years old, he was presiding at the very moment over a looming debacle as manager of a small fish farm in the central highlands of Costa Rica.

An Israeli citizen named Uzi Karlan had wisely located the farm three years earlier downstream from a heavenly, expansive reservoir of high-mountain freshwater covering more than four square miles, Lake Arenal. Karlan's plan was to tap into that freshwater source, raise tilapia—a tasty, inexpensive fish popular in Israel—and export it to the US.

But for some reason Karlan, the founder and owner, had abandoned the business with little notice and zero explanation. He returned to Israel—leaving an empty bank account and an emptyhanded caretaker in Yaacov. "There is no money left to buy food for the fish," Yaacov said. "They'll starve to death in a week."

My entrepreneurial instincts stirred: problems, solutions, opportunity, short-term financing to keep the fish alive. "Maybe there is a way to help," I replied. I had no doubt that I could effectively apply to farming fish the basics of growing healthy live animals that I learned during my years with Perdue.

This business was obviously distressed but not hobbled. It might be available at a bargain bid. I had to investigate.

Yaacov had learned after his two years in the Israeli military how to grow tilapia with as little water as possible. Fresh tilapia was the most

Yaacov at a Tilapia farm, Canas, Costa Rica

popular seafood among Israelis. If I can find a way to keep this fish farm's finances viable long enough to stabilize, then perhaps I could build the business just like we had done at Handy.

We talked animatedly over the next hour about keys to growing live animals. One of them is edible protein, or the amount of protein remaining for someone to eat after nonedible parts of the animal are trimmed off. About 50 percent of a fish is considered edible protein after the head, tail, and scales are removed. For chickens, it's 73 percent.

As we spoke, I contrasted Yaakov's methods with tilapia to what I knew from growing chickens at Perdue—and, perhaps even more importantly, what I knew about salmon. I had just become familiar with the intricacies of raising salmon as board member of a Maine salmon farm. Raising tilapia, I gathered from listening to Yaacov, was much simpler than salmon.

The US was an untested but potential growth market for chilled fresh tilapia. You rarely found chilled fresh tilapia in the States. It wasn't available. Most tilapia sold in the US was imported frozen from China.

Grown in small algae-infested ponds, the fish was cheap but had a muddy taste in North America.

He eagerly described more about the operation as we walked around parts of the twenty-acre site. The warm freshwater supply from Lake Arenal was particularly stunning. The lake, situated near the Arenal volcano about fifty minutes from the farm, is nourished by a dazzling, twenty-foot-high waterfall and several small streams.

The natural lake had tripled in size about a dozen years earlier when a new hydroelectric dam generating 70 percent of Costa Rica's electricity supply was finished. It was a stroke of good fortune for the tilapia farm because the dam sends water from the lake flowing through turbines down to a concrete canal in such volume near the site that water in the farm's dozen fishponds can be replenished every twenty minutes.

This was unheard of. Most aqua farms have a terrible time getting enough water. Ponds become muddy and rife with algae. But tilapia raised in clean freshwater has a unique taste. "Let's have dinner tonight," Yaacov said. He jumped into one of the ponds and hauled out three fish for our meal. "We'll cook tilapia, and you'll see."

At dinner with the howler monkeys sounding off high above us in a canopy of tall trees, we dined in the kitchen of a delightful three-star rural resort on the Pan American Highway where I was staying, the Hacienda La Pacifica.

Instant gratification. The taste was mild and sweet, not fishy at all. The texture was lean and firm. It reminded me of grey sole, an expensive North Atlantic fish served in high-end restaurants along the East Coast. This is fantastic, I thought. Even kids would love this fish.

Given what Yaacov had told me and what I knew about seafood, I had little doubt restaurants in the US could offer tilapia at a price point lower than other species of fish and much lower than grey sole. The fish might appeal to casual diners in restaurants as well as for meals prepared at home. Yaacov obviously was dedicated to the farm, a knowledgeable manager who might be eager to stay on. If we can get seafood buyers to taste this, we can sell it.

Still, I needed to know what had gone wrong. Why had Uzi Karlan abandoned the project? The simple explanation was operations were not integrated like Perdue with a genetics program, feed mill, and processing plant, pushing costs too high by giving profits away to middlemen. The farm was buying too much loose mash for young chickens rather than operating its own feed mill to make cheaper, soft floating pellets. Live fish harvested at the farm were not eviscerated and iced at the site after being pulled from the ponds. They should have been. Processed and chilled filets could have been trucked in insulated boxes three hours to San Jose, flown overnight to Miami for distribution to restaurants and grocery chains along the East Coast as far north as Boston and the Gulf Coast as far west as Texas.

Instead, live harvested tilapia were loaded into insulated containers big enough for seventy-five pounds each, then trucked to San Jose for processing into filets *the next day*. No efforts were made to keep the fish alive. Instead of the fresh taste I was marveling over at dinner, the taste and flavor reputation of this tilapia served in Costa Rica was, in Yaakov's words, "less than great."

A SITE TO FARM AUSTRALIAN CRAWFISH? NO LUCK

It was only by chance that I had found Yaacov. I had come to Costa Rica that week in 1992 at the request of a pair of investors to search for a suitable site to farm northern Australian Redclaw Crawfish. The pair thought importing them to the US could support a profitable startup. (This crawfish grows unusually fast, can weigh well over a pound, looks similar to a lobster, and is considered a seafood delicacy.)

An engaging teak farmer, a middle-aged American with a weathered face, the only person we knew in Costa Rica, drove me around flatter parts of the central highlands for three hours. I was hoping to find a site with freshwater supplies that could accommodate a large pond bigger than two football fields, abundant vegetation for crawfish to eat, and space for low fencing to keep the crawfish inside.

We spoke with several landowners willing to sell. No luck. None could meet my criteria, which also included multiple one-acre ponds, reliable workers, and a clean building to extract meat and prepare it for air shipment.

Well, my driver said, an Israeli citizen had started an aqua farm in the area. Maybe he would point us to a possible site.

"Let's go have a look," I said.

"IF WE REACH A DEAL, YOU HAVE MY VERBAL COMMITMENT TO FUND."

I wanted to move as quickly as possible. A British-accented lending officer in San Jose representing the London-based investment firm Commonwealth Development Corporation told me the next afternoon after my dinner with Yaacov that they had foreclosed on the Karlan loans and were looking for a potential buyer to limit the firm's losses.

I sketched out the crawfish farming concept that brought me to Costa Rica in the first place as representative for a pair of investors, and then I reviewed highlights of Handy's one-hundred-year history in seafoods, my experience growing live animals at Perdue Farms, and strategies for building a brand.

He listened closely as I detailed the changes necessary to make operations profitable and the working capital we would need to execute.

"What is your estimated cost to rebuild the business?" he asked.

"About three million US dollars," I replied.

The lending officer was intrigued but wanted to see Handy's operations firsthand, which required a flight of more than two thousand miles. I was optimistic. Before his Crisfield trip, he advanced funds so Yaacov could continue feeding the tilapia.

At our site, the banker was impressed by what we had—the renovated processing plant, sales teams for marketing fresh and frozen crabs domestically and internationally, and our brand strategies in retail and foodservice centered on high quality and innovation. He even interviewed an inspector with the US Department of Commerce.

"If we reach a deal for you to buy the tilapia farm, you have my verbal commitment to fund the working capital," he said confidently shortly before leaving.

I had to ask myself: *Do I really want to go through with this reinvention of another seafood business in Costa Rica?* I still had the commitment to Handy, plus I enjoyed my new opportunities to pursue fitness, family, and leisure time.

Thinking about the big picture, I asked myself: How could Rain Forest Tilapia, our name for the new enterprise, go wrong? The plans appeared to have all the right elements for success:

- Superior mild-tasting fish with a low grow-out cost
- Opportunities for a feed mill and processing plant to integrate the business
- Experienced general manager in Yaacov
- Fantastic source of warm, clear water from Lake Arenal
- Financing with Commonwealth Development
- Abundant, inexpensive land for expansion
- A short flight to Miami and US markets for fresh shipments daily
- A welcoming country in Costa Rica seeking jobs and foreign exchange

I had the experience to succeed at this: salvage the farm, quickly translate what I knew from Perdue about growing live animals to fish, and build a brand.

OWNERSHIP OFFER SPLIT THREE WAYS, BEARING MY RESERVATIONS

I did have the means to buy all the Karlan equity, but to be totally ethical, I believed I should propose to include the pair as partners who had sent me to Costa Rica in the first place. I had not found a suitable site to raise Australian crawfish, the mission they paid my expenses for. I developed the tilapia farm opportunity independently.

I was convinced that mutual trust was possible by being an ethical, capable, and reliable president, establishing a track record for profitable growth. Was that naïve? As a practical matter, I knew from my Touche Ross and Laird years that partnerships can turn sour if partner objectives change. These two men were friends, and I didn't know either very well. Even though I would have by far the biggest role in guiding the tilapia operations, I would always be the odd man out in partner discussions.

The three of us discussed briefly at the outset how we would operate the company, with the three of us as directors with equal ownership stakes.

I made it clear that I would not divert any of the farm's cash from operations to any form of compensation—stockholder dividends, fees, commissions—and business expenses before we became profitable. None of us knew how long that might take, but they agreed without discussion or qualification.

I added what I considered normal for any business organization like this—hire an outside auditor after getting an accountant in place. They had no comment.

With me as point man in negotiations with the Commonwealth officials, the three of us soon reached a deal to buy the bankrupt company for $260,000. The price was quite reasonable, a bargain if I executed my plans. I kept telling myself, *You couldn't make this up if you tried, but here it is.* Our ownership was split three ways.

I was immediately on scene, moving fast to double the number of ponds, introduce a more efficient floating feed system, and begin processing chilled filets near the site in a vacant, city-owned building. We prepared budgets and forecasts, hired an accountant, and then hired a part-time marketing consultant to prepare point-of-sale materials.

Our tilapia pitch to seafood brokers was similar to when I needed customers for Handy's rising output of soft crabs in the mid-'70s. "We have a superior product; give us a try." Brokers who agreed to an initial tilapia order of perhaps ten pounds would call back within two weeks: "You are right. That's a great taste. Send me two hundred pounds."

I grew even more confident we could accelerate Rain Forest's sales, and we did. Rain Forest Tilapia lost money only in the first month and turned a profit in the second. I was excited, wondering if Rain Forest might become one of the most profitable seafood companies of this era. Net profits at 45 percent of gross sales flowed consistently.

A FEW DAYS IN CALI—AND NOT A DAY MORE

Two years after "go," I began to wonder if we might soon need more sources of tilapia beyond our capacity in Costa Rica. My operations consultant said a new farm and processing plant in the highlands near Cali, Colombia, was worth a look.

The consultant, Israel Snir, and I went to Cali, a four-hour flight south of Panama with a stop in Panama City. As we toured four large ponds and a modern processing plant that was about to open outside Cali, I could visualize its possibilities, and I immediately began mulling how this arrangement might work.

On our way back to the city, chatting with the farm's general manager, a friend of Israel's, our Jeep was halted by soldiers in combat fatigues carrying rifles. Twice. Israel's friend jumped out each time and, after some quick conversations, we moved on.

"It's the end of the month," the general manager said nonchalantly. "They probably had run through their salaries and needed some cash."

Maybe, but we realized the next morning that there undoubtedly was more behind the story of armed soldiers manning checkpoints. Fear. Anger. Greed. Retribution. Brutality.

At breakfast, Israel was dejected. "Fifteen bodies were pulled out of the Cali River yesterday," he said. "Today it was twenty-five."

Those years, 1993 to 1995, marked the peak of shockingly violent warfare between Colombia's two notorious drug cartels. The cartels shipped hundreds of tons of cocaine annually into the US and Europe, generating vast sums for high living. The larger was in Medellin (nine hours to the north by car); the other and more ascendant of the two was there in Cali.

The Justice Department estimated that the Cali organization alone was generating $7 billion a year from trafficking. The rivals each thought they deserved all those US dollars flooding south. They competed ruthlessly.

Israel added: "I suggest we forget about any involvement here."

I would have preferred to spend a few more days relaxing in Cali. The climate at 3,300-feet elevation was pleasant, and the people we encountered (not wearing military fatigues) were gracious, friendly. But I was of no mind now to place a Rain Forest bet on Cali.

We booked the next flight out of Colombia to Costa Rica's capital, San Jose, and never returned.

THOSE CONCERNS CONFIRMED: DOUBLE-TEAMED, THEN OUSTED

Now is a good time, I reasoned, to work out the compensation formulas we had agreed over the phone to set *after* Rain Forest was profitable. My work as president and CEO was taking more and more of my time. Profits were rolling in faster than any of us had anticipated. I proposed what I considered reasonable terms for these responsibilities: an annual salary of $50,000. I was shocked by their response. They refused without explanation to pay me anything.

"What! Don't you recall our agreement that there would be reasonable compensation when Rain Forest turned profitable? Don't you remember how this opportunity was found, and how quickly it has turned profitable?" There was no acknowledgment of the agreement.

They appeared to be double-teaming me with sharpening elbows. "We're in charge now."

I was still president, a director, and a one-third owner. What was I going to do? I had to stay involved to protect my investment. But that wasn't going to be possible for three reasons.

Rain Forest was paying a brokerage sales commission to a company owned by one of the pair. This violated that pact we had agreed to orally but never put into writing, given the rush to close with Commonwealth. Then I learned of an outrageously exorbitant bill one of the pair had charged to Rain Forest for a Boston hotel suite. The charge was reimbursed, but our wrangling over the bill was contentious.

Finally, the pair became agitated by inquiries Commonwealth had asked me to make about adding other sales brokers to either augment or even replace the service owned by one of the two partners. Still our lead financing source, Commonwealth was raising doubts to me privately about Rain Forest's sales capacity; in other words, could the one owner with rights to Rain Forest distribution in the US deliver? Could he stimulate enough demand and build sales rapidly enough "to achieve the farm's potential"?

I reported back to Commonwealth some days after their request that I didn't see any advantage in a possible alternative broker and had stopped looking. But the relationship damage from those calls with my co-owners was irreparable.

Within days, the pair forced me out as president. Although I was still a one-third owner, they banned me from setting foot on the Rain Forest site. Outrageous. I could only think, Hey guys, where did this fantastic opportunity come from? How did it drop into your laps? Was a net profit of 45 percent not satisfactory? I asked for an explanation. There was none.

I planned to remain a director and one-third owner, but they pulled an old trick to dilute my ownership, calling for a suspicious equity cash call, with no discussion of reasons or specific use of the funds. If I didn't participate, which they anticipated, my one-third equity would fall, and they would hold larger rights to whatever price the company fetched in a sale. There was no doubt in my mind that this was their plan: sell Rain Forest and turn a quick profit. If they could squeeze my share of the equity, they would take a bigger share of the profits.

I did put my cash in on time, to little avail. Our disputes first went to arbitration. Then I settled a nuisance lawsuit they filed against me for the price of a parking ticket; this avoided months of litigation activity and mounting legal fees.

Ultimately, we sold Rain Forest, each of us banking a substantial check from the buyer, AquaChile, on a payday in 1996, but that number had the potential to be twenty times greater if we had stayed on course. After all my efforts, this was quite a disappointment. Too much money left on the table. If we had held the owners' stake another fifteen or twenty years to when US tilapia sales reached a peak, who knows how much more Rain Forest Tilapia might have returned?

In 1992, the year we introduced Rain Forest Tilapia for the first time to the US, total US tilapia sales amounted to less than $15 million, according to annual data compiled by the National Oceanic and Atmospheric Administration's Fisheries unit. By 2014, the year of peak sales, tilapia was the nation's fourth most popular seafood, after shrimp, salmon, and canned tuna. Sales topped $1.7 *billion*.

China still ranked highest in total tilapia imports, but chilled freshwater tilapia imports led by fish farms in Honduras, Ecuador, and Colombia had become increasingly popular in American restaurants and grocery stores.

What about imports from tilapia farms in Costa Rica? I can't say because I gradually lost contact with people there in that industry. For its part, citing accumulated losses of $36 million,, AquaChile sold its Costa Rica operations—including the ponds and surrounding lands we once prized as Rain Forest Tilapia—to Martec for $6 million in 2021.

Had AquaChile over expanded, become uncompetitive, failed to innovate? I have no idea. We know the pandemic put a damper on tilapia demand starting in 2020. Market forecasts for recovery later turned optimistic. They put annual global tilapia demand rising to $22 billion by 2033, from $14.1 billion in 2021. Will Martec's timing prove prescient? Will the market recover and rise beyond? Who can say?

HARD KNOCKS, BUT LESSONS TO STRENGTHEN FUTURE PARTNERSHIPS IN ASIA

What I do know is that if I had not shown up when I did, those fish would have died. The market value for the bank of empty ponds would have been slashed. Commonwealth's British lending officer seemed grateful, willing to keep the fish alive until we completed the sale and I could get to work.

Overall, I was more than gratified as the stemwinding entrepreneur in making Costa Rica tilapia appealing to thousands and thousands of American families, creating jobs throughout our supply chain for Costa Ricans as well as Americans. And I enjoyed getting to know generous, reliable, and pleasant people who became associates and colleagues in making Rain Forest so successful.

While the hard lessons I learned in Costa Rica about putting precise details into contracts with prospective partners were difficult to swallow at the time, they were extremely valuable. That experience made me much better prepared to build the types of positive, lasting partnerships for Handy operations in Asia, where the stakes and rewards would be much higher.

There were principle takeaways. First, know your prospective business partners' experience and reputation. Next, be diligent in gauging their agendas—both agendas as articulated and, given human nature, agendas that are hidden.

Then, too, be diligent in preparing agreements with stockholders, vendors, and sales prospects. Finally, as you surely have anticipated by now, insist that these agreements are in written form, conform with all applicable laws, are vetted closely, and are revised as needed by experienced, trusted lawyers.

SEVENTEEN

IN NIGERIA: THREATENING INTERROGATORS, WELCOMING VILLAGERS

I knew as my flight approached Africa's most populous country that few nations could rival Nigeria's recent history of political turmoil: five military coups dating to the mid-'60s. Yet as I landed in Lagos in October 1993, I hadn't given that much thought.

Two months earlier I had enjoyed a cordial meeting with Nigeria's ambassador to the European Union in his Brussels residence. The introduction was arranged through a Maryland trade official with good EU connections who was impressed with my Rain Forest success in Costa Rica.

The ambassador was intrigued and encouraged me to visit his country and offer advice on fish farming. Specifically, could a tilapia farm in his native village in the country's northwest succeed?

This had the makings of a soul-satisfying mission. I might be able to lend a hand to villagers in a remote part of the country. Maybe I could, but . . .

Ooof! Will I ever be able make the analysis? As soon as I stepped from my British Airways plane onto the tarmac, two armed men in full military uniform grabbed my arms, one on each side. They marched me off quickly, hustling toward a stone-walled interrogation room.

I tried to remain calm but was extremely anxious. Alone with these two, I was at their mercy. *What will happen if I'm detained?* I wondered. *Who can I call? How am I going to get out of this?*

The soldiers questioned me again and again. For thirty minutes, menacingly. These guys were muscular, about five feet, six inches tall, with deep tribal scars on their face. They were suspicious, threatening, dismissive of my replies, but I couldn't detect any motive.

"Who are you? Why have you come to Nigeria? Are you CIA? What's in these papers?"

"I'm here at the invitation of the Nigerian ambassador to the European Union," I said, over and over. "The Ambassador is interested in setting up a fish farm in the north. Those papers are all about fish and crabs. Please check them out. The ambassador's representative is in the waiting room outside, probably with a small sign reading 'Conway.'"

Finally, one of them walked out to the waiting room, where my driver was easy to pick out, holding that sign, "Conway." Without comment or apology, the other soldier returned my passport. I was freed and quickly connected with my host.

He was wearing a colorful Taqiyah skull cap. I've forgotten his name, so I'll refer to him here as Kwame.

"What was this all about?" I asked him. "Why me? Any idea? Did the soldier say anything to you?" Kwame shook his head. No. But he cautioned that airport security had been on high alert for months. The results of democratic elections in June had been tossed out, and an interim president had resigned under pressure from the military in August. Nigeria again was under military rule. Rumors of coup plotting by dissident army factions were rampant.

The streets we drove through in Lagos seemed relatively quiet, at least on that morning. Kwame couldn't explain why I had been targeted and handled so roughly.

He drove us toward the ambassador's village, a four-hour journey into Nigeria's northwest not far from the Niger border. Rolling hills there without any level terrain was at first glance not the ideal topography

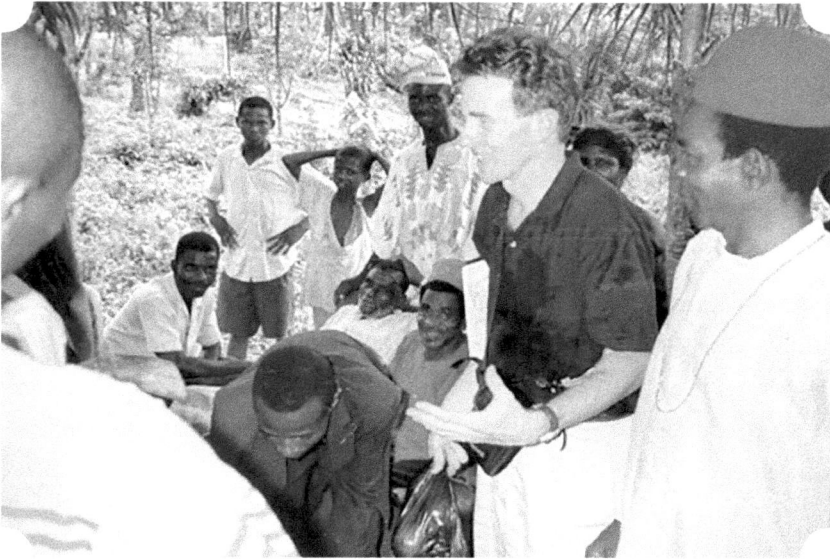

Northern Nigeria

you'd want for a fish farm. But there was a freshwater source, a spring-fed stream.

About fifty villagers greeted us warmly. After we settled in, an elder offered me whiskey. I smiled to show appreciation but waved off the glass he had extended to me.

Still shaken by the morning interrogation, I was glad to have a reason to walk around that evening, clear my head, and survey prospects for fish farming. The villagers moved in unison as a group, mirroring each step I took. I walked ten feet to the right; the group walked, silently, ten feet to the right.

I was flattered, touched. No one spoke English, but it was obvious they knew why I was there. They appeared keenly interested, eager for an upbeat outcome. A fish farm could offer more employment and income. Before dark, about thirty men donned festive masks and danced rhythmically. A friendly ritual in my honor? Seemed so.

The water in the spring-fed stream was clear, but because it was the only water source and just eight feet wide, the setting would not be workable for raising tilapia. There also was that issue of topography: no level areas for digging large ponds. Moreover, I figured, the air temperature likely would be too cool for tilapia. Catfish farming? I explained that possibly this approach had possibilities.

I wish I could have been more encouraging in my conclusion, but the facts as I saw them that day didn't cooperate. I still remember the veiled disappointment in those men's eyes.

After dinner Kwame led me to a wooden bunkhouse nearby with no electricity. I was assigned a bunk in an open room with no door. "No need to worry," Kwame said. "There's a guard outside." The guard was friendly but unarmed. I doubted his ability to stop an intruder but, given the peaceful surroundings, I wasn't concerned.

LESSON: BE MORE CAREFUL SELECTING OVERSEAS PARTNERS

I didn't sleep well. In the morning, we had no news about political plots and tensions. Worried about troubles that might lurk along the roads, I wanted to get back to Lagos as soon as possible.[19] My main thoughts were to pass through ticketing and security check-ins at the airport there without incident—and not miss my flight.

"Let's go directly to the airport," I told Kwame.

We weren't in the car for long before Kwame pulled over, stood outside, and said to me, "Let's pray together." Pray? Okay. I bent over and bowed silently with him. Did he know something he hadn't told me about dangers ahead? No, but there was something else. He asked me to give him my two-zone Timex watch. Letting me reply Kwame upped the ante. He wondered if I would like to "make an investment in my new enterprise"—meaning, I suppose, the village fish farm.

---

[19] *The New York Times* would soon describe these months as "the most turbulent period in Nigeria's history since the 1967 civil war."

Nigerian Doll

I expressed my appreciation for his hospitality but declined both requests.

No hard feelings. When we pulled to a stop by the British Airways entrance *twelve hours* ahead of my scheduled departure, Kwame handed me a souvenir doll made of twigs, a gift. (I liked the design and still have it on display in my home.)

With plenty of time on my hands and no commotion in the passenger boarding area, I drafted my report to the Maryland trade officer who had befriended the Nigerian ambassador in Brussels. Conclusion: insufficient water, air temperatures too cold for warm-water fish, not enough flat land for large ponds.

Three hours before boarding—as soon as procedures allowed—I asked a British Air agent for my boarding pass. It was not forthcoming . . . until I offered a $10 bill in exchange. I then was able to check my bags with the agent.

As our plane lifted off the runway and its big wheels folded up into the fuselage, I felt the tension in my body begin to release as I eased back into my British Air coach seat. *The ordeal is over. I am not in a Nigerian jail.*

Later, back in Salisbury, I discovered my luggage had been opened before takeoff and a pair of my size 11½-narrow shoes was missing. Nigerians have wide feet. I wondered to myself with a chuckle, *Who would ever be able to wear them?* Then I waved it off with the same feeling I had when that flight rose into the African skies toward London.

I heard later that the villagers, presumably including Kwame, did develop a catfish farm. Sadly, the effort failed for all the reasons I had flagged in my report. Those rumors of another coup? Those were well-founded. A month after I was in the country, yet another army general took over Nigeria's presidency. It apparently was the last, at least for thirty years. There have not been any Nigerian military coups since.

This trip produced no value directly for Handy. For me, I never made any effort to discover why those soldiers in Lagos had targeted me. I simply was immensely relieved to put that episode behind me. The lesson, though, was hard-earned, enduring: I must be more careful in selecting potential overseas partners.

EIGHTEEN

"KEEP GOING. DON'T YOU STOP AND REST."

Some of the Appalachian Trail's most difficult hiking terrain along the two-thousand-mile passage from Georgia to Maine is in northern New Hampshire's White Mountains. The route becomes so rocky you have to concentrate carefully on each next step or risk a fall.

As you rise into the clouds above the tree line, along the highest peak in the Northeast, Mount Washington, the going gets even tougher. And then, those sudden rain and snow squalls!

Susan and I discovered with two dozen friends, after I had downshifted to Handy consulting, that the blend of panoramic mountain views, rustic bunkhouse evenings, and group camaraderie along the trails spiced with personal stories, reminiscences, and silly jokes was captivating. Best of all? The après parties atop a mountain or below a waterfall.

Like the thousands of people who rush to reserve their bunkhouse nights every year—thirty thousand, according to *The New York Times*—we became regulars for five days at some point during the May–October season.

Susan's first sampling was in 1989, and after her subsequent feast of lively anecdotes for me, I was eager to join the next year. We light-heartedly dubbed our group of thirty the "eastern shore Mountain Goats," a spoof because we lived on the flats of eastern Maryland (a sandbar, topographically) near the Atlantic Ocean. We would make this delightful, recharging pilgrimage annually for nearly thirty years.

"COUNT ME IN!"

My hiking comrades included medical professionals or staff specialists at our local hospital. One year, our de facto leader, Dr. Bernie, declared that since we all were obviously so advanced in our physical fitness, we should enter Salisbury's sprint triathlon the next spring: three races shorter than a standard triathlon: 750-meter swim, 12-mile bike, and 3.1-mile (5-kilometer) run. "Terry, how about you? Will you commit?" he said.

"Of course," I replied reflexively. "Count me in."

I bought a road bike, took swimming lessons at the Y (dedicating hours to regular workouts), and ran in the neighborhood twice a week. Then, in May, the race. Not another eastern shore "goat" in sight. Well, never mind. I competed in my first triathlon and was so gently intoxicated by the experience, with endorphins abounding and happy feelings of accomplishment, that I told myself, *I will gladly do this again.*

Dawn first appears in the night sky on the west coast of Hawaii's Big Island shortly before six o'clock on October mornings. By then, on what would be a magical day for me in 1995, I was registered, my credentials verified.

After finishing sixth out of sixteen in my age group in that abbreviated Salisbury triathlon two years before—something of a lark, laced as it was with pain and exhaustion—I never envisioned being part of this scene: one of 1,500 of the world's elite triathletes gathered in Kona, Hawaii, for the Ironman World Championship. This was two months after that Salisbury race, when I won my triathlon age group at a competition in Delaware—the first time I had won *any* athletic competition. Yet the Kona starting line was where superior coaching and serious training discipline landed me.

Those events were fun—inspiring to participate in—and I was eager for more. As I became stronger physically and more energetic in my daily activities, I grew increasingly serious about triathlon fitness training. How serious? My swimming coach was Terry McLaughlin, the legendary college coach and creator of swimming's Total Immersion regimen. At his camp, I learned Total Immersion's two key elements: use only arms for propulsion through the water, with no leg kicks, plus swimming with your head fully in the water to maintain pressure on the sternum to keep the body balanced and flat. The concept was to position your body and stroke as if you felt like swimming downhill, with the sternum as the fulcrum point.[20]

Remarkably, when I had competed at an Ironman regional qualifying event for the Kona world championship in Wilkes-Barre, Pennsylvania, I was awarded the only slot in my 55–59 age group for Kona. When I told Terry McLaughlin the news, he immediately replied, "You need an Ironman coach. Troy Jacobson is the best."

Five times longer than any triathlon I'd entered, the Ironman is 140.6 miles: an ocean swim of 2.4 miles, a bike race of 112 miles, and a running marathon: 26.2 miles. I had *only thirty-five days* to prepare for this grueling test. The thought turned my stomach.

To my great good fortune, Jacobson lived in Baltimore, less than two hours from Salisbury, and responded immediately when I called him.[21] His best piece of advice surprised me at first: *avoid* intense training drills and any impulses to race aggressively during the Kona competitions on October 7. "The Ironman is a long event. If you try to race, you won't make it. Learn to find your cruise pace in the training, then just cruise—hang out there," he said.

For swimming, the first Kona event, Troy set my daily workouts at an hour, working different muscles with segments in freestyle, backstroke,

---

[20] The headline of *The New York Times* obituary on Terry McLaughlin, in 2017, captured his basic insights: "Terry McLaughlin, Who Taught Swimmers Not to Struggle, Dies at 66."

[21] Residing in Tucson in 2024, Jacobson remained a preeminent Ironman coach.

breaststroke, and backstroke. On the bike, the second event, I gradually extended daily training rides to a peak of forty miles.

I was happy to let go of my crazy idea to train for the marathon, the final event, pressing hard to match a Boston qualifying pace. I had over-trained badly that summer, attempting in two marathon races to run a pace fast enough to qualify for Boston in my age group: eight minutes, twelve seconds. (A full marathon at that pace would take three hours, thirty-five minutes.) I "bonked" both attempts at the eighteen-mile mark. Accumulating lactic acid turned my legs to stone; I could barely move them. It would have been disastrous to stubbornly attempt that Boston pace again as part of my buildup for Kona.

My goal for Kona simply would be to finish ahead of the dreaded midnight disqualification. I had to avoid bonking. I worked out a revised race plan. Run at cruising speed the first ten miles, then alternate walking and running a mile to the finish line.

THAT MYSTERIOUS AUSTRALIAN SURFER AT MY SIDE

Standing there on the Kona beach, we all waited for the signal to enter the water and swim out to deeper depths where the race would begin. A hundred and forty miles of nonstop racing was about to begin. I'm sure everyone was thinking, as I was, *Am I ready? Can I do this?* It was eerily quiet. The atmosphere was tense, but I felt surprisingly calm. I'd taken it easy the day before, laughing through three straight *Police Academy* movies in my hotel room and eating a big steak dinner. "That's what the Germans do and they're the best triathletes," Troy had counseled earlier.

I did have a sense of urgency. As I just indicated, everyone had to finish by midnight, seventeen hours later, or be disqualified—a DNF affixed for posterity next to our names: Did Not Finish. My goal was to complete each segment faster than the maximum time for each. (A slower time after any of the three segments would trigger immediate disqualification.) That would guarantee I would beat the midnight dead-line and make me a winner, in my own mind at least, regardless of where I ranked in my age group.

When the horn sounded at 7:00 a.m., I watched . . . and *watched* . . . as the crowd of athletes treading water suddenly came alive, thrashing and splashing. "Just hang back," Troy had advised. "Let them all climb over each other, wear themselves out," he said. "Don't even get into that mess. Start a little late, then go at your own pace."

This was shrewd advice, for two reasons. I did avoid the pileup of arms flailing and legs kicking. More importantly, shortly after I began my stroke, a wholly unexpected savior appeared by my left shoulder, an Australian lifeguard on a surfboard.

"You're getting off to a slow start. You're having trouble," he shouted.

No, I explained. The slow start in part was because I had waited until the pack was fifty yards ahead, but also because my back was slightly lop-sided (I had developed a mild case of scoliosis when I was eleven), I found it difficult to swim straight without lifting my head often to correct the drift. This course was a straight out and back to the beach, with a turn-around at a dock at 1.2 miles out.

"If you can stay to my left and keep me on course, I'll be able to see you and swim a straight line," I said.

"Okay," he said. "Let's do it."

For 2.4 miles, this fellow paddled right next to me on his surfboard, with frequent chirps of encouragement. Surfers are renowned for their lithe strength as well as their love of the ocean and joyful competitions. Keeping my head down, except for left-side breathing, I was delighted when I spotted NBC's underwater camera crews filming us stroking along. At one point, with my upper arms aching badly, I picked my head up and said to my surfboard companion, "I have to stop and rest."

He would not have it. "Oh no. You keep going. Don't you stop and rest."

I finished with eight minutes to spare before the swim cutoff. I don't know if it was possible to have made it without him. Probably not. I was so grateful, exhilarated, and then I looked all around to thank him. But I never saw the Australian again.

As I walked quickly through the shower area, changed into my riding clothes, and grabbed my racing bike, I thought to myself, *That guy now has a crazy yarn to share: nudging me along the entire 2.4 miles and helping me beat the cutoff.* More than ten thousand people come as volunteers for the Kona Ironman and to party late into the night. He checked the first box, and perhaps the second as well.

Next, onto two wheels. I had followed Troy's plan, cycling for twenty-five miles on different sections of the bike course on each of the four days I was in Kona before the event. The out-and-back course was fifty-six miles northward along main coastal roads, then a turnaround to the south. A strong crosswind, about fifteen miles an hour, slowed my pace. I wasn't concerned, figuring those high winds would give me a boost after the turnaround.

Not so. As I wolfed down a peanut butter sandwich for a protein hit at the turnaround, the winds reversed direction. Adjusting again to the stiff crosswinds as I cycled back, I glanced often at small mounds and hardened rivulets of dark lava that dotted the incline rising to the active Hualalai Volcano (last eruption: 1801) opposite the ocean.

Up ahead, as we neared a cove opening to the ocean, I was alarmed to spot cyclists ahead of me toppling onto the road. Truly dangerous crosswinds. *Better lean into those winds, or that will happen to me too,* I thought. I would learn later that NBC clocked those gusts at forty miles an hour. Concentrating on keeping my balance, not maintaining speed, I kept going. Once again, I finished comfortably ahead of the cutoff time after the cycling stage . . . remarkably, the same eight-minute cushion as with the swim. The cutoff after cycling had been ten hours, thirty minutes from the starting horn; I was ahead by sixteen minutes.

EXECUTING THE PLAN, FINAL STAGE

One more event to go—the marathon. Sunset was upon us. Gazing up at a steep incline, the overture for this run, I was surprisingly relaxed thanks to the modest time cushion I had banked through the swim and biking segments. But there was more work to do.

Don't bonk. Finish, I reminded myself. I could run these 26.2 miles in six hours or less. If I stayed true to my plan—run the first ten miles, then alternate a steady walk for a mile and run for a mile for the remaining sixteen miles—I would make the midnight deadline.

After trekking up that steep initial incline as Troy had coached, and not running, I made my way across ten miles on flat terrain along the coast into a sequence of rolling hillocks and level jaunts. At mile eleven, I took a deep breath, inhaled, and reminded myself: *Focus on getting to mile twelve, repeat progressively, and keep going to the finish*. Unconventional, I know, yet this worked well for me.

As I made the last turn in mile twenty-six onto the Ironman's celebrated home stretch, the time was fifteen minutes past 11:00 p.m. . . . forty-five minutes ahead of the deadline. These remaining four hundred yards along Ail'i Drive before me were bracketed by throngs of cheering volunteers and partiers behind small barricades on either side of the runners. Thousands. What a thrill! I was extremely happy, joyful, grateful—and under control. I had to be mindful that any acceleration in response to this adrenaline surge might pull me down. *Don't turn on the afterburners*, I cautioned myself. *Just get to the finish line*.

When I made it, a booming voice rang out through the loudspeakers: "Terry Conway. *You're an Iron Man!*"

Susan found me seconds later. Exhausted and staggering, I threw my arms around her. We hugged, made our way toward a tent with massage tables. I clambered onto one of them, soon attended by one of the strong women—Russians, as I remember. They immediately began kneading my arms and legs. "Why don't you sit up?" one said.

Day after finishing the Kona Ironman Triathlon

That is the last thing I remember . . . until I awoke apparently just moments later, bouncing along on a stretcher into the medical tent. My sodium count was microscopic, a routine ailment among long-distance athletes after hours-long events. After two bags of intravenous saline solution, I revived.

Now Susan was in my face, her nose pressed against mine. "Terry, you scared me. Please do not do this again!" I heard her clearly but was respectfully noncommittal. The issue turned out to be moot, although we didn't realize it at the time. I did try to qualify again for the Kona event in each of the next two years, failing both times. My Ironman heroics were consigned to the 1995 Kona results.

The Ironman championship experience was fabulous. The precise time etched into the back of my prized finisher's medal reads: 16.20:57 (or, 16 hours, 20 minutes, 57 seconds). With only thirty-five days to train seriously, I completed my Ironman World Championship challenge slightly more than thirty-nine minutes before the midnight cutoff. In my 55–59 age group, at age fifty-six, I ranked thirty-second out of forty men; one more finisher in my age group made it before midnight. The other seven participants were DNFs.

After taking in a lively awards party exclusively for competitors the next night, Susan and I flew together to San Francisco, then she to Baltimore and I to Boston on direct flights, my body feeling mostly numb and my brain buzzing and excited. My flight was taking me back to work, and that was fine too. The National Fisheries Institute annual convention was happening in Boston, an unparalleled networking event for me that I rarely missed even during the Taiyo ownership years.

I had given little thought before or after the race to how much time I might need to recover physically after putting so much energy and effort into that long day of the Ironman. Back in Salisbury, I resumed a mild exercise routine, assured by some of those new friends at Kona that I would recover after two weeks. How long did it take? Nine months . . . until I matched my normal pre-training time for my routine three-mile run around the neighborhood.

Not that any of that mattered. I still remember every minute of that race in Kona.

NINETEEN

BEACHHEAD IN THAILAND

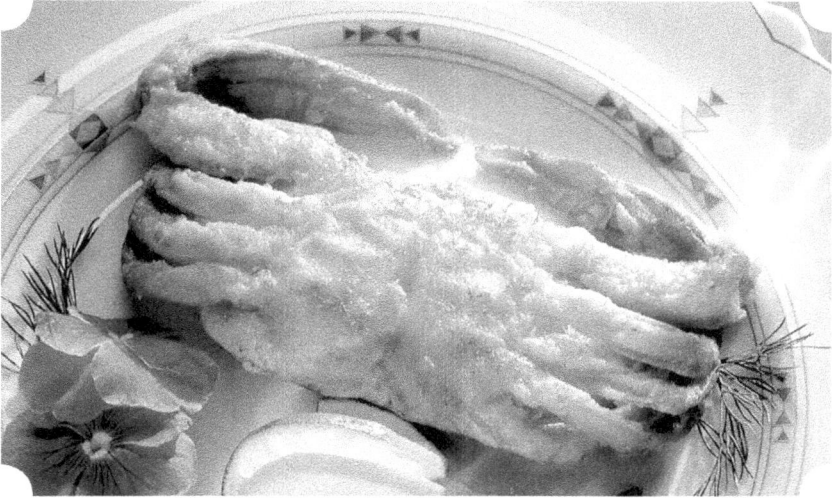

Soft Crab

At the thought of buying Handy back from Taiyo Oil, I was anxious and excited. Sleep was elusive. Here was a once-in-a-lifetime opportunity for another startup, an unexpected gift as I turned sixty to take what was still a cottage business onto the world stage. Annual sales had increased by a million dollars under Taiyo's control, but I was excited about what an unleashed international strategy across the Pacific could achieve.

Taiyo had left Handy's structure essentially intact during its ownership, and the company had continued to flourish under Carol's leadership. Now, we had an opportunity to open up even more international markets. We had several factors in our favor. First, the Asian soft crabs are superior, with fewer missing legs and claws, and they can be produced at significant savings. Second, the crab cake market was expanding rapidly, and Handy had no more space in the Crisfield plant, so Asia might also be a good place for producing this ever more popular product.

My vision for an Asia expansion would soon have three simple elements: Process better quality soft crabs at lower cost; ramp up production of crab cakes from the plentiful supply of fresh crabmeat; and, when timing seemed right, expand the product line to process the best quality pasteurized crabmeat on the market. My team was enthusiastic as well, eager to put these plans into action.

I booked my first flight to Asia less than a month after closing the deal to reclaim control of Handy. A US sales representative for a large seafood broker in Hong Kong, Tony Tsang, was the catalyst for this move.

Making the rounds at our most important industry networking event, the Boston Seafood Show, he had approached me and said, "I've got a large volume of excess soft crabs from Thailand I'd like to sell you."

"We're in the market now for that," I replied. "We need to establish new soft crab sources." Here I was . . . receiving an intriguing overture that perfectly matched one of my highest priorities.

"I'll put you in touch with my agent in Thailand," Tony said. "You should meet her." Within three weeks, I was on my way to Bangkok.

I celebrated quietly in coach economy, my habitual fare for every flight, during two long airborne segments spanning seventeen hours from Washington DC's Dulles Airport to Bangkok through Japan. I was glad to stretch my legs after traveling those nine thousand miles, walking quickly to claim my baggage and then stepping outside the terminal shortly after midnight . . . into humid, stifling air. It was April 15, 2000. The heat index was above 100 degrees.

The seafood agent in Thailand, Saisamorn Poupanthong, greeted me with a small gift the next day—a sweet gesture, emblematic, as I came to appreciate, of gracious Thai hospitality.

As Saisamorn (pronounced *SIGH-suh-morn*) described to me her connections in the thriving fishing and seafood processing industries of Thailand and neighboring Burma (soon to be renamed Myanmar), Tony's characterization of her as a savvy adviser appeared well-considered. Her English was excellent. Yet I couldn't shake the question that crowded my thoughts throughout the long flights: Was this journey going to lead to my lucky day, a new wellspring in Asia to help drive Handy's growth, or another dead-end adventure?

Then it was my turn for a first impression. I noted briefly for Saisamorn my return to ownership, highlights of Handy's hundred-plus-year history, our financial strength, growing customer demand, and my quest now to accelerate imports of soft crabs by sourcing shipments from international waters. I was excited, I added, to investigate Thailand under her wing as a potential beachhead for our Asia sourcing strategy.

One of my highest priorities was to sign supplier partnership agreements with established seafood processors to avoid building and owning our own plants. A brick-and-mortar investment would tie up Handy capital for years. We didn't have that kind of money, plus we didn't have the management capacity to learn and comply with local labor laws and other regulations. If this reconnaissance didn't work out, Handy would not lose much money.

"A processor named Kantang Seafood in southern Thailand might be a good fit for you," she replied. "They told me they have space in their Trang facilities if Handy would buy the soft crabs and handle all the processing there." If we decided to move forward, we'd have the ability to finance the operation with cash flow.

Trang, population sixty thousand, was situated about 450 miles south of Bangkok on Thailand's southwest coast across a small inlet from Phuket. The immaculate white beaches and turquoise waters of that resort island are world famous.

"It's just a little more than an hour to get there by plane. We can book a flight for tomorrow," she said.

I nodded enthusiastically. "Absolutely," I replied. "I'm looking forward to it."

Perhaps I was on the cusp of capitalizing on the insight that excited me more than two decades before, in those early days after buying Handy, that soft crabs ought to thrive in brackish waters virtually anywhere in the world. That this small business on the eastern shores of the Chesapeake truly had global potential. Here I was in Southeast Asia, about to take the measure of an unanticipated opportunity to put in motion my plan to expand Handy's supply and processing operations.

THIS COULD WORK.

With a coastal expanse of two thousand miles, Thailand has ranked among the world's largest seafood exporters, as high as third by some measures after China and Norway. Saisamorn explained during our eighty-minute flight the next morning that Kantang Seafood was among the large regional processors and exporters, handling a variety of seafoods. It had export licenses for all twenty-five European Union countries at the time as well as for the United States. The licenses were an all-important necessity.

Looking for crabs in Trang, Thailand

Companies such as Kantang Seafood knew how to schedule the large container vessels that crowd into the world's major ports and contract with shippers to have them load freshly processed seafood as often as two or three times a week. They took care of all of this, which meant that if we agreed to work together, Handy could keep its focus on sourcing crabs from local watermen, building a reputation as a reliable buyer, and monitoring quality of processing and packaging operations at every step.

"The owner, a Mr. Kriengsak, says his space is limited, so you'll have to judge if it will be adequate for what you need," Saisamorn told me. "He's willing to sign a confidentiality agreement and quote you a per-kilo fee based on the volume of soft crabs he processes weekly." She added that he was willing to help locate and introduce us to soft crab farmers in the area, and that he had no problem with our requirement to hire, train, and place Handy quality control staff in his plant.

Everything here matched items on my checklist.

This could work, I told myself, *if the processing fee they have in mind and payment terms are reasonable.* Still, I had to be cautious, guarded. *Is this too good to be true?* I wondered. *Is Saisamorn someone I can trust?* I had connected with Saisamorn only because someone I didn't know based in Hong Kong had approached me at the Boston Seafood Show. Tony Tsang did seem sincere and legitimate. He was an employee of Sun Wah, a large Hong Kong trading company. But I didn't know for sure. In my large network of business connections, he was only a minor contact.

I had few facts and no experience in a foreign country. I was reliant on Saisamorn and Mr. Kriengsak. I understood the abundance of risks. But it was a place to start without a huge investment; I made the decision to proceed.

Even so, I had to keep focus on Handy's pressing need for new sources of soft crabs and not let it cloud my judgment. Trust in business partners was implicit in my core principles. Whatever business partner I would commit to work with in Asia, halfway around the northern hemisphere from Crisfield, had to be one I believed down deep would be trustworthy.

Mr. Kriengsak and his plant manager, Supote, walked us through the processing plant, answering my questions along the way. Their site was on the mouth of the Trang River, fifteen minutes from the city center. Kriengsak, slightly built and about fifty years old, was all business. He did not speak much English, but his plant manager did. "We haven't worked with soft crabs before, but we can just set up as if we were doing another kind of fish," Supote told me.

As best I observed, adding to what Saisamorn had covered during our flight, their capabilities and standards met most of my specifications. The plant was old and hot, with poor lighting and a slight odor, yet clean. Space in cabinet freezers for Individually Quick Frozen soft crabs was adequate. Tables for workers to clean and process soft crabs, small weighing scales, and cold storage were available.

Kriengsak pointed to a darkened corner. "This is the space I would have for you," he said. It was small, barely enough to process crabs and store in cold storage daily. That was what we had to produce to assemble enough boxes of frozen soft crabs to fill a twenty-foot-long ocean container every two months. Even that would not be enough frozen soft crabs when combined with Crisfield production to meet projected sales. But it was a start.

That was the opportunity, take it or leave it. The fee and other terms were reasonable. I took it.

Within two months, our head of operations in Crisfield, Ben White, and a supervisor skilled in soft crab processing, Arlene Wharton, were on location in Kantang, diagramming how to set up a processing line and locating Thai vendors to provide supplies for the processing that they would ship by truck to Kantang. (These supplies included food-grade cellophane sheets for wrapping crabs, scissors for trimming and cleaning crabs, portable thermometers, and aprons and hairnets for the processing staff.) After another two months, we had hired staff for processing and for assuring that any new product in Thailand matched our Crisfield standards and quality.

Hiring quality assurance staff for Kantang was crucial for a successful ramping up of this first beachhead for Handy in Asia. It was our responsibility, and keeping with our good business practice, to assure consistent high quality and meet or exceed every government regulation. I never wanted to be in a situation where I learned of a competitor doing a better job in any aspect of quality products and customer service. And I never wanted to be in a situation of having to renegotiate pricing with customers or clash with government regulators who disputed the quality of Handy seafood.

"TERRY, WHAT ARE YOU GOING TO DO?"

Our confidence in the new partner's operations grew quickly after we started. Crabs arrived in a trickle at first. We were not surprised—local crab farmers had never worked with Handy, and most knew nothing about us. Ben White and I rented a shallow-water longboat powered by a noisy air-cooled engine mounted on a long drive shaft and set out with for two long days to see farmers along narrow rivers in mangrove swamps.

We found eight. One of our first quality control hires, Supote, handled introductions. As I had encouraged watermen on the Chesapeake in the early '80s, he asked them to "give us a try." In each case the farmers seemed receptive, happy to have another potential buyer for their catch. On a third day, after traveling two hours by truck on single-lane, clay-packed roads, we added more.

Their added supplies helped, but the Kantang operation would need more if our sales projections proved accurate. When I mentioned this to Saisamorn, she said we should consider pursuing more local fishermen on our own. "There are some soft crab farms not far away, but they are accessible only by boat," she said. "Do you want to visit?"

"Of course," I said. We had to find more soft crab sources. Carol Haltaman, in Kantang at the time, reminded me of another reason we needed more crabs: orders from food brokers and grocery chains in the United States were surging "above expectations." She added, "Can I come along?" Of course.

Saisamorn rented a skiff powered by a small outboard engine for the excursion, a forty-five-minute trip on a quiet, scenic, wide river to meet the soft crab farmers she had in mind. Most were pleased to learn they might have another potential buyer in Handy, possibly a large one, and said they would "send a few." That was all we wanted.

As we climbed back into the boat, I was relaxed and delighted by the afternoon's quarry. More soft crabs to fill rising orders back in Crisfield. I noted that the skiff had no oars or life jackets but shrugged it off, thinking the trip back was a short one. It wouldn't take us very long.

After about twenty minutes, the wind picked up as dark storm clouds approached. Without warning, the engine failed. Within moments we were sitting motionless on the water, uneasy as the sun sank slowly and those dark clouds loomed. *Out of gas.* Where are the life jackets? And the oars?

"I can't swim," Saisamorn said softly.

"Neither can I," Carol said, adding: "Terry, what are you going to do?" This was long before any of us had mobile phones to call for help. We glanced back at the boat operator sitting behind us, now apprehensive, subdued, and clearly nervous. He had no backup fuel. He couldn't swim either.

I looked around, water lapping quietly against the wooden boat. The shore was a good two miles away. No boat was within sight that might give us a tow. "Come on, Terry!" Carol repeated, sounding a bit panic-stricken. *"What are you going to do?!?"*

What indeed. Jump in and start swimming—with one arm . . . and push the boat with the other. My feet couldn't find the lake bottom, but I had no fear of water and I definitely could swim . . . thanks in part to those Ironman competitions a decade before and their mandatory 2.4-mile ocean or lake swims.

With three people in the boat and my dog-paddling with one hand and feet kicking under water, we were barely moving. The *African Queen* movie scene with Humphrey Bogart attempting to elude German soldiers, pulling a small steamboat with the engine turned off through a leech-infested swamp, came to mind.

"We need to move faster!" Carol exclaimed.

I retorted in an uncharacteristic, hard-edged command voice, "Put one arm in the water—and *pull!*"

I soon saw shore lights ahead. Thank goodness! That welcome sight provided navigational guidance and a hint of progress, such as it was, as we struggled forward. After what seemed like hours straining against the elements, but was less than one hour, my shoes found the muddy bottom, the water now chest high. From there, I knew I could press ahead more easily toward the shore, one step at a time, as the water became shallower. We were going to make it before dark.

Once we had all scrambled onto land, Saisamorn paid the hapless boatman—first with a terse comment in Thai and then in Thai baht cash. We climbed back into our vehicle and headed back to Trang, not that much worse for wear. The bay water was warm; the air was warm as well. I would have sore shoulders and arms the next day, but no cuts, bruises—or leeches. We dried off within minutes.

Looking back, I would do it all again. The fishermen we introduced ourselves to that day were exactly what we were hoping to find: an accommodating, reliable, long-term source of soft crabs. We became an accommodating, reliable, long-term source of demand and cash. Plus, we came away with a good yarn—with an abiding course of action emblazoned upon our memories: Insist on a readiness checklist briefing before stepping onto anyone's hired boat for journeys in remote waters.

CONFLICT IN KANTANG

We soon knew that we had a higher quality of soft crabs coming from Thailand than Crisfield, and we knew we were comparable or better than other soft crabs farmed in Thailand and elsewhere in Asia. These Asian crabs had a consistently soft texture. They looked a little different, with more white body meat, yet the taste when cooked was identical to American soft crabs, and became extremely popular at high-end seafood restaurants especially on the West Coast.

Two weeks after I returned to Crisfield after the two startup months in Trang, the plant began processing live crabs, sending them cleaned and frozen by the thousands onto container ships destined for Norfolk. Each container ship would carry nearly 200,000 frozen soft crabs. The line workers we hired were diligent and picked up details of their tasks quickly, traits I came to appreciate as characteristic of Thai people generally.

I was elated and grateful as frozen soft crabs processed and packaged in Kantang began arriving in Crisfield via truck from container docks in Norfolk. This was only two months after we signed the Kantang agreement . . . only three months after I regained ownership of Handy. It is difficult to picture how all the pieces came together by simply focusing step by step on each item on the Thailand checklist we had drafted in Crisfield. But it actually happened.

I kept in touch with my new Kantang partners often by phone and email and even flew back to visit the Trang site five times. With Trang getting into gear, we were operating two businesses at the same time: processing, packaging, and shipping in Crisfield, and this startup for soft crabs in Trang. I had often advised small clients at Deloitte and Laird to stick to their knitting, to avoid losing focus from over-reaching, but we had no choice.

It was exhausting at times for all of us traveling between Crisfield and Thailand, yet we kept pace. Quality and efficiency measures in the Trang plant were high. Local fishermen were harvesting healthy crabs with a clever, enhanced molting process that produced remarkably high yields. I was delighted. High quality, higher yields, lower costs.

Then what we should have expected to happen for a small American business planting a flag for the first time in a foreign country happened. Conflict. Kriengsak decided one day he would void our written contract and *triple* the agreed processing fee we were paying. I protested, diplomatically, that this was not how legal agreements work. We both had committed to terms. "That contract was agreed to months ago," he insisted. "My expenses are going up. I need more money. The fee needs to be higher."

It struck me then that contracts in Asia might not be enforceable in ways American law requires. Maybe they were more like temporary memos of understanding. I soon learned that while international contracts can be litigated in Thailand, cases typically drag on for three years as legal expenses mount. Filing a complaint made no sense in my opinion unless you are a big company seeking to recover tens or hundreds of millions of dollars. Challenging Kriengsak legally was not a realistic option. And arbitration in Singapore would take months. A Thai court might take three years before issuing a ruling if we filed a lawsuit in Thailand.

A GAMBLE IN RANONG

I hated confronting the possibility that our first overseas processing operation would collapse. It was stressful, disappointing. What was possible to replicate the successful operations we might be abandoning? How much would it cost? How long would it take? But I couldn't agree to Kriengsak's demand. If we allowed Kantang to triple its fee, wouldn't more demands soon follow? Even worse, the closely knit community of seafood processors soon would catch wind of our caving in. That would be a problem for our reputation in the years ahead, not only in Thailand but neighboring countries. Once the word got out that we tolerated breaking contracts, I figured we'd be dead.

I assumed Kriengsak wagered I had no option but to accept the higher fee. Maybe he had toiled in this vineyard before, hiking clients' fees sharply—a standard operating procedure. No matter. I didn't want the higher costs. And I didn't want to risk losing sales momentum in the United States by raising soft crab prices for my customers.

I decided to walk away.

We had no backup plan. We would have to start over, with these pressing unknowns: As outsiders still finding our footing in a foreign country, was it possible to locate an empty building nearby and start the business from scratch? Was there a similar seafood processing plant with space available to support a faster transition? The Crisfield city council had implausibly rejected our plan to expand processing there, but should we try again?

"We've got to figure this out," Ben White said.

Who might help? Members of the National Fisheries Institute, our industry trade organization, might operate or work with similar processing firms in Thailand. Would our contacts at the institute know? "I'll call them. It's a start. We can't quit until we find the best solution."

We wondered, what about Saisamorn? It turned out she had a friend who had inherited a seafood plant 240 miles north of Trang in an isolated coastal fishing port called Ranong. Saisamorn learned from her friend that the plant had space and working plate freezers for Individually Quick Frozen crabs and available storage. "It looks like our only option for now," I told her from my hotel room in Kantang. "I'll meet you there."

The six-hour drive to Ranong through monsoon downpours was exhausting, but I had not been in any mood to wait for a day when the skies cleared. (Ranong's rainy season spanned eight months.) My bias for taking action again paid off; a tour of the aging plant late in the day buoyed my spirits. The building was clean with no fishy odor, had flexible space for efficient operations, and offered plenty of room to relocate everything from our Kantang space . . . and for us to expand.

Moreover, the location was on a port near the Andaman Sea shoreline, two miles by boat south of Burma's southernmost border. "Handy can export directly from Ranong," said Duke, my tour guide and the general manager. "You would have your own entrance, with receiving dock and private space in connecting rooms for processing and packing. Office space is on the second floor."

The lighting was too dim for close inspections of the crabs, but better lighting was fixable. Overall, what I saw looked far better than what we would be leaving behind in Kantang. I was excited.

RISKY BUT POSSIBLE

Organizing the relocation moves from Kantang for all our equipment and simultaneously setting up a new business entity, Handy Thailand Ltd., was daunting. This is risky but possible, I thought. We remained mostly clueless on work rules, cultural mores, and government regulations for foreign-owned companies. Nor could we speak more than a few words of the Thai language. Did we have the skills and energy to make this work?

Our expanding Thai brain trust made sure that we did. Saisamorn huddled with her Bangkok friend and plant owner, Jarashporn Eaimimjit ("Jit" to us), and her husband, Duke, general manager, to draft a contract for the lease in English. They introduced me to experienced professionals who guided us through incorporation laws, permits for export-oriented businesses, and rules for tax filings.

To give me confidence that all Handy soft crabs shipped to the US from this new Ranong facility matched our high quality in Crisfield, one Crisfield processing team leader—Wanda Marshall—agreed to long stints in Ranong to train new workers. I never wanted to be negotiating with customers or a government about the quality of Handy's products.

In effect, I was orchestrating another complete startup, only this time it was located nine thousand miles away from Salisbury. For Gina, taking the role of lead instructor, and Wanda, supervisor, the flights to Bangkok were their first ever on a plane. Two other team members who excelled in packing crabs in Crisfield came too.

Within a month, our recruiter for quality assurance teams initially in Thailand and later everywhere we operated in Asia, Holly Mattos, signed up two eager college classmates who had been trained in food science.

It was their first job. Through Jit's connections, we found an accountant to make sure soft crab farmers and workers were paid fairly and on time as well as to track and prepare financial reports to make sure soft crab farmers and workers were paid fairly and on time as well as to track and prepare financial reports.

HOLLY'S GIFT: HIRING TALENTED FOOD TECHNOLOGY GRADS

Susan and I first met Holly Mattos on a hundred-mile Backroads cycling tour in northern Thailand from Chiang Mai to Chiang Rei. A native Californian living in Thailand, Holly was our guide: athletic, knowledge-able, and enthusiastic. Her principal job at Backroads was researching good hotels and the best restaurants and designing tours in Southeast Asia. She had a delightful personality. Soon after our cycling journey finished, we heard that Backroads planned to eliminate its Thailand cycling tours. "Terry, you should hire her for Handy," Susan suggested, and we did.

Holly became a major contributor to Handy's successful first decade in Asia, attracting forty talented students who were graduating with food technology and fisheries degrees from top universities in Thailand, Indonesia, and neighboring countries. She screened candidates who were smart to ensure that anyone we considered was able to speak and write English well. (Most Thai children study English in grade school.) For some of these students, landing a job with an American company in their home country was a dream come true.

I have found that over time, when you hire good people and support them in developing valuable skills, growth happens at every level in a business.

Those young people have become Handy's bedrock across Asia for maintaining rigorous compliance with US regulations and our rep-utation for quality products from Asia. No customer has ever raised a concern about any imported Handy shipment quality or refused payment for that reason. Very few seafood companies can say that. I don't know of any. One of Holly's recruits is now our operations manager in Bangkok; another runs one of Handy's big operations in Surabaya, Indonesia.

Duke tapped his years of experience to help hire local supervisors and workers who became valuable members of this new team. He offered employment to dozens of experienced crab workers who had worked at a Ranong plant that one of our Maryland competitors, Phillips Foods Inc., was closing. He and one of Holly's quality assurance recruits, Suradet Chobmee, spread the word of Handy's arrival and our desire to pay quickly and fairly from future harvests to the local crab farmers.

TWENTY

GENTLE, HARDWORKING PEOPLE

Thailand is a wonderful country with a distinct history and culture, never colonized. The people and government are inviting for foreigners interested in living or working there. Bangkok is a bustling modern city of more than six million people. Office and residential towers dominate the cityscape amidst ancient yet active Buddhist temples along the busy Chao Phraya River.

Buddhist culture and religion run especially deep in Thailand. Our partners and advisers in Thailand highlighted practical differences in American and Thai culture, differences we highlighted for Crisfield employees who helped us get started in Kantang. To cite the basics: Anyone raising their voice is viewed as lacking self-control; keep calm in conversations. Pointing a finger at anyone is rude; don't do it. Pointing your feet directly toward an image of the Buddha when sitting nearby is disrespectful; be sure to avoid this.

And here was a potentially serious hurdle that impacted non-Thai soft crab marketers: observant Buddhists do not kill animals or insects. The American practice of trimming away a live soft crab's nonedible parts such as the eyes and chewy apron on the back would not work in Thailand; that method causes a crab to expire. "If we are going to do business with you, you need to change this. Otherwise, we are violating our religious values . . . we are sinning," Sumpote told me in our first weeks in Kantang.

We had to find a different way. With his help, we quickly learned that immersing Thailand's indigenous warm-water soft crabs in cold water slows their metabolism to the point where they die naturally. In time, we made this change everywhere in Asia, eliminating all cutting of live crabs on our processing lines and respecting local beliefs and mores. In addition, one crab farmer's innovative solution to induce and monitor molting more humanely and efficiently gave us a brilliant solution to improving quality, matching the fresh taste of Chesapeake Bay crabs, and lowering costs.

We also had to abandon in Asia the American method of harvesting molting peeler crabs from their habitats before a new hard shell forms, the method waterman Eddie Daniels used. Asian crabs give no indication of when they are about to molt; they aren't peelers. We could not abide by induced molting, the standard practice then in Vietnam and Indonesia . . . and copied for a while in India.

Farmers there induced molting crudely, forcing the crab to release its claws and cutting off a live crab's legs at the joint, leaving only a paddle fin that crabs need to maneuver in shallow water. The cutting shock jolts a crab's survival instinct into action, with stubby new claws and supine legs soon emerging without enough time or food sources to fill in the body.

This lower-cost yet unnatural molting forced the crabs to absorb much more water than any method I had ever encountered. The frozen crabs shipped to restaurant kitchens in the United States bore little meat in the shell cavity. Worse yet, the extra water absorbed during shock molting spoiled cooking oil. The resulting taste was disagreeable, to put it mildly. Restaurants did serve these low-grade soft crabs—we dubbed them "water balloons"—but customers complained. Orders plunged.

Something had to be done.

COCONUT MONKEYS TREATED WELL? I THINK SO

The day I first met Sumpote, one of our new food technology hires in southern Thailand's Surat Thani province, he told us he was delighted to have found a good job so quickly in his home province near his family. His eagerness was infectious.

He drove us past lovely beaches to remote villages where we might locate fishermen who could supply live crabs for a new plant in Chaiya, the local urban center, where we planned to add production.

Sumpote's tour along the narrow Thai peninsula between the Gulf of Thailand and the Andaman Sea took us into a dense rainforest with tall limestone mountains and rubber trees. Around one bend, to my astonishment, I spotted a pickup truck ahead full of coconuts with a muscular monkey hanging on the back gate. A coconut monkey.

Coconut monkeys, Sumpote explained, are trained to rapidly climb trees, pick ripe coconuts, twist the stems, then drop the coconuts to the ground. The monkeys then descend swiftly and load coconuts onto a pickup truck. They are excellent workers. Male monkeys can average a thousand coconuts per day, females six hundred—both much higher than the eighty a day an experienced human climber can shake loose. It's a dangerous job for people.

In Thailand coconut monkeys go to a "school" for six months where, Sumpote assured me, they are treated with patience and kindness as they practice their trade. Their owners pay a thousand dollars for the training, a big investment in rural Thailand that gives the owners serious incentive to treat their monkeys well. Some coconut monkeys become family pets, similar to how some clans embrace their elephants in northern Thailand.

I saw one monkey riding on the back of a motorcycle, arms wrapped around the driver's waist, just like a teenager. That monkey on the truck ahead was finished for the day, enjoying a ride on the back gate, probably to either a street market or his owner's home.

Training intelligent animals to perform human work has been practiced for centuries. Asian elephants, horses, guide dogs, donkeys, and sniffer dogs are current examples. Most owners of working animals believe it is possible for intelligent, trained animals to enjoy having a job to do. I am one of them. The coconut monkeys seemed eager to show off their climbing skills, and especially liked riding on the back of the truck. When working in and around trees, the monkeys are tethered for reasons similar to why we keep pet dogs on a leash.

PETA, an animal rights nonprofit, has protested the treatment of coconut monkeys, persuading some retailers to avoid stocking any products harvested by coconut monkeys. The organization contends that these monkeys are treated as miserable slaves. That is not what I have observed during my trips to Surat Thani. And I have been traveling there for nearly two decades.

A BRILLIANT INVENTION: CRAB CONDOS FOR PLUMP CRABS WITH MORE MEAT

A Thai soft crab farmer in eastern Thailand near the Cambodia border was gaining a following for his plump and tasty crabs among Saisamorn's clients in Hong Kong. The new, more economical system he had invented for molting soft crabs was unique in Southeast Asia. With orders compounding, the farmer, Jumnong, was expanding operations rapidly and encouraging Saisamorn to spread the word. This sounded too good to be true.

Was this a far better soft crab at a lower price? What was the magic in this new molting method? How soon could we visit? With Saisamorn's brother at the wheel and her favorite American country music on the radio, we traveled three hours from Bangkok to Chanthaburi, a river town of 23,000 people near the shores of the Gulf of Thailand. Jumnong's processing plant and his home were perched on poles above the tidal Chanthaburi River close to his farm.

Entering his home, we removed our shoes. Saisamorn introduced us to the family, including Jumnong's wife, daughter, granddaughter, and father, who later, with a smile, handed me as a gift the small wooden boat he had been carving. Jumnong picked this location for processing crabs and for a residence because it was across the street from a large Christian cemetery. Most potential thieves, wary of menacing ghosts, preferred other marks and kept their distance, he said. Angels might have been abundant in the neighborhood as well, home to the century-old Cathedral of the Immaculate Conception.

The dozen ponds of Jumnong's sprawling farm featured a dazzling expanse of his invention, hundreds of ventilated plastic boxes. The boxes were small, some fifteen by thirteen by ten inches, floating in water, half-submerged and tethered to long PVC poles. He called them a one-crab condo.

Every day Jumnong and his farm workers dropped morsels of cut-up small fish into the condos. Within two to four weeks each crab fills up its shell, becomes fully packed, molts, puffs itself up with water, and begins the hardening process for its new larger shell by absorbing calcium from the water, something every crustacean must do to grow. To keep pace with this ballet of nonstop molting, Jumnong's workers inspect the condos every four hours, extract the recently molted, and determine if the crab is too soft or hard. If left in the water too long, the crab will become stiff in six hours and totally hard in twelve.

Yes, Jumnong said, the condos are expensive to keep free of barnacles and require manual inspection every four hours to pull molted soft crabs out of the water. The crab's weight from a condo is so much heavier than one whose legs and claws are cut to induce molting before becoming fully developed that the economics favor the condos. WOW! A plumper crab with its full craws and legs as nature intended at a lower cost! Plus far less moisture compared to half-empty induced crabs, which spoils cooking during the cooking process. This was a breakthrough.

I was enthralled. When you find a better product, you need to run hard. We quickly began ferrying Jumnong's live soft crabs by truck to our new Ranong operation. The cost of the eleven-hour trip was negligible compared to the higher yield. The taste was surprisingly comparable to the sweet Chesapeake Bay soft crab when cooked, and it had more white meat. Handy enjoyed a competitive advantage wherever we shipped them to Europe and the United States.

No one could match the taste at the price we charged. We opened up a brand-new market. I persuaded our soft crab farmers at the time and in the years ahead to convert to Jumnong's crab condo system. No one anywhere in the world I've encountered has developed a method to surpass his. Twenty years later, Jumnong remains among our most preferred soft crab farmers.

KEEP MOVING, DON'T LOOK BACK

Things might have worked out very differently after I refused the demand in Kantang for the steeper processing fee. We could have stumbled badly and eventually retreated entirely from Thailand and maybe Southeast Asia entirely. Perhaps the sting of such a setback could have persuaded me to step back from my plans for global expansion.

Yet by now I had no doubts that brackish estuaries with prolific crab habitats were out there and would be essential to keep building Handy. We had to stay the course. "Just move head, keep moving," I reminded myself once again as we sorted through how to put the Kantang disappointments in the past. "Keep moving, and don't look back."

This impressive team overcame multiple obstacles. We created operations in Ranong and later Surabaya in Indonesia that were fully integrated, similar to what I had seen decades before at Perdue Farms. Having control of supply, processing, packaging, and shipping all the way to the final customer without relying on costly middlemen enabled us to monitor and adjust quickly when necessary to ensure that every step met our quality standards.

It was remarkable to me that the entirely new Ranong operation opened for business only two weeks after we halted operations in Kantang and began loading equipment for the 240-mile journey north. I am as elated and grateful now as I was at the time. More than twenty years after that all-hands-on-deck rally, a pivotal moment in Handy's history, we still operate the Ranong plant. It continues to ship high-quality frozen soft crabs and now other crab food products thousands of miles across the oceans to customers in Europe and the United States.

BOLSTERING MANGROVE FORESTS

Since 2007, we have closed the Ranong operations for a day each year so teams of Handy workers can spend time together planting mangrove trees nearby along the western shores of the Andaman Sea.

It's a contribution that helps support stability and growth for the local crab population, a vital practice for fisheries that is also important for the local economy. Moreover, mangrove forests improve air quality by converting carbon dioxide to oxygen.

Mangrove forests are a balm for crab habitats because their trapped sediment and underwater root systems extending several feet out into the water provide shelter that protects especially young crabs from fish predators and invertebrates such as squid, clams, and earthworms. Muddy waters contribute to the defenses as well.

The forests also can limit or prevent coastal destruction from tsunamis and storm surges because they can withstand the battering on land by absorbing wave energy from the towering first waves of seawater and limiting erosion.

Ranong escaped mostly unscathed, largely due to a smattering of small islands offshore that absorbed the blows, when a massive tsunami in 2004 devastated parts of two popular tourist destinations, Khao Lak and Phuket, between one hundred and two hundred miles to the south. More than five thousand people died, and thousands more were injured.

It wasn't long after the tsunami disaster that Thailand's Department of Marine and Coastal Resources organized a mangrove planting campaign that included a location near Ranong. The agency halted large-scale cutting of mangrove forests there by locals who were clearing coastal land for shrimp farming.

"All our employees live in the area, so this was a fitting project," said Jay Ivancic, our vice president for international operations. "We wanted to give back to the community. It's also an educational resource because our workers teach their children and spouses, some of whom are local fishermen, about the importance of the mangroves."

The Handy planting day typically is in late November or early December. Thai Environment Day is December 4.

"We try to start work early in the morning before it gets too hot. Weather conditions range from hot and rainy to scorching heat and high humidity, with temperatures well into the nineties," Jay said. "Then we'll usually finish the day with a dinner and appreciation party for all the employees."

Nearly 800,000 trees were planted in the Ranong area from 2010 through 2024, with Handy teams accounting for 24,000 across the eight years Handy has participated. Some 80 percent of trees planted survive, according to government records. And the mud crab, or Scylla serrata species, population has increased.

Several years later after we joined the Thai mangrove project, we had a role in starting a related program to teach local fishermen in the Philippines and Indonesia best conservation practices for swimming crabs. The goal: to prevent over harvesting and habitat declines in established or emerging areas of high-volume crab sourcing.

More than thirty fisheries in the United States, convened by the National Fisheries Institute, set a standard in 2010 of not accepting crabs with smaller carapaces (defined now as ten centimeters or less) or female crabs dredged from nutrient-rich mudflats. Trawling gear was banned.

The program is managed through the NFI's Crab Council, which Handy helped initiate; we later added Thailand, India, Sri Lanka, and

Vietnam. It disperses $1 million a year to local fishermen that the NFI companies raise collectively in what is known as a pre-competitive collaboration.

MOST OF MY TIME IN ASIA, WELL INTO MY SEVENTIES

Success comes at a personal price—and with unfailing commitment. I had to spend an enormous amount of time getting the plants in Ranong and Bangkok started. Thailand was especially difficult because it was the first time Handy operated outside of Crisfield as a food processor with the crab cakes and later other specialized variations such as shrimp wraps and tempura soft crabs. We had to become more than a seafood processor.

For more than ten years, from 2001 well into the 2010s—and well into my seventies—I was in Asia more than Maryland, often thirty weeks a year. I am sure my habits of staying fit, exercising when possible, and eating reasonably well enabled me to be strong enough physically and mentally to do this work. Of course, I also was highly motivated.

I planned five multipurpose trips to Asia each year. The normal pattern was to work two to three days at a location and take a direct flight to the next location at night. Most trips were between four and five weeks. The agenda for each trip included a variety of stops: processing plant openings, first production of a new product, first and second visits to new sourcing and processing opportunities, and visits from American and European customers. Each location included a delightful luncheon with Handy's quality control staff and an update on "what was going on at Handy worldwide."

The purpose was always to find high-quality and dependable sources of supply. In all, I visited twenty-five different countries in Asia and Africa. Most were referrals from existing suppliers. I made several trips to very remote areas where I grabbed my Indiana Jones hat. A quick glimpse of my passport stampings from Asia and Africa provides a testament to this endless search. In Indonesia, I toured harvesting farms in Java, Sumatra, Sulawesi, and Borneo as well as five more in Thailand (beyond what we found) that didn't work out. The Philippines became a good source. I came up emptyhanded, either quickly or in the long run, in Vietnam, Cambodia, Malaysia, China, and Sri Lanka. Trips to Africa led to take-a-pass results in Madagascar and Mozambique, but Tunisia in recent years has been fabulous.

Each trip was followed by four days of recovery to clear my head from jet lag after I landed at Dulles and drove three hours to our home in Salisbury. In my absence, Carol Haltaman ran the company office in Salisbury, and Ben White managed the operations in Crisfield.

COMMODITY BUSINESS IMPERATIVE: ALWAYS PURSUE LOWER-COST SOURCES

Seafood is a commodity business. That means we need to always keep our eyes on potential new sources of crabs that are available at lower costs. In other words, we were always chasing low-cost producers of soft crabs. A huge soft crab farm in an isolated area of Burma, now called Myanmar, turned into a windfall for us.

Investors in Malaysia had backed a Thai soft crab farmer who had created a thriving operation copying Jumnong's crab condo methods. It was thriving in production but not sales. A seafood broker in Los Angeles called me and said, "You are the soft crab leader in America. A new soft crab processing farm in southern Burma has a lot of product but not enough customers. Are you interested?" I soon hopped onto a ninety-minute flight from Yangon to Myeik and was driven to a very poor, isolated area. The operation had both soft crab farming and processing. It was fabulous, at least twice the size of Ranong.

The sanctions affected fishermen living in remote regions working from small sampans. We had been buying by the hundreds of thousands through the big farm. We just had to wait it out. Those sanctions were lifted in 2012.

Years ago, our international vice president, Jay Ivancic (pronounced eh-VON-chick), said it was a good time to investigate prospects for buying soft crabs in Bangladesh. He discovered an excellent, largely untapped source along the southern coast: the world's largest mangrove forest, the Sundarbans.

The Sundarbans is the Bengal tigers' natural habitat, a United Nations World Heritage Foundation site encompassing more than forty thousand square miles. It spans the borders of Bangladesh and India along the brackish coastal waters of the Bay of Bengal.

We opened a processing plant there in 2020. The crabs are cold and hard, and molt for only a very short period. Our Bangladeshi farmers know how to stay on top of this. They also use the crab condo method, which as we know keeps quality and yield high.

"It's very remote," Jay said. "I fly two and a half hours to Dakar, the capital, take another flight to Chittagong, a port city to the south, and then drive five hours in a van to get there. Along the way, you pass huts of mud and straw where most people live. They are very poor."

We hired and trained two hundred people from local communities when we opened the plant. I hope this has helped them live a little better, something I have always believed is true for employees of well-run businesses. Strengthening local economies and communities was a motivation I had when I was young and wanted to one day own my own business.

A SOFT CRAB'S LIFE

The soft crab fishery is the most wondrous of the world's fisheries. The mating process is romantic. The struggle to molt is incredible to watch. The soft crab with all new and larger parts is one of nature's wonders. And the soft crab must be clever enough to locate a place to hide from predators while patiently waiting for its new shell to harden.

When the female crab senses the last of her eighteen molts is approaching, she searches for a male crab willing to carry her around for protection until molting, mating while she is temporally soft, and carry again until her new shell hardens.

Crab molting to grow a larger shell

She develops a sponge that holds two million tiny, fertilized eggs. When they're released, the winds and currents gradually move them to the saltwater coastline, where they feed and molt frequently. As the crab's legs and claws gradually take shape, the crab swims toward brackish water and begins growing larger. The crab reaches adulthood in one year.

Watermen catch crabs in chicken-wire pots. If the paddle find indicates molting is within a week, crabs are placed in open-air tanks, where they absorb water to open a crack in the shell, molt by using all of their strength to back out, and absorb calcium in the water to start the hardening process. It's fascinating to watch.

A CRAB IS NOT A CRAB

A note to the reader: The crab that you eat is not a crab. Yes, the process starts with live crabs, but these crabs are separated into three crab products, each processed in a specialty plant.

In the passages above, we reviewed soft crabs from the first day in Crisfield to Ranong, Thailand, and subsequently in Myanmar and

Bangladesh. The second crab product—crab cakes—also began in Crisfield and is now processed at specialty food plants in Thailand and Indonesia. The third crab product—pasteurized crabmeat—was first processed in Tuticorin, India, and is currently packed in Indonesia and the Philippines as well.

TWENTY-ONE

CRAB CAKES: INNOVATIONS, GUINNESS WORLD RECORDS

Hand-made Crab Cake

At Handy, we were always eager to seize opportunities, and that meant having several irons in the fire at once. So, while I was scouring the world in search of high-quality, low-cost suppliers, we were simultaneously thinking about taking the next step in the company's growth. With our soft crab sales still rising in the United States and new markets in Japan and Europe buzzing, I wondered with Carol if timing was right to introduce something new to build on Handy's hundred-year-old brand.

A product extension, a second seafood offering to complement soft crabs, seemed the safest approach. "Let's think about crab cakes," she said. "Everyone in town seems to have a secret recipe. I have a simple one."

Good idea.

Crab cakes were prized as a delicious regional specialty. Fresh crabmeat had been plentiful in decades past along Maryland's eastern shore. I thought back to that festive meal of soft crabs and crab cakes my family enjoyed before I bought the company. Why weren't these local delicacies better known?

Here was an opportunity to change that, but not without challenges. With Chesapeake Bay's annual soft crab harvest slowing, more crabmeat was being shipped from nearby states or imported. At some point, crabmeat supplies might be constrained and production costs increased if we succeeded in building a market for a quality Handy crab cake. What then?

Moreover, ensuring food safety and quality consistency with crab cakes is more complicated, far more complicated, than processing soft crabs.

PROCESSING EARLY CRAB CAKES IN CRISFIELD

We knew that to succeed in crab cakes we would have to be constantly experimenting, innovating, and investing, especially in the first years. A first try, with outsourcing in 1985, eventually failed; crab cakes made by a company within an hour from Salisbury with our recipe had great taste but flopped. Customers couldn't see crabmeat even though crabmeat comprised 70 percent of volume. The flecks were too small. A typical remark: "It tastes pretty good, but we can't see it."

Then, too, the cakes punched out by this company's automated machines looked like hockey pucks, not the handmade quality we had in mind. Crab cakes currently on the market that we sampled for possible alternatives barely had any crabmeat at all, only 5 percent, and a flat taste. Who would want to buy a second time?

By the mid-1990s we became determined to do crab cakes ourselves. Big visible chunks of crabmeat . . . 65 percent of total volume.

Small bits of shell in local crabmeat had to be spotted and removed with small forceps. We needed black lights for this. Adding and mixing ingredients, such as mayonnaise and spices, had to meet FDA standards. A mayonnaise maker in California shipped an all-natural fresh product we needed to have a shot with Whole Foods and other grocery chains with no-preservative policies. Serving sizes needed to be uniform, handmade with a scoop just like the scoops you use to make ice cream cones. We wanted a handmade, authentic, "back of the house" look.

To prevent contamination, all staff in our clean rooms had to be attired in head-to-toe protective gear, from hair covers and facemasks down to boots they would wear on production lines after walking through a shallow bath of sanitizing fluids. Then, to make sure it all worked, we would need quality control specialists to monitor everything. The soft crab processing steps we knew so well were so simple by comparison that we needed only one QC specialist.

Food technology was more complicated too. We needed nitrogen freezers to keep steam-cooked lumps of crabmeat intact and quickly lock in fresh flavors and colors once new crab cakes were formed, scales to ensure consistent portion weights, and freezer storage with tightly calibrated cooling gauges. Temperatures too high or too low would ruin a batch. And with all our existing equipment and space designed to process soft crabs in high volumes, we needed to organize a separate space dedicated to processing, making, and packaging the crab cakes.

The early going was slow. Shipments for food shows and among wholesale buyers for the grocery chains drew some interest but no orders.

Then, a breakthrough with Costco. The Mid-Atlantic group of Costco's Northeast division agreed to offer a small shipment of Handy crab cakes, four pallets, during the 1999 holiday season. With nearly five hundred stores across the United States at the time, Costco was on its way to becoming what by the early 2020s was the world's fifth largest retailer. Its distinctive strategy: curating choice and restaurant-quality foods for shoppers at lower prices in a grocery superstore setting.

The head of our retail sales division, Nelda DeLauro, made the first sales pitch. Nelda was trusted and respected by Costco and the other big membership clubs, Sam's Club and BJ's. Trusted because she had a reputation for always delivering what she promised—deliveries on time and quantities and pricing as agreed. Respected because she held firm during pricing negotiations. (Buyers called her "The Velvet Hammer.")

That initial order sold out quickly. Consumers could see the crabmeat. This innovation of ours finally was changing the game. Costco's

Northeast buyers placed more orders and made Handy crab cakes a permanent item, not seasonal. Buyers in Texas, San Diego, and Los Angeles soon followed. Costco has seven regional buying centers. The organizational structure enables regional division heads to stock brands popular with their shoppers that might not sell as well elsewhere in the country.

You can imagine how excited we were when all Costco divisions independently began ordering Handy crab cakes. Their competitors soon followed Sam's and BJ's, as well as large regional grocery chains along the Atlantic coast such as Whole Foods. Handy was the first to offer quality frozen crab cakes that foodservice wholesalers and retail warehouses sold to their consumers. Within five years, higher-quality crab cakes were on the menus of top restaurants in Japan, Great Britain, continental Europe, and Australia.

Crab cakes, of course, had been on restaurant menus for decades in Baltimore and along the Chesapeake coasts. These servings were handmade, typically with secret ingredients cultivated in house. And the servings could be stunningly huge, especially in sports bars: two six-ounce patties on a plate! (We packaged ours in three-ounce servings.)

NEED FOR MORE PROCESSING CAPACITY

We were achieving two of my criteria for business success: an increasingly superior product and a profitable market, but we had yet to expand our capacity in Crisfield enough to complete the third one: processing at a competitive advantage.

We created a very small space for crab cake production in the recently renovated plant I mentioned before and then proceeded to immediately add a seven-hundred-square-foot addition, the size of a one-bedroom apartment yet big enough to handle all those elements that we needed.

As sales took off, we advised our Taiyo owners that setting up crab cake production in Asia might be the most efficient way to quickly accelerate output to keep pace with demand, but they turned down the idea of Handy production in Asia. "Just keep doing what you are doing," they said.

We had initially thought, when Carol and I came up with the idea, that a product extension into crab cakes might be a low-risk way to build longer-term profits for Taiyo. We wanted them to be delighted with their Handy ownership, and they wanted all Handy production to remain within the United States. As crab cake demand from both wholesalers and retail warehouses continued to surge by early 2000, we tried again. Same answer: "Don't change; stick with what you are doing."

Okay, I thought, we'll need to build more capacity in Crisfield. An architect designed a $4 million state-of-the-art plant for turning out crab cakes and other special products for US customers. We had in mind acquiring a vacant lot owned by the town next to a Dollar General store. Most of our associates lived nearby and walked from their homes. We estimated these operations would create sixty jobs initially and perhaps two hundred over time. Local planning and zoning officials unanimously approved the plans.

All was well. We organized a hiring campaign to bring dozens of new line workers to Handy, bolstering the local economy. But then, dismay. Crisfield's five-member city council, including the state-appointed county official overseeing economic development, unanimously *turned down* the project. I asked one of the voting council members why.

"Just . . . wanted . . . to," he said, flatly, with no explanation. As years passed, I never picked up any local gossip about what was behind this. The logic baffled us then as it does now.

KICKSTARTING OUTPUT IN ASIA

I didn't have time to plot the kind of protest we had mounted years before, when we blocked a Maryland governor's plan to put state funds behind an ocean vessel painting business nearby using chemicals that would have poisoned soft crab habitats and harvesting. We had to react quickly.

Luckily, under the Taiyo radar, we had been researching ways to produce crab cakes in Asia before Taiyo rejected the idea and the city council blocked our expansion plan in Crisfield. These visions for expanding crab

Kuhn Prasan and Terry Conway 2025

cake production in Asia took wing quickly after we reacquired Handy ownership from Taiyo that summer.

Saisamorn connected us with the managing director of a prospering, well-established seafood and commodity processing company near Bangkok. His name was Prasan Tanprasert. His company was TEP Kinsho.

The TEP Kinsho operations, with three thousand employees in seven buildings, were humming. They included a range of activity we would need for crab cake production: processing lines, nitrogen freezers, and a laboratory for testing and complying with international food safety rules. His teams were producing a variety of handmade seafood for export to Japan. Other Japanese companies had their own operations in leased space.[22]

---

[22] Nitrogen freezers are essential in processing high-quality crab foods. We use them to freeze crabmeat quickly at –75 degrees Fahrenheit after the food is processed. This prevents ice crystals from accumulating, preserving a fresh texture. If ice crystals do form, thawing crab foods become mushy.

But how could we get started? He had no space, nothing unoccupied by his teams or those of his clients. The only possible space, Mr. Prasan said, was to give us access to a small test kitchen, the size of a small bedroom, but that would be only after 5:00 p.m., when employees of a Japanese seafood company had left for the day. Was that acceptable? It had to be.

Even that small test kitchen was not adequately equipped when Carol Haltaman and Gina Brown arrived from the States within days after Prasan and I signed a two-year deal. Prasan's staff had to set them up in a small room close to the plant site without air conditioning.

The Thai heat and humidity were draining for our native Marylanders. "It was so hot in there," Carol remembers. "We were standing all day on a cement floor doing these recipes. At the end of the day, we were just drenched, all the way through."

Their move into the air-conditioned Japanese test kitchen brought welcome relief. "It was spacious and modern, with everything we needed, including an office," Carol says.

Prasan later dedicated a large section in one of his buildings for us to produce the crab cakes and, soon, mini crab cakes, tempura soft crabs, and other specialized crab items. We shipped the black lights required for his team members to spot and remove tiny pieces of soft cartilage in golf bags with hard plastic shells. We discovered (the hard way, from experience) that the golf bags were an effective way to protect the lights from shattering during trans-Pacific flights.

Carol and Saisamorn were rushing with me in Kantang, and others pitching in from Crisfield, to locate suppliers for the same all-natural ingredients to match the taste in the recipe Carol had crafted for Crisfield's crab cakes years before: Old Bay Seasoning (a blend of herbs and spices), all-natural mayonnaise, panko breadcrumbs, yellow mustard, fresh eggs, and fresh vegetables. Our only missing piece after a month of inquiries and agreements was a vendor for all-natural mayonnaise.

"It took a long time to figure out," Carol says. "Getting the mayonnaise right in Asia was a huge challenge for us." We made a list of vendor prospects by buying all mayonnaise brands at a Bangkok grocery store, then called their suppliers on the phone. Most protested that they didn't have ways to keep mayonnaise without preservatives cold and fresh during deliveries. Or that our initial orders would be too small to be worth the trouble. Or, most often, "We don't do that. Just buy our stuff."

A large Unilever plant in Thailand did agree to deliver shipments of chilled mayonnaise with no preservatives. Initially, crab cakes with all these local ingredients tasted fine, a perfect match to Crisfield's best-sellers, but then we had a problem. "Something has changed," we told Unilever. "We can't taste the crabmeat."

They were defensive at first, so we organized a series of simple spoon-sized taste tests, contrasting crab cakes made with our US-sourced mayonnaise with Unilever's current version in Thailand. The latter somehow erased the crab cakes' spicy taste and masked the sweet crab flavor. Unilever's Thai food scientists did come around, acknowledging flavor gaps. They soon discovered that their production team had switched to a different food oil supplier. When they reverted to the original supplier, problem solved—at last. This mayonnaise stumble took a month to straighten out.

"WE GIVE HONOR TO EACH OTHER."

As orders grew, we leveraged this slim toehold in the sprawling complex of TEP Kinsho into a more spacious, air-cooled crab cake production center. Handy sourced the crabmeat locally, and TEP Kinsho workers, under our quality team's supervision, made and packaged the crab cakes. As I mentioned earlier, crab cake production is much more complicated than soft crab production. We needed six full-time quality control specialists for crab cakes in Bangkok; for soft crabs in Ranong, we needed only one.

Handy now had achieved for crab cakes all three parts of our success model—a superior product, processed at competitive advantage, and sold profitably. Just as we had done in Asia with soft crabs.

Within three years, our crab cake processing operation ranked among TEP Kinsho's biggest customers. This was not the case by the early 2020s. The company's other export businesses in rice, sugar, frozen seafood, pork, and poultry products had grown rapidly with rising demand in the Middle East. Even so, for more than twenty years, we have shared a respectful and successful partnership.

"There has been a loyalty all along between us and Terry," Prasan replied when my colleague in developing this book, Tom Hayes, asked him in his Bangkok headquarters what he thought had made the relationship work. I couldn't agree more.

Prasan continued: "We give honor to each other. We both were interested in a long-term relationship when we first started. Even though our work for Handy now is not a big part of our business, we will keep going as far as I'm concerned. The good heart of Terry . . . that is what we like here."

I feel the same about Prasan and his team. Consider this remarkable gesture. A handful of our major retail customers require any company engaged in Handy operations outside the United States to comply with their social audit standards governing how well *all* of that partnering company's workers are paid, their housing conditions, plant safety, and more. This covers all workers in a partnering company, not just Handy's and other US workers. Yet fewer than two hundred of Prasan's two thousand workers work for all his US clients combined.

Putting these rules into practice for all TEP Kinsho workers added between 5 and 10 percent to his costs. If Prasan had not agreed, we would have been forced to take our business somewhere else or lose these large customers. This marvelous relationship would have been severed.

"Sometimes we feel this social audit standard is a trade barrier," Prasan told Tom, calmly. "Terry feels this is unfair to us. But we have always compromised when differences arise. Terry never makes demands. He appreciates what we have done. That is nice for him as a leader, and why we can keep our relationship for long-term business."

TAKING A LOWER-COST,
HIGH-QUALITY OPTION IN INDONESIA

This remained true of our relationship even as we needed, for competitive reasons, to find another large seafood processor with comparable facilities for producing crab cakes and other specialty items.

I couldn't quarrel with Prasan's logic or decision, but that change combined with higher crabmeat prices narrowed our profit margins. Most competitors simply cut back on how much crabmeat they put in their crab cakes, but we didn't. We wanted to maintain quality—and especially our customers' trust in the Handy brand.

We also didn't want to raise prices for our customers, so we asked ourselves: "Is there a similarly integrated plant in another Asian country with less expensive crabmeat and processing?"

A large international shrimp-processing company in Surabaya, Indonesia, known as BMI, was especially appealing. Their customers included several well-known American importers I knew. They all gave me rave reviews about BMI. The company was founded by a woman. Her four sons were running it. The family's third generation had all studied at American universities—UCLA, University of Southern California, University of Washington—which made it easy for me to talk with them.

We had started buying pasteurized crabmeat from a new division at BMI and were aware that they had abundant crabmeat sources near their location on Indonesia's northern coast: three and a half hours by air from Bangkok and four hundred miles east of Jakarta. They had no experience with crab cake processing, but we agreed those details would be similar to shrimp products that BMI handled in high volumes. They had the right equipment and space for us to begin quickly, and we soon had a deal.

Onsite crabmeat production gave BMI a slight competitive edge over TEP Kinsho for two reasons. One, prices were lower because BMI had its own expanding crabmeat supplies. Two, we could avoid the added expense we had in Thailand for shipping crabmeat by truck eight hours nightly to Bangkok after cleaning and processing in Surat Thani, the coastal province more than two hundred miles away.

TWO THRIVING PARTNERSHIPS: HIGH VOLUME, SALES, AND PROFITS

It took us only three months to replicate our TEP Kinsho facilities with BMI. The half dozen college graduates in food technology whom Holly Mattos recruited from a prominent Jakarta University quickly identified reputable vendors for recipe ingredients, trained production workers, and then took responsibility to ensure product quality met our high standards. (One of those hires today manages one of the Indonesia plants.) We flew in key leaders of our crab cake teams in Crisfield and Thailand, tapping their expertise during the ramp-up. Taste and quality of Handy crab cakes from BMI were immediately indistinguishable from our two existing sites . . . a perfect match.

Within three years after starting in Bangkok, by 2006, we had sold more than ten million crab cakes shipped from our TEP Kinsho operations alone, mostly half-ounce minis. Costco remained our biggest customer, selling the bite-sized half-ounce minis through seven of its eight regional distribution centers. Sam's Club and BJ's also added Handy minis to their stores.

The semi-competitive situation with TEP Kinsho and BMI has kept costs reasonable without creating any material strains in relationships. Prasan was used to having customers move on entirely after a few years of operations with TEP Kinsho. We, of course, have been eager to continue the relationship.

These two plants are both major success stories for us. They brought to life my long-delayed vision for Handy's major expansion into Asia, a vision I harbored for fifteen years before I could begin chasing it after the buyback from Taiyo. Here's an important lesson for entrepreneurs: having multiple suppliers for the same product often is a good strategy.

Our overseas operations have been growing while the Crisfield employee count has remained stable for several years, around thirty in 2024. We have three hundred or four hundred people in the largest facilities—in Surabaya, Indonesia, and about two hundred in Bangkok. Those two Handy partnerships produce the largest volume, with more employees, and contribute more to sales and profits than all other Handy operations.

Looking back, that jarring vote by the Crisfield city council to block our plans for the crab cake production plant may have been a good business outcome for Handy. Our crab cake operations in Southeast Asia became Handy's lifeblood.

GUNNING FOR THE GUINNESS *BOOK OF WORLD RECORDS*

If Handy could bake the world's largest crab cake, how big would it have to be? How would we do it? Why would we do it?

Those questions had never crossed my mind until one of our customers, Bally's Casino Resort in Dover, Delaware, proposed we do this for a summer event they planned for 2009. "We'll invite the Guinness Book of Records. It will be good publicity for everyone," Bally's general manager said. "You can scoop off portions, sell crab cake sandwiches to cover your costs, and donate the rest."

One of our respected competitors had taken a pass, but we didn't hesitate. No doubt in my mind: this could boost the Handy brand.

After checking Guinness records, Carol Haltaman and Ben White projected the ingredients, colossal quantities, and outsized cooking equipment we would need to what we agreed would comfortably set the crab cake record: *three hundred pounds*. Their plan:

- 220 pounds of crabmeat for picking out tiny shell fragments under black lights at Handy, mayonnaise, mustard, and other essentials
- Fifteen-pound batches of ingredients to keep taste consistent and lumps intact

- A custom outdoor cooking rig big enough to hold a stainless steel pan (like a huge pizza dish) measuring thirty inches in diameter and seven inches deep from its base

For even cooking, the pan would need to be rotated 90 degrees every ten minutes under three round burners fueled with propane that could be raised or lowered. Estimated cooking time? Ten hours at a temperature of 145 degrees Fahrenheit.

A first test in Crisfield failed because the baked crab cake didn't hold in one piece, a Guinness requirement. "Try different mustard," our consulting chef suggested. Presto! The second test worked to perfection. In Dover, we fired up the burners and began cooking at 3:00 a.m.

By 11:30, our fifteen-inch thermometer recorded the internal temperature at 150 degrees F. "Ready to serve," affirmed the health department. We unbuckled the oven lid, turned the pan upside down, and slowly lifted the lid. Our crab cake was in one piece (!), weighing in at 285 pounds . . . enough for the Guinness record.

Armed with ice cream scoops, the Handy team served up four-ounce servings for sandwiches at eight dollars each. In two hours, the 285-pound leviathan was gone. We donated proceeds exceeding our costs to Bally's designated nonprofit, the Boy Scouts.

This was so much fun and such a success for Handy that we immediately laid plans for a sequel. Go for three hundred pounds, break our new record at Crisfield's annual Clam Bake, an event that draws thousands of tourists as well as a must-attend "see and be seen" opportunity for politicians and contractors.

The sponsoring Crisfield Chamber of Commerce embraced the idea. One of Handy's respected competitors agreed: this would be a big international draw, further bolster Crisfield's claim to "Crab Capitol of the World," and stoke demand for crabmeat and other local seafood. But then, Murphy's Law. Another of our local rivals objected—"too much publicity for Handy"—and persuaded Clam Bake organizers to scratch the plan.

I wasn't discouraged. We'd find another appealing venue. How about the Maryland State Fair in Baltimore County? Yes. With only six weeks to spare, we were in.

We again loaded the refrigerated Handy truck, drove three and a half hours, and set up on the fairgrounds. Guinness supervised the weighing, on September 1, 2009, and confirmed a new record: 300.5 pounds. Our Handy crab cake sandwiches sold out again, and we donated $3,000 to Future Farmers of America.

What fun! Both times. A wonderful team-building experience and a testament to Handy's mastery of the art and science of crab cakes.

How many companies can boast an enduring listing in the *Guinness Book of World Records*? Fifteen years later, as I write now in 2025, Handy still holds the record.

C R A B M E A T S T A R T U P ,
B O R N I N I N D I A

Jumbo Lump Pasteurized Crab Meat

BUILDING TRUST WITH SOFT CRABS

The aisles at the Long Beach seafood show were crowded with Handy customers. I had a smile on my face.

Back in Crisfield, Carol was anticipating the arrival of the first container shipment with Handy's newest product, frozen soft crabs from Thailand. "Seafood shows are the best way to launch a new product," she had noted. "I'll have colorful sales flyers prepared for Long Beach. We'll cook samples for buyers to taste."

One after another, Handy's soft crab customers were taking my samples, scanning flyers, and asking me about these imported soft crabs from Thai waters. One visitor picked up an empty carton, reading the front and back repeatedly as he flipped it over several times. His badge read: Paddy Ranjan, Chennai, India. He was about thirty-five years old, well-dressed.

"I'm a broker representing Red Lobster, here to evaluate shrimp processors in India," he said. "We have this same crab on the east coast of India. Tell me more about soft crabs."

Within twenty minutes, I had that feeling again, the same one I had had initially about Thailand. With Handy's imported soft crabs from Thailand selling fast, we soon would need a second source of supply. Might that be India? I accepted Paddy's invitation to visit—my first ever trip to India. Dozens were to follow. For the next eighteen months, more than 80 percent of my Handy agenda would be dominated by detailed planning, lucky breaks—and nimble reactions to surprising twists and turns—that became the story of our small company's remarkable passage to India.

As I stepped off the plane's walkway in Chennai around midnight, a dense odor told me I was in another country. Long lines had formed at immigration, where security officers scrutinized each passport. It was nearly midnight. Big crowds as well at baggage claim and customs passage were signs that several international fights had arrived at about the same time.

Two hours later, I waded into a crowd of people, shoulder to shoulder, twenty deep. They were straining for a first glimpse of friends and family. Contract drivers waited for assigned passengers with names marked on homemade signs. Spotting a small "Handy" scribbled on one of them at the back of the crowd, I made my way forward to greet the driver from my hotel, fending off multiple offers along the way—closer to pleas, it seemed—to pull my roller bag or take me to my destination.

My senses on alert, I gazed out at heavy bumper-to-bumper traffic, horns honking from all sides as my driver jockeyed to openings briefly appearing and disappearing across unmarked lanes. (Lanes? There did not appear to be marked lanes on these highways.)

"You must be experienced," I said to my driver. "This looks confusing to me."

"In India," he replied, "you need a good horn, good brakes, and good luck."

I believed him, and I made a mental note: *If I am not able to drive in my elder years, I should interview drivers from India to hire.*

Our destination was the Chennai Taj, a five-star hotel that Paddy recommended that was a five-minute walk to the Bay of Bengal beach and only ten miles from the airport. Paddy's family had once been minority owners of Taj hotels in India. As I soon discovered, the Chennai Taj Hotel—known among local cognoscenti as Taj at Fisherman's Cove—was outstanding.

ONE OF INDIA'S MOST PROMINENT INDUSTRIALIST GROUPS

Paddy had arranged for me to meet key executives in Chennai at the headquarters of Waterbase Limited, a publicly traded shrimp processor with several international customers such as his brokering client, Red Lobster. Waterbase was controlled by the Thapar family, which for over six decades and three generations had assembled a highly respected, innovative group of businesses in multiple industries in India.

The Thapar Group had interests at one time or another in banking, paint, paper, textiles, coal, pharmaceuticals and food, specialty chemicals, and several other industries. It was one of India's largest conglomerates before it was split into different companies in 2000. An engineering and technology institute, now known as Thapar University, was founded by the family's entrepreneurial patriarch, Karam Chand Thapar. After Karam's death in 1962, his four sons continued to expand the business.

One of Karam's grandsons, Vikram, was my first contact with family executives in 2002. At the time, Thapar Group operated a successful shrimp processing plant in a remote place on the coast of the Bay of Bengal, three hours north of Chennai. Over lunch one day weeks before at a white tablecloth restaurant near Thapar's headquarters in New Delhi, I had described to Vikram how we might organize and build a soft crab business. His interest never flagged. At a board meeting the next day, he was ebullient and enthusiastic. Our new partnership with Waterbase was unanimously approved.

Back in Chennai on my first day of activity, I was greeted by Paddy's father-in-law, Ashok Nanjapa, in a sparse, one-story office building, close to the road, with a cow tied up near the entrance. Inside, small offices were separated by aluminum and glass partitions. Lighting was dim, and the walls were bare. Not a setting to bring to mind a vision of exalted rajahs, I thought, favorably. Waterbase seemed to be both a savvy *and* frugal prospective business partner.

At age fifty-five, Ashok was tall, athletic, energetic, and focused crisply on our business at hand. Sipping homemade tea, we exchanged historical information about Handy and Waterbase. "Tell me about your soft crab operation in Thailand," he said. "I'm very interested in the details." We continued the conversation over lunch, a delicious mutton (goat) entrée at a nearby restaurant. The dining areas inside and walkway to the entrance were clean, but piles of discarded food and other trash lining the walkway caught my eye as we entered, detritus feedings for the cow and other animals that might happen by. I wondered, *Will the shrimp plant we are about to see be like this?*

ROAMING CATTLE, WHITE-ROBED HINDU PRIEST, LOW CRAB HARVESTS

The plant turned out to be a large processing complex in a remote coastal area situated more than three hours north by train from Chennai to Nellore, a city of half a million people. At the Chennai train station, porters steadied with one hand the luggage balanced on their heads. At the Nellore station, I spotted muscular monkeys climbing downspouts on buildings along the tracks and peeking into windows. *Looking for food*, I thought.

We rode from the Nellore station for more than half an hour in a rugged, tight-springs Ambassador sedan toward the Waterbase complex. Our driver maneuvered slowly to avoid potholes along a dirt road. We passed dozens of one-family mud huts where children and adults appeared cheerful as they played near the road, an impression I relayed to Ashok. "The government provides family groups with a cow for milk and nutrition," he said.

The four-bedroom guesthouse on the complex was stark—white and clean, with Hindu icons on the walls. A fried chicken dinner was tasty but tough, probably because the chicken was only hours removed from being a freelance bird. I relaxed as Ashok and I swapped stories about the shrimp and soft crab business, enjoying our after-dinner beers. *He is quite impressive*, I thought. With his dynamic leadership, not to mention the Thapar family's solid finances in the wings, quality soft crabs here for Handy might work.

Cattle roamed around the seven-acre site when we arrived for a plant tour the next morning. "Watch your step," Ashok cautioned. In its twentieth year of activity, the plant was clean inside, suitable for raw seafood, and government-approved for exports. Most workers, housed in dormitories on site, came from rural villages. Supervisors examined each of them for cleanliness and any skin problems as they entered each day.

Just outside the plant, Waterbase had erected a small, one-room Hindu temple where the villagers could pray and receive a priest's blessing as they began or ended their workday. It was only ten feet from the plant entrance. "The temple and entrance face exactly east to greet the morning sun," Ashok explained, adding, "You should have a look one day."

Intrigued and curious, one day I did. Entering the temple, I quickly made eye contact with a priest in a white robe who was standing alone in the room decorated with Hindu icons. He assumed I was there not as a tourist but for a private religious ceremony, and he immediately began speaking in Hindi. He motioned me forward, dabbed a small spot of moist red powder on my forehead for good luck (as was explained by others later), then offered me a small ladle of holy water and motioned with his hand that I should drink it like a shot of whiskey.

I had until then followed the ceremony's symbolic elements, but I had clearly missed that last critical detail. Without much thought I proceeded to splash the contents on my forehead just above the red dot. The holy water streamed down my face. What a mess. The priest, bemused now by this odd American, chuckled. I thanked him for the ceremony, left a small donation, and took my leave.

Ashok showed me the space he had in mind inside for Handy's soft crab operations. "We must keep it separate from shrimp processing. That will prevent cross-contamination. Plus, it meets government require-ments: cooler for live crabs, separate areas for processing and packing with weighing scales, and its own blast freezer." The space was compact but, as I told Ashok, it seemed adequate for a low-volume startup.

We agreed that I would assign a loyal, knowledgeable manager on Crisfield's staff to teach the same quality assurance practices we employed in the Maryland soft crab plant to workers here. As we saw for Thailand, ensuring that high quality was a Handy principle was essential for our international expansion and the only way to consistently deliver a high-quality product from multiple points of supply.

Alas, crab supplies in the waters adjacent to the Waterbase shrimp-processing complex proved to be too low to sustain profitable operations. Less than a year after we began operations there, we decided to close them. For the near future, Handy would continue to rely on supplies from Thailand.

PLANS PASTEURIZED CRAB MEAT VENTURE BEGIN

But as we've seen, failures offer keen learning opportunities. In truth, that soft crab business for India had been a new product experiment.

The foray gave Handy and Waterbase valuable new insights about each other. Our values. Our judgment. Our principles. The execution of our assigned roles matched the commitments of our word. We developed trust. For an American entrepreneur still finding his way in Asia, in India, this was priceless.

One of our competitors on Maryland's eastern shore, Phillips Foods Inc., had a plant for pasteurizing crabmeat on the subcontinent's south-eastern coast by the Indian Ocean, twelve hours by train to a remote coastal region south of Chennai. I hadn't known about their Indian operations until Ashok described them to me. "It appears to be working," he added. "Maybe we should look into it."

For a competitor in Chesapeake Bay to have located a processing plant in that area immediately suggested to me that the crab population might be substantial, perhaps prolific. *Bingo!* I thought. *There must be crabs there.* I envisioned us buying crabs by the thousands from local fishermen.

Still, I had to temper my enthusiasm. The crab population in that area might be too meager to supply more than one existing plant. For all I knew, that crab supply at that moment might even be below what that one plant required to operate. We might be building a second plant as plans were in motion to shut the first one! We didn't have the faintest idea of the crab population's size there. We would have to guess. We just didn't know.

CAN A 50-50 JOINT VENTURE FUNCTION AMICABLY—AND ENDURE?

I was troubled in some ways about agreeing with Waterbase to a fully equal joint venture—that is, with each of the two partners owning 50 percent of the enterprise. Ideally, the two equal partners need to be in total agreement when their pact first takes effect and able to amicably sort through differences that arise in the future.

Our circumstances for shaping a crabmeat partnership overflowed with uncertainties and unknowns. I had no prior experience with Indian companies, and no professional advisers to review plans or guide me in negotiations with Waterbase or fending off unscrupulous vendors or competitors I might encounter. I had gained confidence by sourcing soft crabs in Thailand, but starting from scratch with sourcing crabs in India for crabmeat production raised a whole set of separate challenges.

We would have to manage fluctuations in crab supplies, shipping operations, and customer demand What difficulties might arise? Would Waterbase and Handy be capable of handling their respective defined roles equally, or would one partner have to carry the other? If the latter, that probably would erode trust. (My troubles with those two Rain Forest Tilapia partners, who teamed against me, while not entirely analogous, were a factor in why I was cautious here.)

A legal claim filed in India's judicial system involving Indian and non-Indian partners takes six years to resolve. An arbitration process conducted in Singapore was shorter, less than a year usually, but preparing documents can churn up endless hours and distract you from deftly managing inevitable ups-and-downs in operations.

In sum, I had no way to assess how big these risks would prove to be. If I went ahead with Waterbase to form a 50–50 joint venture, I knew I would have to rely on my capacities in wits and stamina to outrun the risks.

One option in structuring a joint venture can be adding a third investor to the group, someone who is respected and highly trusted by the two lead partners. Their ownership percentage might be small, such as 15 percent or less, but their vote can be a tiebreaker when needed to resolve any material disputes between the two lead partners.

Ashok and I considered this. I met with one recommended prospect, an industrialist. But he demanded a 15 percent minority owner's role, seeking an active co-equal voice in decision-making. Plus, he was from India. Those realities likely would put Handy at a disadvantage in potential conflict scenarios that I pondered.

This option held little appeal for me. Recruiting a person who is respected, highly trusted by both partners, and able to sustain that respect and trust through thick and thin is difficult. "I do not see the feasibility of a tiebreaker," I told Ashok. "We'll have to keep working on building the trust between the two companies we have built."[23]

One other concern I had is that producing quality crabmeat is more complicated than processing soft crabs or crab cakes. In part, this is because crabmeat must be pasteurized to make it safe to eat and to lengthen the shelf life. Pasteurization typically kills most bacteria in food products such as goods, milk, and wine.

I thought we should do better. One way was to test the shelf life of crabmeat under refrigeration to make sure Handy had the healthiest crabmeat with better taste and a shelf life of eighteen months, beyond what competitors offered. We would need equipment to heat cans to a specific computer-controlled temperature, for a precise period, then bury the cans in ice until the temperature fell to 34 degrees, when the cans would be placed in a room cooled to that temperature.

Another major task would be training and supervising new workers to carefully pick meat from crabs. The workflow would be like this: Each morning, fishermen would bring their overnight catch and unload nets onto beaches of coastal villages. Workers would steam-cook live crabs, remove decaying soft meat. In the plant, other workers would use black lights to visually detect pieces of shell still in the meat, remove the shell pieces, and then pack the crabmeat carefully in small cans.

In time, as the plans for our crabmeat processing plant came to life, all these essentials became manifest.

---

[23] My good years with Waterbase have convinced me that 50–50 partnerships with large, established companies with good reputations can be fair and effective. I still avoid equal partnerships with individuals I don't know well. I've seen companies ruined when one partner runs off with the cash or refuses to contribute much of value.

TWENTY-THREE

CLEAR ROLES, VIRTUOUS FEEDBACK LOOP

I met P. K. Ramachandran ("Ram") for the first time in New Delhi at Thapar headquarters. Tapped by Thapar executives to lead the Waterbase side of Handy–Waterbase in Tuticorin, he was trim, dressed smartly, and well-spoken at age thirty-five with a degree from one of India's most prestigious graduate business schools.

"Handy and Waterbase have worked well together," I said to Ram, as everyone called him, aiming to set a tone quickly of admiration, optimism, and focus. The relationship with Waterbase to that point truly had been honest, cordial, and respectful. "We have the same standards of high quality," I added, then turned quickly to what I saw as the main challenges for the new business.

"But neither of us has any experience with a fresh pasteurized seafood product. That is a far more complicated business than frozen seafood like soft crabs. Plus, we're going to have to create a better product than seventy competitors on the market. We've got to set a goal of being the low-cost, efficient producer to have a competitive advantage. And we must sell profitably with seasoned marketing and sales professionals who know how to close deals. How do we get to the top of the heap? We have a lot to do. Let's build a business plan, present it to the Waterbase board, and ask them to approve it."

Ram and I agreed quickly on the basic concepts. Waterbase would arrange financing to cover costs to develop and manage costs associated with crabmeat inventories and shipping. They would locate a contractor to build a processing plant, provide skilled personnel to operate the plant, and acquire whatever operating equipment we needed that was available in India, such as backup generators, freezer alarms, and water purification systems.

Handy would craft recipes and other details for a superior, Handy-branded, ready-to-eat product. We would manage shipping, sales, and marketing in the United States and elsewhere with the goal of quickly establishing Handy crabmeat as a premium offering in North America and Europe. Moreover, Handy would design and oversee construction of the production plant. We could control all specialized materials and equipment for the plant because we could purchase everything from manufacturing companies we knew in Maryland from our Crisfield renovations fifteen years earlier. Better yet, we could import these exceptional production goods on an ocean container to Tuticorin under a ten-year, duty-free agreement with the Indian government.

The provision, negotiated on the joint venture's behalf by Waterbase, waived all taxes on profits generated from our crabmeat exports for the first ten years. (Business taxes in India amounted to about 20 percent of profits.) In practice, this meant we would be able to retain all profits, netting us a bigger cash flow. We could redeploy those funds into expanding operations in India, building a market to add customers more rapidly in North America and Europe and harvesting rising sales and profits. A virtuous feedback loop.

I knew I was taking quite a risk. How were we actually going to produce a crabmeat product superior to anything my future competitors were selling in the United States and Europe?

I didn't know much about crabmeat, but I knew people who did. The most important one turned out to be Tom Rippen, a crab industry expert at the University of Maryland's Sea Grant College located just twenty miles from Crisfield in Princess Anne. Tom walked me through all aspects of crabmeat production: pasteurization, canning, quality control, and processing equipment. His wisdom here cost Handy absolutely nothing. He was providing a valuable consulting service supported entirely by Maryland taxpayers.

Waterbase had for decades operated a shrimp processing plant in India. Tapping Ashok's contacts in the construction networks around Nellore, Ram penciled in total costs at $2.5 million for plant construction and working capital to set up operations and begin production. How would we fund that? Again, our India partner had answers.

"I'll take care of this," he said. Bolstered by Waterbase's stellar reputation and financial strength, Ram quickly arranged bank loans. Terms were extremely favorable, beyond anything that would have been within Handy's reach if we were acting alone as a foreign investor in India.

The banks did require presidents of both owners to personally guarantee more than $2.4 million in project loans, plus commit $35,000 each, or 11 percent of the full package, as an equity investment. I was delighted by Ram's initiative and legwork with his contacts. This was wonderful financing. I had no doubt we could quickly tap into Handy's conservative and flexible finances for the $35,000 equity investment due without denting our cash flow. Our personal guarantees for the loans? If the project failed, the banks had pledges from the two crabmeat venture owners to cover any unpaid debts.

The impressive Waterbase board responded favorably as we covered details in the business plan. The board included several outside directors (as India requires for publicly traded companies), including one from a major coffee company.

This is a sensible group, I thought. They asked good questions. I imagined they must have reviewed pitches from entrepreneurs that might have sounded promising but later fizzled. Maybe they had taken the bait. If I now was reading the room accurately, ours might have looked better than most. An American company with an established brand and market. Deep knowledge of the business.

They liked the fact that I was a CPA, a signal that they could trust financial reports from this prospective joint venture and perhaps a credential that struck a harmonious chord. Their founder, Karam Chand Thapar, was a CPA. So was the chairman, Vikram Thapar, the founder's grandson. Some board members were especially curious about Handy's long history, and the three core principles that I emphasized to them had helped us prosper since I first acquired the business twenty years before: superior products, processed at competitive advantage, and sold profitably.

I was delighted. The board approved the plan that day. Summing up, Vikram said, "Let's give crabmeat a shot."

AN EXCEPTIONAL PLANT, BUILT TO LAST

Ram soon acquired a piece of land in an industrial park outside Tuticorin. It took us twelve hours by train from Chennai each morning after I flew in from the United States to get to the site, which was on a dirt road with electricity and water and little else.

My observation at the time was that industrial plants in India looked tired and old just six months after they were built. Everything was painted. It was not long before the air turned paint dark. Tile was ubiquitous and colorful inside seafood plants, but the grout harbors bacteria that is impossible to clean and impossible to remove. A foul stink pervades the air forever.

Our plant was an exception. The contractor that Ram hired really knew his stuff, another example of why pursuing high-quality local partners was essential to build and grow Handy's production in Asia. We had poured, polished, and coated concrete floors with a small slope to aid water runoff, interior walls with clear fiberglass, and no paint, tile, or exposed pipes. External walls were a flaky type of stone. We installed air conditioning, applying another lesson from renovating the Crisfield plant fifteen years before. Everything was beautifully engineered. Construction was finished in four months.

I remember spotting local women wearing perfectly clean saris in bright reds, blues, and yellows as they climbed ladders at the two-story site, hauling bricks and other materials balanced on their heads.

That plant in the coastal town of Tuticorin still looks new after more than twenty years. Built to last, for the ages. Another way I like to do things.

SUNDAY DRIVE TO MEENAKSHI TEMPLE

During construction of the crabmeat plant, one of my colleagues at Waterbase suggested we take a Sunday excursion to visit the historic Meenakshi Temple in Madurai, eighty-five miles and two and a half hours by car from Tuticorin. His wife and son would join us.

The famous temple is a major destination for Hindu pilgrims and tourists. The dazzling stone complex was built originally by what ancient texts describe as a poet-saint king to honor goddess Meenakshi in the sixth century, and later expanded and reconstructed by other rulers into the sixteenth century.

Tens of thousands of people visit daily. During the annual ten-day Meenakshi festival, more than one million visit.

Some take a plunge in the Vaigai River that flows nearby in the belief that the Vaigai waters will cleanse them of all past sins. (I didn't take advantage.)

My companion hired a classic Ambassador model car with a driver to navigate the journey. These Ambassador cars were everywhere in India. The vehicles, manufactured by Hindustan Motors of India, are close copies of the British 1956 Morris Oxford sedan. Calibrated to maneuver along rugged Indian roads, the design was unchanged since 1957. Our Ambassador featured the original puttering engine with a horsepower of thirty-seven, about one-third what you'd find in a small American car and another reason why we averaged less than forty miles an hour on the eighty-five-mile trip.

My companion said buyer demand for Ambassadors was inexhaust-
ible. "The wait time for a new Ambassador is nine months," he noted,
a thought that immediately brought to mind for him this popular joke.
"As the recently departed were awaiting entrance to heaven, the next in
line told his story: 'I was an industrialist: I made the Ambassador cars
for India.' 'Come right in,' was the welcoming response. 'I receive thousands of prayers every day about Ambassadors.'"

As we headed back to Tuticorin, I was made aware of the real reason
for our trip. My companion's son was anticipating an arranged marriage
in the coming weeks . . . with a bride-to-be he had never seen. "We were
hoping to get a peek at the bride during the tour," his father told me with
a sigh. Alas, a glimpse of the young lady was not in the cards that day.

During the drive back to Tuticorin, he spoke more about the value
of arranged marriages. The primary motivation is the joining of two
families, rather than two people who have fallen in love freely choosing
to make a life together. Arranged marriage remains very common and
accepted in India; 90 percent of marriages in India are arranged, usually
within the same caste.

India has become one of the largest exporters of crabmeat, behind
Indonesia, now with those ten competing production plants in all
(including Handy) in the Tuticorin area. Yes, we did have good luck. Crab
supplies there were abundant, enough not only to support our new plant
and the existing plant of Phillips, our Chesapeake Bay competitor, but
eight more! Several of these competing plants are managed by onetime
members of our Tuticorin operations team. When you develop talent
in a growing industry, you can't keep people locked in. That's the way
the world works. After they leave, I found, they never quite get it right.
We kept our competitive edge in quality.

One reason for that is Ram recruited an outstanding plant manager
at the outset, a PhD in fisheries who held that position for two decades

before retiring in 2022. Finding highly qualified professionals in remote areas is not always easy, but Ajitha Kumar was exceptional. For our part, we recruited a fellow in coastal Virginia, Mike Taylor, who managed seafood plants during the summer and was available because when I came knocking on his door it was between seasons. "Sure, I'll go," he said.

Pasteurization, as we knew, is difficult, but Mike knew what he was doing, getting the plant organized and running well. His accommodations during those four months were a two-story hotel that, in all candor, looked like a wooden shack. The doors didn't close. Light fixtures didn't work. Toilets were "squatters," without seats. I had a room there for fifteen nights on my first visit. Mike never complained about it. Just a wonderful guy.

NUMERICAL GAUGE: THE TRANSFER PRICE

The beating heart of any joint venture is mutual trust. Our corporate lawyer reminded me as we laid plans for the Waterbase pact that building trust requires "clearly written contracts that preserve the balance between both parties. No detail is too small, yet no agreement can anticipate and address all circumstances that inevitably arise. The best conditions for successful partnership are when both parties continue to be mutually dependent, and able to work out minor differences without resorting to arbitration or the courts."

I asked myself, what might trigger minor differences (or worse) for us with Waterbase? We had neatly defined our roles, I thought, but one crucial element in business dealings would be determined by forces beyond our control. The element was money . . . shrouded in an accounting convention known as the transfer price. The forces beyond our control were supply-demand dynamics in the market.

The transfer price was what Handy and Waterbase would charge each other within the joint venture financial structure to cover costs for supplying a service or product to each other. This is the work of accountants. Here's the rub: Charges would fluctuate according to whatever price Handy would be charging customers for Handy crabmeat in the market.

Transfer pricing can make or break a joint venture. Are these internal charges fair and equitable? For Handy–Waterbase, both parties would need to be comfortable about the level at which the market price is set for any given month. By being comfortable, I mean a belief that a specific price is optimizing the business strategy, given all factors in that strategy, and not favoring one partner or the other.

Our finance and accounting teams would collect pricing and cost data always at arm's length from various sources in the market (such as other companies, traders, brokers, government data). Handy would buy crabmeat from other producers in the market. Handy–Waterbase had the resources to check around and determine what other buyers were paying. Together, both parties agreed to a fair transfer price that could be justified by an auditor.

This follows the "arm's length" principle for determining transfer pricing. Prices agreed by two parties should be similar to what independent companies would have set and accepted in comparable circumstances. We document every container price before shipping and encourage all our suppliers to do the same.

Each country's method of collecting income taxes includes a provision on transfer pricing. Some hire an independent legal and tax professional to verify if a given formula is equitable. In our case it's the arm's length principle—legitimately reflecting market pricing. That happened in 2016 when the government of India reviewed our Handy–Waterbase formula. The resulting *eighty-three-page* report verified for Indian officials that our practice generated fair taxes.

Our general manager in Bangkok, Jay Ivancic, directs these negotiations with suppliers and the Waterbase team for Handy. It was fairly easy to come up with transfer pricing charges that teams representing both owners in the joint venture could agree were fair and equitable. Mutual trust built over time is the key. Jay was trusted. He's very effective and won't hesitate to hold the line at the existing market price if he can't find evidence the market has moved to a higher price at the time an order is placed. Container shipping prices are set at the time an order is placed.

LITTLE DETAILS BOLSTER A PREMIUM BRAND

I had chosen Thailand for my crash course to learn crabmeat operations: what separated the best from the rest and what we needed to do to top the best. Several Handy contacts in soft crab production and marketing at Thai seafood companies were in the crabmeat business. Seven or eight of them invited me to visit their plants when they heard of our plans in Tuticorin. Each struck me as having a particular expertise in one aspect of crabmeat production.

I was astounded at how welcoming and forthright the eight whom I approached were. Maybe they figured, *This guy could be a new customer.*

Most people want to impress you, if you listen, with how much they know. And I listened, taking a flurry of notes on the smallest details: quality, taste, processing techniques, and plant layouts. For example, packing crabmeat in cans. You'll recall that some companies added lower-grade pieces into cans marked as "jumbo" lumps into pieces, mixing those lumps with smaller ones. *We can do better*, I knew. Use only whole lumps. With whole lumps, you can place them more attractively in the can, one piece at a time, in a circular way with the knob on the outside until the can meets the specific weight marked on the outside of the can.

We soon set up more buying stations in these villages for the fishermen's nightly catch along the coast near Tuticorin. And kept buying and buying—but only live crabs. Other companies were mixing live and dead crabs, a sure way to sour the taste. Using only live crabs, Handy delivered a fresh, sweet taste. That's the way we have always done things. We were the premium brand.

We were shipping 100,000 cans each time in oceangoing container vessels on the five-week journey to North America, which remained by far our largest marketing region. Most buyers operated along the

East Coast of the United States, in the Florida panhandle, and westward along the Gulf Coast.

Our sales teams fanned out quickly, bringing Handy fresh crabmeat samples to restaurant locations. Hundreds of restaurants. One sales rep in the Florida panhandle told me, "If I can get them to taste our crabmeat, and compare it with what they had before, they buy it on the spot." This simple taste test, replicated hundreds of times, sparked a rush of orders.

Our first shipments to the United States were an immediate hit. "This is really beautiful crabmeat," food brokers and buyers for restaurants and grocery chains told us. "Better than anything we've seen."

As I envisioned, Handy had started at a very high level. All those little details we pursued and perfected had added up. You are as you start. We had the best crabmeat product on the market, the top of the heap, and sales took off. In that first year, sales for the Handy–Waterbase crabmeat startup registered $2 million.

This continues to be more than a great partnership. Waterbase runs an efficient, effective operation with high standards and talented leaders. Together we employ some 250 people in the plant and villages near Tuticorin. The Waterbase team is responsive to any suggestions we bring and has become one of our primary suppliers.

SIMPLER, HIGH-IMPACT PACKAGING

It wasn't long before our graphics designer, Robin English, created a wall poster for restaurants showing cutaway illustrations of Handy crabmeat cans with the theme, "What's in Your Can?"

Here was another way to reinforce Handy's reputation for trust and quality. Competitors generally packed different lump sizes in their cans. Each image on our poster depicted the precise number and size of crabmeat lumps we packaged in a can. We printed the number of lumps on the lid of each can, such as fifty-five to seventy-five, a step the industry had never taken before.

"This is the dumbest thing I've ever seen in the seafood business," one major competitor complained, accosting me at a trade show. He argued that lump sizes must vary with crabmeat costs—smaller lumps especially when costs rise—to maintain profit margins and pricing. I ignored him.

When you enter a market for the first time, you've got to do whatever you can to get to the top of the heap. Customers were entitled to know what they were buying. With Handy at least, what they were buying would not change. This was my strategy to set Handy apart quickly from the seventy companies selling crabmeat.

Our sales teams offered the posters to customers at no cost. Hanging on kitchen walls with the eye-catching Handy logo, the posters became a huge promotional win for us. "What's in Your Can?" continues its long run as one of Handy's most important innovations.

Another packaging modification we introduced for crabmeat was the six-can carton. The norm at that point was a twelve-can carton. Sounds simple, but restaurants could turn the product faster, have less crabmeat spoil before it could be served, and invest fewer funds in excess inventory they might not use.

We also introduced different colors for different grades of crabmeat. Again, sounds simple, but for kitchen staff this was an immediate hit. All competitor cans at the time had blue lids. The restaurant staff didn't take time to read labels, or couldn't read well generally or anything in English. They might pull a Jumbo can instead of a Prime, or a Prime instead of a Whale. With six grades of crabmeat, and a dozen cans in a case, orders often were mixed up. Handy's varying colors made it simpler and faster for kitchen staff to match the right quality of crabmeat with a specific customer order.

Our motivation was to reinforce Handy as the most trusted brand for seafood quality and bolster our position as the chef's choice. Handy products should be simple for their kitchen staff to prepare and serve correctly to diners.

TWENTY-FOUR

INDIANA JONES, EMPTYHANDED

LETTING GO IN MADAGASCAR

I always walked the aisles at the annual Brussels Seafood Show to meet Handy customers and encourage their connections with our exclusive European importer, Chris Champion. One year I heard about a promising site for soft crab farming on the northwest coast of Madagascar, four hundred miles offshore from southeast Africa.

"There's an abundance of mangrove crabs along the west coast," a Waterbase agent at the show named Gayathri Rao told me.

I regularly encouraged our partners in India and Thailand to pass along tips they might have about new sources for crab supplies. Sales agents were in a position to pick up timely intelligence that might give Handy an edge over rivals in tapping into these new sources.

I was always eager to book a flight and see for myself any time they offered a tip, and I made it a best practice to do so. I enjoyed the discovery and business analysis, seeing new parts of the world, meeting people, and absorbing surprises, delights, and emotions of new cultures. More often than not, these were quick trips to dead ends for Handy. But I became savvier, sharpening my approach and insights with each one.

Our success in rapidly moving and reigniting our Thailand soft crab production to Ranong from Katang buoyed my confidence. We now had

what seemed to me a workable template: find a financially sound partner, rent space from a seafood processor with export licenses, and hire
a capable manager to oversee Handy's soft crab production within the
partner's seafood operations.

Madagascar. More than four thousand miles and a nine-hour flight
from Bangkok. More than thirteen hundred miles south of the Equator.
Handy's next frontier?

"It might be a good source for Handy," Gayathri continued.
Madagascar is an island nation with central mountain rainforests, coastal
plains, savannah grasslands, and brackish waters. She introduced me to
the chief executive of Unima, a major French shrimp importer that had
a large shrimp processing plant near those soft crab habitats at the country's northern tip.

"Several rivers flow from the mountains to flat areas with tidal estuaries and mangrove trees," the Unima executive, Amyne, told me. "Five
Chinese companies with export licenses are buying crabs from local fishermen there. My shrimp plant has extra processing capacity. You should
come and take a look. It could work out for both of us."

It didn't.

I was uncertain from the start if we would have enough soft crabs
to make the operation economic or whether the government would
cooperate with us, so I designed a pilot program mirroring our Thailand
model. Create a network of reliable soft crab fishermen in their small
sampans. Train local soft crab farmers to molt crabs naturally with the
crab condo method. Recruit people from nearby villages to process the
crabs for shipping back to Crisfield.

Within weeks I was buoyant. The pieces were coming into place.
Holly Mattos had found a young French-speaking Thai college graduate, Opal, a food science major, who was primed to relocate and work
with the fishermen in Madagascar. I had the last piece of the project—a
French-speaking general manager who knew the seafood business.

Then Amyne decided to close his plant—with no advance notice
or consultations with me. I now had no place to process soft crabs, no

established partner with an export license and influence with local politicians and bureaucrats—in other words, no Ranong equivalent, and no general manager.

My hunch was that Unima's wild-caught shrimp harvest was falling too fast for that plant to recover. In truth, looking back, I was more eager for this partnership to develop than Amyne. Even if a new pact with Handy was agreed, Amyne likely was losing confidence before we met that the plant could again be profitable. He consolidated the Unima shrimp processing to a larger plant one hour away to the south.

I had no desire to try to go it alone, make a much bigger investment than planned, and in time hope to draw in one or more partners to off-load some financial risk. Plus, as I said, we had no assurance the soft crab harvest would be what Gayathuri first described to me in Brussels—"an abundance"—to support the investment.

Meanwhile, Handy's operations in Thailand and India were prospering. It was a quick, clear decision: Let go of Madagascar. Stick to our knitting. Build further into Southeast and Southern Asia from solid footings.

IN MOZAMBIQUE: A VORTEX OF LEGERDEMAIN

We achieved such speed and volume in exporting frozen soft crabs from Thailand to the US and Europe that a favorable storyline spread quickly there, and accurately, among our traditional customers and competitors: Handy was tapping into a mother lode others had not recognized, building new sources of supply that might more than offset alarming declines in Chesapeake Bay harvests.

If I could advance our core objectives by gaining a toehold in other countries as we were doing in Thailand, I should continue to investigate. Where to go? I remembered receiving a call years before from a State Department official about soft crab habitats in Mozambique. Madagascar had not worked out, but maybe Mozambique, four hundred miles to the west along Africa's eastern coastline, was worth a look.

Possibly, we could build more local crab processing and ship from there as we were doing in Thailand.

I tracked down that State Department official I had met long ago in Washington. His name was Bill. When I reached him by phone from Bangkok, he told me he had left the government, moved to Mozambique, and was setting up a business—crabmeat processing.

"I'm developing a picking facility for crabmeat in Mozambique. It has huge potential," Bill said.

He had read articles over the years about awards Handy had received. "I think you'll be interested in the crab supplies, or even in buying me out. I want to retire and move back to America." When he mentioned that large habitats of mangrove crabs were in the area, this sparked for me the idea of processing soft crabs there too— potentially. We could molt them as we were doing with crab condos in Thailand.

Within days, I was on my way again to southeast Africa.

Our business model required us to keep pressing for lowest-cost crab supplies. It is the hard truth for any commodity business: stay in the hunt at all times for lower-cost supplies. Handy soft crab products were of high quality and premium-priced. To maintain or increase profit margins and stay true to our brand promise of great taste and high quality, we had to continuously reduce operating costs.

Raising prices always was an option, of course, but I regarded this warily; doing so could trim Handy's market share if customers switched to competitors with lower quality and lower prices—which I was certain some would do, at least in the short term. I preferred to innovate with lower-cost supply systems. Finding new sources of abundant low-cost soft crabs stood out.

Business is simple once you figure it out: Offer increasingly superior products, process them at competitive advantage, and sell them profitably. I had not wavered, remaining intensely focused on those three strategic rules for building Handy, and the tactical arts of keeping them in balance. At every step.

A HUGE, POSSIBLY DANGEROUS, MISCALCULATION

Mozambique is even farther than Madagascar from Bangkok—more than five thousand miles and more than eleven hours by air. Why would I even consider this? I still held the thought that Madagascar might have worked if I had found a good partner and a bigger crab habitat. It was 2005. Business was expanding nicely.

I could not shake the serious concern that our soft crab supplies might soon fall short of accelerating demand. The total Chesapeake soft crab harvest had declined *more than 80 percent* from when I first bought the Handy business more than twenty years earlier. Handy shipped products to customers across North America and Europe, plus Japan and some Asian countries. To keep the wheels turning, I had to locate more supply.

Mozambique was a Portuguese colony for four hundred years, dating to the sixteenth century. After winning independence in 1975, the country's government turned communist, sending thousands of young laborers to East Germany in exchange for machinery, funds, and soon, military support during a long civil war against pro-democracy forces.

Peace came in the mid-1980s, followed by a democratic constitution. Its principal architect, Joaquin Chissano, was in his final years as president when I arrived. The economy was in bad shape. Healthcare was marginal and rates high for infectious disease, notably malaria and HIV/AIDS; only three doctors for every 100,000 people.

Bill might have been on Chissano's payroll, an adviser on trade matters. He had boasted during our first meeting at some restaurant in Washington years before that he knew Chissano. "He was at a meeting during one of my development workshops at the State Department. I had lunch with the president just the other day," he crowed. I had an inkling at the time that Bill's nature was to guild the lily. That luncheon with Chissano? Probably more than two hundred people attending some official function.

The Maputo Holiday Inn, where I spent the first night, was the only modern building in sight. On the taxi ride from the airport, the

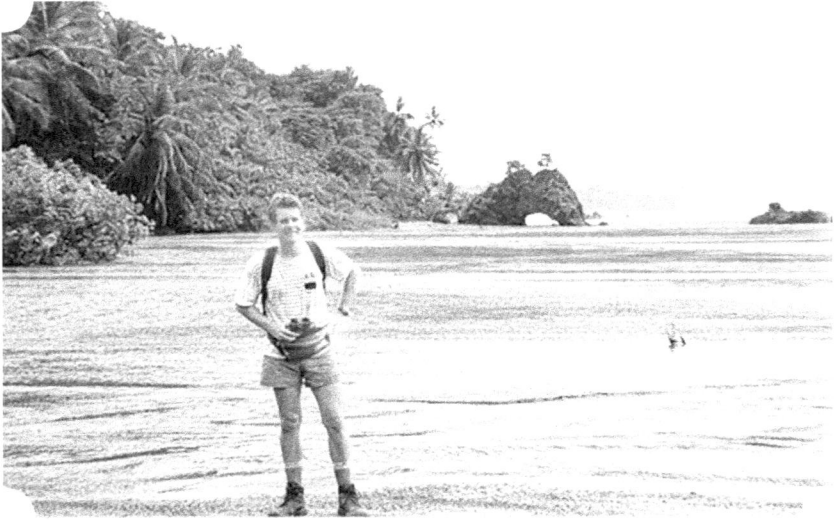

Beach in Mozambique

roads were lined with skeletons of broken-down vehicles. *Looks like the Demolition Derby here.*

The next morning, Bill and I boarded his new Cessna Caravan cargo plane for a two-and-a-half-hour flight northward to a remote area south of the country's second-largest city, Beira. Our destination along the Indian Ocean coastline was not far from a large estuary at the mouth of the 250-mile-long Pungwe River. Brackish waters. Beautiful beaches. Warm breezes. Relaxing temperatures. Promising, I thought.

About sixty years old and overweight, Bill seemed initially to have an engaging personality, but I was being too generous. It didn't take me long after we were airborne to realize that, in my zeal to find new crab supplies in Mozambique, I had made a huge, possibly dangerous, miscalculation. The bad, remarkably bad news began to emerge shortly after takeoff.

"My new bride and I purchased a cabin cruiser and motored along the Mozambique coast," he began. "One night a group of rebels boarded, looking for food. They stripped the boat and let it drift onto a sandbar."

"What?" I exclaimed. "Why?"

"There is a civil war going on, mostly to the north of where we're going. It's been peaceful recently, but the boat is not serviceable. I do have a devoted dog there."

Hardly reassuring. Our two pilots, who normally flew full-time for South African Airlines, were on a busman's holiday, hired by Bill. Their plan was to pick up cargo for another client and return—*after three days*.

"DO NOT TRUST BILL."

I was trapped. There would be more unsettling revelations once we landed, but I knew then that I should never have agreed to the trip. *Nobody knows where I am.* I had no communications, no way of sending an SOS to our team in Bangkok. My only option was to keep calm and stay safe until boarding the return flight.

I saw Bill's boat on a sandbar after we touched down on a narrow landing strip—nothing more than a small field of packed sand—and began walking around the grounds. A dog ran straight to me, tail wagging, zooming past Bill. *Hmm, maybe not so devoted*, I thought.

A concrete wall, some twenty feet long, six feet high, faced the river. It appeared to have some function, but I couldn't fathom what that might be.

"Why is this here?" I asked a lean, strong fellow standing nearby. He was about forty, with an intense gaze and weathered visage.

"This is a barricade," he replied in a British accent. "My job is to protect this community from rebels." A mercenary, most likely, he added that he was from neighboring Zimbabwe to the west. "We built this here because this is where the last invaders crossed the river. There was a skirmish. They took food and left—but one of our men was killed." The shootout happened not recently . . . sometime within the last year," he said. "We're better prepared now . . . for the next time."

My predicament now was looking seriously dangerous. Scary. Bill and I turned to walk away, but before I had taken steps, the mercenary pulled me aside. "Do not trust Bill," he said emphatically.

I nodded knowingly, as if to say, "I've come to that conclusion."

I did brighten briefly moments later when we toured the crab processing facility. The taste of the crabmeat Bill's team was making was quite good. But the "huge volume" Bill had promised? Not close. At less than twenty-five pounds per day, this would be far too little to support the facility we would need to make a Handy project feasible. We would have to produce much more volume—a thousand pounds per day.

The makeshift compound was primitive, with minimal infrastructure. I would have to create nearly everything for a crabmeat operation plus a much larger crabmeat facility. The cost? Perhaps $200,000. There was no electricity, no housing.

Roads were too dangerous for delivering fuel for generators; robberies at gunpoint and various assaults were frequent. Those fuel deliveries came in on the waves, literally. I watched the next morning as large vessels two hundred yards away dumped fifty-five-gallon drums containing either gasoline or oil into calm waters. I was amazed, watching the huge drums float into shallower waters near the beach and then being pushed to shore by swimmers. This fuel was essential. It ran generators providing electricity in addition to powering land vehicles and aircraft.

A dozen of us watched movies on DVDs at night as the sun set behind the country's highest mountain peak to the west, above eight thousand feet elevation, and a dazzling canopy of stars began to appear across darkening skies. Along the beach during daylight, I saw a flock of seventy-five pink flamingos picking at the sands for tiny algae and crustaceans to eat. This was a lovely setting.

HOW DID I EVER GET HERE FROM WALL STREET?

One of Bill's associates, chatting casually with me, mentioned that resort developers had considered the area for a tourism project but ruled it out because malaria was too prevalent.

Malaria? *Why didn't Bill tell me this before I came?* I was disgusted, an unusual (for me) surge of anger. My blood pressure ratcheted higher.

Bill had needlessly put me at risk for contracting a miserable, occasionally fatal disease. *I could have taken malaria pills before leaving Thailand.*

My lodging was a tent with high-quality mosquito netting, thankfully. Sitting on a comfortable bed inside, massaging my forehead and lightly scratching my arms and legs, I asked myself, *How did I ever get from Wall Street to this dangerous, remote place?* Gradually, I fell asleep to the calming sounds of local villagers singing and chanting around a campfire and ocean waters lapping along the beach.

Finally, the day came for the return flight with our pilots, me, and Bill to Durban in South Africa. I relaxed after takeoff, visualizing reentry to modern civilization. But first, the pilots had other ideas. An hour into the flight, one of them turned to me, removed his headset, smiled, and said eagerly, "My friend has a wild game preserve ahead. Would you like to land and take a tour?"

I was rested, in good spirits, eager to see this animal preserve. "Of course."

The pilot's friend was not at home when we arrived on foot after landing on a packed dirt runway nearby. "Never mind. We'll take his open-air Jeep and drive around," the pilot said casually. He noted that the gas tank was reading "empty" before we drove off but, foolishly, was unconcerned. "Let's go anyway."

The tour was fun, memorable, but we did run out of gas a mile away from where our plane was parked. "We should be okay," the same pilot said. "It's a twenty or twenty-five-minute walk. Let's form a tight group." It was sunny and warm, about three o'clock in the afternoon. "The lions usually are sleeping now." Lions?

We hustled, making as little sound as possible. We did hear lions along the way. A small pride had stirred with what sounded to me like a muffled roar. The lions were awake. We never saw any . . . presumably they didn't see or hear us. We kept moving silently, making as little sound as possible. We did come across a giraffe carcass, a grisly sight, one of the lions' recent kills. I was immensely relieved when we climbed into our aircraft and soon lifted off, heading to Durban.

I would have to see Bill one last time, the next morning, for a meeting with a banker he knew. Bill appeared to be thinking, *We can figure out how to refinance my one-million-dollar Cessna, get you some working capital, and we'll be ready to make things go.* We never discussed any details or even objectives for the conversation with the banker.

In the meeting, I was passive, pleasant but just going through the motions. I had no use for a million-dollar plane, no interest in being part of Bill's Mozambique hallucination. The banker apparently knew Bill, perhaps from the Cessna transaction. Bill had the Cessna title with him. The conversation was strained, perfunctory. The banker was cordial but seemed to conclude quickly that Bill's setup was a sham. After less than twenty minutes, the conversation drifted off to nothing.

I never saw Bill again. Never confronted him about his legerdemain. There was no point. Later that day, I was extremely relieved to be sitting in my coach seat on a thirteen-hour flight back to Bangkok.

CHOOSING SUPPLIERS

Choosing reliable foreign suppliers is essential. After analyzing past successes and failures, we noted the following important criteria for future affiliations:

> The owner and family are engaged in a multiple-generational seafood business.
>
> The suppliers' customers must be known to Handy as demanding high quality and integrity and willing to provide reference checks.
>
> The supplier must agree to
> 1. Accept Handy's quality assurance personnel on site.
> 2. Provide a high rating from a food safety inspection agency such as BRC (British Retail Consortium).
> 3. Provide a social audit acceptable to Handy's customers.

4. Speak English well enough to understand Handy's requirements for product excellence.

Handy requires an executed supply agreement that outlines the responsibilities of Handy and the supplier including responsibility for FDA clearance. The comprehensive and detailed agreement must be reviewed by Handy's attorney and signed by the CEO of each organization.

A LURE IN DUTCH HARBOR

I'd helped engineer acquisitions during my ten years at Perdue Farms, including that pivotal, fast-moving Esmark deal.

Once at Handy, I looked at potentially buying several small seafood companies, but most, such as the colorful case I'll describe here, shortly had problems with sales and money. Oddly, perhaps, for someone who once contemplated a career in Wall Street investment banking, I have never acquired a company of any size in more than forty years with Handy.

I always kept an open mind. A strategy of buying premium and specialty seafood companies could add market share or, through our financing strength and seasoned management, bolster sales by taking a promising brand onto a higher trajectory.

The closest I came was in 2008. A company in the Pacific Northwest, Harbor Crown, harvested and processed a premier crab delicacy, Alaskan Red King crabs, and way out on Alaska's Aleutian Islands in the major fishing port Dutch Harbor.

The company was in financial distress. Bankruptcy loomed, and the company was looking for a buyer. The preseason fixed price it was under contract to pay boat captains for their catch of red Alaskan Crabs turned out to be too high because market prices for Alaskan Crabs were down.

This is a risk smaller companies often take. Their gamble is to tie up supplies with price commitments to boat captains, and then sell crabs at what they hope will be a higher price. Not this time. Harbor Crown was losing money on every sale. Buyers were paying less than anticipated, around 25 percent less than what Harbor Crown was committed to pay.

I was intrigued by the opportunity to possibly add Harbor Crown to Handy's product line. These crabs may deliver the best, healthiest meal of any crab, with a sweet taste, lean protein, and higher omega-3 fatty acids. The red Alaskan crabs were preferred and slightly larger than golden Alaskan crabs.

At a first meeting in a small sales office in Coeur d'Alene, Idaho, I was told by Ken Dorris, one of Harbor Crown's lead owners, that his business might be profitable again if it could get past the current cash crunch, so I accepted his invitation to tour Harbor Crown's operations in Dutch Harbor.

At the time, Dutch Harbor was the base of fishing-fleet operations for the Discovery Channel's popular reality series *Deadliest Catch* that ran between 2005 and 2014. Episodes showcased the fishermen's extraordinarily dangerous—and occasionally lethal—line of work.

The next day I boarded a twin-turboprop plane, large enough for thirty passengers plus cargo, for the three-and-a-half-hour flight from Anchorage to the lone landing strip at the isolated Dutch Harbor airport. The landing strip, only 4,500 feet long, was surrounded by deep, frigid waters on three sides.

The crab processing plant along the waterfront was clean and well-organized. Repair parts and supplies arrived by air freight flown in as needed from well-stocked warehouses in Anchorage.

This appeared promising. Walking around the grounds, I noted a row of thirty-five eagles perched below an overhanging roof. What a sight! "They're drying their feathers," Rocky Coldera, the manager, said, anticipating my question.

A positive omen? No. Rocky, a savvy operator, told me candidly that revenues for any future owner would be limited by the small harvest quota Harbor Crown was allotted by the state. Moreover, the plant had no room to expand into processing other plentiful Alaskan seafoods in these waters, such as cod.

He graciously took me to dinner that night at a rustic hangout for local fishermen in the Grand Aleutian Hotel. With a warning before we entered.

"Fights break out here frequently and become random. No one will know which side you are on," he cautioned. "Memorize the exits. You should be okay, but be ready to move instantly and then run as fast as you can."

When the cook asked for my order, I replied, flippantly, and slightly unnerved, "How about a soft shell crab from Chesapeake Bay?" Without a flinch, he opened the freezer and began preparing the meal. I was amazed. Not what I'd expected. How did soft crabs from the Chesapeake get all the way to Dutch Harbor? Answer: a seafood distributor in Seattle.

Driving to the airport the next morning, Rocky pulled into a weathered bar. "We must stop for a shot," he said.

"I don't drink that much," I replied, intending to beg off.

"You must," he insisted. "It's mandatory for good luck to get around the mountain after takeoff."

No argument there. The mountain peak looming above the short landing strip, Mount Ballyhoo, was 1,700 feet above the tarmac. I sipped my shot and, with Rocky, examined the number of passengers who had climbed on board and how much cargo was loaded. The plane had to elevate quickly.

The twin-turboprop engines revved up; then the pilot suddenly released the brakes. We zipped ahead, the Bering Sea to the north . . . Pacific Ocean to the south. I sat wide-eyed after takeoff at the sight of Mount Ballyhoo rushing toward us. Our pilot then veered to the right, urgently, into open skies.

Back in Anchorage, I weighed the negatives. Our Handy sales force excelled in products from swimming crab but not red Alaskan Crabs. With future pricing difficult to gauge, we would have to make wagers similar to Harbor Crown: commit to paying boat captains a fixed price in advance when the actual market price could drop. The annual catch quota limit set by Alaska would restrict sales growth.

Finally, who would run the plant? Rocky told me he was weighing leaving his post and campaigning against the powerful Republican lawmaker, Ted Stevens, for one of Alaska's seats in the US Senate.

I knew this wouldn't work, so I did not waste time before putting in a call to Ken Dorris in Coeur d'Alene. "Thanks, Ken, I appreciate your time, but we're not going to move ahead."

Harbor Crown ceased operations a year later and was sold in 2010 to Copper River Seafoods.

DATELINE MOSCOW: IN SEARCH OF AN EXCLUSIVE IMPORTER

Handy's strategy for international sales is to find exclusive importers who can develop their local markets without competition. It worked well for us in Japan, Europe, Hong Kong, and Taiwan.

Now in late summer 2008 there was another opportunity: Russia. The US Department of Commerce had granted subsidies for Maryland's Department of Agriculture to exhibit products at an upcoming three-day food show in Moscow. Handy was invited to participate.

The federal funding covered a full range of services, including an interpreter, discounted booth space, free shipment of products and literature, and special invitations from the US Embassy staff to likely buyers in Russia of Handy's products.

I thought it unlikely, but maybe, just maybe, we might locate an exclusive importer willing to develop the Russian market for us over the long term. It was worth a try. I found a direct flight from Chicago to Moscow's main international airport, Sheremetyevo, and booked it.

The food show was in a clean, well-ventilated exhibition hall, more polished than what I was accustomed to in Germany or England. As visitors arrived, we noticed that most were much more interested in checking out our attractive Russian interpreter than learning what Handy had to offer.

After one day, only two companies showed any interest in Handy's products, and those visitors were not decision-makers able to negotiate a deal. The second and third days were a repeat. The embassy staff followed up with potential buyers after the exhibit without any activity. They suggested that visits to individual places of business would be necessary to secure a sale or an exclusive agreement.

I liked Russia. The late September temperatures were mild. No coat necessary. People were well-dressed. Our hotel was a four-star. The country was clean and orderly, and the food was good. Most people did not want to speak to us, but my guess is this had little or nothing to do with the fact that we were Americans; they probably were not comfortable speaking English.

There was one incident that I won't soon forget, a flash of violence and political intrigue that often catches the attention of US news reporters in Moscow.

The US Embassy hired a bus to take us from our hotel to and from the exhibit site. Returning in early evening the second day, the bus was snarled in a small traffic jam, motionless, in front of the British Embassy near the Kremlin. There had been a shooting: A man in his Mercedes just ahead had been killed instantly. A US Embassy official the next day identified the victim as Ruslan Yanadayev, a former Chechen leader living in Moscow. Yanadayev had been a member of Chechnya's parliament and, according to *The Guardian*, "a bitter rival of Chechnya's pro-Kremlin president."

Was this an isolated incident? We had another day ahead in Moscow. Our embassy official was reassuring. "Don't worry," he said. "You are not in danger; assassins shoot straight."

On the flight home I thought about what our embassy had advised before we headed to the airport, emptyhanded. We should have researched Russia's established seafood importers before the trip and made appointments to meet them directly in their places of business ahead of the event. Food shows were not the place *to find* serious importers.

Face to face, in their comfortable quarters, we would have been better able to gauge their interest and, if encouraged, outline specifics we had in mind for an exclusive agreement. If we had invested those four to five days upfront, the food exhibition and trip overall might have been more valuable.

PASTEURIZATION PUZZLE IN VENEZUELA

"Look at all the pounds of fresh crabmeat imports coming from Venezuela," a Handy operations director in Crisfield exclaimed to me one day in 2009. He had just finished looking through a new Treasury Department report on seafood imports the previous year.

Could Venezuela be another good source of crabmeat supply? I immediately thought, *I'll call the largest exporter and maybe go for a visit.*

Lake Maracaibo, the largest lake in South America, is massive—a surface of more than five thousand square miles and greater than Chesapeake Bay. Lake Maracaibo actually is an inlet, fed by Atlantic Ocean saltwater in the north, where depths are shallow, and by fresh river waters into the deeper southern and middle regions. Both Maracaibo and the Chesapeake are about 50 percent brackish water.

When I contacted Luis Dao, an executive in the Miami office of his family-owned Standard Seafood, he told me his potential for orders in the United States was limited to fresh crabmeat packed in ice. Worse yet, some of these shipments contained a saltwater bacteria, vibrio, and had been rejected by FDA inspectors.

"Please come to Venezuela," he said. "I need your advice on my pasteurization problem."

I was more than willing to do this. Effective pasteurization should solve Luis' problem with fresh crabmeat imports to the United States by eliminating vibrio contamination. And, as he emphasized to me, high-quality pasteurized crabmeat held potential for him to open new markets for Standard crabmeat across the United States.

Handy excelled in pasteurizing crabmeat. We had to because food safety is a cornerstone of our quality reputation with customers.

Pasteurizing crabmeat begins with a rapid heating process, followed by an ice bath to drop the temperature so cold the bacteria stops growing.

I thought that if I made an effective pasteurization process work for Standard, I might develop an appealing new business partnership in the Americas—a reliable crabmeat—and broaden sources of supply beyond the Chesapeake and Thailand for our booming new line of Handy crab cakes.

On the scene at Lake Maracaibo, my impression was Luis' company executed pasteurization processes very well. Yet, for some strange reason, their pasteurized canned crabmeat carried a foul taste when cans packed for sale were opened in the States.

"I have the latest pasteurization equipment made in America and the same cans," Luis explained. "The problem is the off-taste after my good fresh crabmeat is pasteurized. No one can figure out why."

I couldn't either.

His operations were located at the northern end of Lake Maracaibo, where saltwater from the Caribbean Sea flows through an inlet into the freshwater of Lake Maracaibo.

My conclusion was that the bad taste probably was caused by oil-industry pollution in Lake Maracaibo. More specifically, a large oil refinery along the lakefront might be involved, with chemicals seeping into groundwater. Perhaps the rapid heat escalation during pasteurization caused some residue from these chemicals to react badly with metals in packing cans.

The next day Luis and I talked through the differences in our fresh crab businesses. They were profound, starting with his vibrio problem and extending to the rapid distribution system required for fresh crabmeat *after* the FDA completed inspections.

I noted that vibrio problems could be overcome with expensive high-pressure-processing equipment. But Handy was not set up for a high-volume rapid distribution of a chilled, ready-to-eat product requiring frequent deliveries. It was a completely different business.

I was disappointed. Blue crabs in the Chesapeake and Lake Maracaibo had the same sweet taste. And of course, Venezuela is much closer to Crisfield than TEP Kinsho in Asia.

I called Luis soon with my decision: We would continue to rely on our fresh crabmeat sources in Asia for our crab cakes because the economics there for us were more appealing. He understood. We agreed to keep the dialogue between our companies open, willing to explore other opportunities if they appeared.

Maybe someday Standard will develop a pasteurization process for canned crabmeat that will preserve the great taste.

In 2024, Luis' company continued to distribute fresh crabmeat through its own rapid distribution system: from picking out shell fragments and packing fresh meat in ice at their plant in Venezuela, to shipping by air to Miami, Baltimore, and Chicago, and trucking to customers.

Fresh crabmeat has a great taste and continues to be popular and in high demand in these parts of the country. It just wasn't the right business for us.

WINDOWS INTO THE ARAB WORLD: BAHRAIN, DUBAI

I got a tip during one of my six-week-long trips to Asia that seafood companies in Bahrain in the Persian Gulf were harvesting significant volumes of live swimming crabs. Bushels of them were seen sitting unloaded on beaches. As always, I was always looking for new sources of crab and eager to know more.

Similar to Luis Dao's Standard Seafood in Venezuela, one of those companies was eager to learn better pasteurization methods so it could ship globally and open new markets. "I have so many crabs," Mr. Noaimi, owner of the local National Fish Company, told me over the phone. "I need to know all about pasteurization."

Why not? An eight-hour flight from Bangkok and I could check this out. I was excited. If stars aligned, as a buyer, we indeed might secure for Handy a reliable new source of crab supplies. "Visit any day except a Friday," he said eagerly. I booked a flight.

On the scene of the narrow, thirty-mile-long island off the coast of Saudi Arabia, I learned quickly that Persian Gulf waters are far saltier than the Atlantic. By a factor of *nine*. These crabs were not edible.

Could that problem be solved? Yes, if enough freshwater was available. Soaking live salty crabs in freshwater for three to four hours can wash out the overpowering salty taste. Was enough freshwater for this available in Bahrain? Noaimi didn't know, a response I interpreted as: highly unlikely. Then, too, Bahrain labor costs were 25 percent higher than Southeast Asia.

So Bahrain was not going to work, but I marveled during that brief visit at the expansive reach of American culture. Outside the US Navy's huge base there, you have a choice of two dozen American-style fast-food and sit-down restaurants. A flock of American retailers nearby attracts sailors on leave and tourists from Saudi Arabia who drive across a fifteen-mile causeway.

Dubai, the immensely wealthy emirate with a population of 3.5 million, is only nine hours by car south of Bahrain. Was this a potential new market for selling Handy seafood? Western-style food sought by tourists, ex-pat chefs, and hotel staff living in Dubai arrived by air and container-ship. Might luxury hotels, restaurants, and grocery chains there want to stock our offerings?

The ruling family's exclusive food importer invited Jay Ivancic and me to bring Handy samples and meet food distributors and other potential customers during a two-day food show. At the seafood show, Jay and I were busy both days, chatting and handing out samples we prepared onsite. But in the following days and weeks, silence. No interest.

And no regrets for us. This brief business excursion in Bahrain opened a window for me into contemporary Arab life. In Dubai, the spectacular Dubai Mall, an indoor-outdoor gathering of luxury emporia with its iconic refrigerated indoor ski slope and other tourist attractions, was stunning. Stores were packed with shoppers. Walking past Victoria's Secret, I spotted dozens of ladies in burkas queued up, giggling and laughing.

It was important for me as Handy's chief to learn firsthand, with minimal investment, that crabs are not a popular food in the Middle East. Demand was negligible; plus, importers, expensive to begin with, charged something we would never agree to—high upfront cash payments. (What if they kept our money and produced nothing in return?)

A UK seafood importer, originally from Iran, told me later that doing business in the Persian Gulf is especially difficult for Western companies.

TWENTY-FIVE

CLASHING WITH GOVERNMENT— LOCAL, STATE, FEDERAL

Once you cast your fate into entrepreneurial waters, you've got to anticipate that sooner or later storms blowing in from frontline functionaries, career regulators, or elected politicians will knock you off course. They can be irritating, menacing, or even potentially cataclysmic.

Someone, at some point, for whatever reason, from outside or within, will pressure the government to keep you from making progress. In each case, you have to marshal the facts, be prepared to push back, then weigh trade-offs in gauging the long-term impacts between just taking the hits or fighting back with all you've got.

I carry multiple scars from these government-versus-industry conflicts over the decades.

At Handy, we crossed swords either indirectly or directly with Crisfield's local post office and city council and the county administration, two Maryland state governors, and the federal Food and Drug Administration and Department of Agriculture.

More than once I suspected that competitors seeking or calling in favors might be active in the shadows. Often with a burgeoning sense of outrage, we had to navigate storms of varying intensity. Occasionally we dipped deep into cash reserves to defend our watermen, and once even corralled the attention of a US senator to help break a stubborn bureau-cratic fever that I feared would force Handy into taking on more debt and add significantly to our bank interest expense.

Despite these conflicts, I always was able to move forward with what-ever the situation required, strategically and emotionally, because I was continuing to invest in and sell Handy products that were high quality and in high demand. I had this strong conviction that our customers—the market, if you will—would stay with us if our product quality never wavered until we arrived in safe harbor. They always did.

I'm recounting four stories here, dismaying as they were for me, because I believe they underscore the enduring value through the occa-sionally rough and tumble arena of government relations of that first principle for business success: increasingly superior products.

1982–83: POST OFFICE MALFEASANCE? COUNTY AGENTS LEAKING SECRETS?

It wasn't even a month after I acquired control of Handy that we noticed a dip in sales. One of our employees shared with me an anonymous tip that the local post office was giving names of our customers to local rivals. If true, I surmised that a postal clerk had flipped through our pack of daily invoices, made the list, and given the customer names to our nearby competitors. Tampering with US mail is a clear-cut federal offense. Was the Crisfield post office giving away industrial secrets? *Handy's* industrial secrets?

I learned in coming weeks that some customers indeed placed orders with some of these companies instead of us, but in time these Handy customers all returned. These customers never placed a repeat order with competitors they had sampled after the suspected incident. Several told me Handy was better and they would keep buying from us. The market preferred my product because our quality was higher. Not the other guys'.

It's likely the simplest, clearest case of government failure we encountered. When I reprise this story for friends and acquaintances, they immediately understand. The circumstances indicated how petty motivations and malfeasance can tarnish government . . . part of human nature you may have to confront in running your own business. You can't trust the Crisfield post office?!

I never pressed charges. Instead, I was determined to keep my head down, focusing on the business, especially in these first months. Still, fool me once, shame on you; fool me twice, shame on me. I no longer trusted the Crisfield post office with our daily invoices, taking the invoices home with me to Salisbury instead and hand-delivering them to the local post office there.

This wasn't the end of local officials mishandling—or leaking—Handy secrets.

Financing the renovation of a vacant building in Crisfield with an Economic Development Bond became more public than promised when the county broke its specific promise and published our confidential customer list.

Within two days, all seven competitors had seen the list, and we learned that several were offering to undercut our pricing or take away orders with other schemes.

I knew this because these rivals were calling our increasingly loyal customers. Bewildered and irritated, the customers then were calling me, one by one, asking, "What's going on?" Our attorney said that this time we had flat-out "provable damages" of government malfeasance, but despite the dip we saw in sales likely triggered by this second government leak, I dismissed the idea.

I didn't have any time to pursue a lawsuit, a quick cost versus benefit calculation probably influenced at some level by my dad's courtroom stories over dinner when I was a teenager. I was too busy trying to find new customers. Plus, who could say what future hassles I might stir up with county government?

In general, I consider lawsuits a waste of time and resources. I was never persuaded to file a lawsuit at any time while leading Handy. The Japanese have a serious distaste for court battles, something I came to admire and appreciate as Japan became one of our biggest markets. Japanese companies and the Japanese people generally believe it embarrassing to sue someone; much preferable to work out differences respectfully, privately. My view on this extends to haggling or negotiating with business partners or customers after an agreement is in place. Too much churning of the stomach. Just focus on high quality and let the market decide.

The result? We did retain all ten customers on the leaked list, including some who had taken a flyer on a competitor's bargain offer. One of these rivals took a big loss after shipping a high volume of product to one of Handy's big customers, Chicago Fish, which had been lured by a pricing discount. The shipment was made just weeks before Chicago Fish went out of business.

Again, I just kept going. We were seeing another sales rise because our quality took a leap after the recent renovation of our processing plant. That renovation gave our Handy soft crabs more consistent sizing and improved taste resulting from the new Individually Quick Frozen method. Higher quality. None of our competitors could match this.

I would never shake the belief that these two incidents—first in the post office just down Main Street from Handy and then at the country administration building twenty minutes up the highway in Princess Anne—were encouraged if not prompted by competitors and their allies who did not want this outsider, the onetime Wall Streeter and business adviser from Salisbury, to succeed.

1989: TAKING ON GOVERNOR SCHAEFER

By now, with Handy sales and operations prospering more than ever, a group in Crisfield got the backing of Maryland's powerful governor, William Donald Schaefer, for state funding to support a proposed business to repair and paint commercial vessels along the coastline next to Handy. Only six jobs would be created at a cost to taxpayers of $6 million.

We had to fight this for two reasons. Fish and other sea life along the coast, including crabs, were unable to tolerate contamination from paint and other toxic chemicals released into the bay. We knew this because a vessel repair and painting operation in Newport News had devastated fish life there. Then, too, poisoned water at Crisfield would be sucked into the shanties on our property, just one hundred yards away, and kill peeler crabs by the thousands (half of our total crab supplies, by our estimates) that our fifty watermen at the time had harvested and were in various stages of molting.

A respected lawyer we hired, a professor in the renowned environmental law program at the University of Maryland Law School named Scott Burns, complained to state fishing officials. "This is a ridiculous project," he said. "They are talking about creating only six jobs, but these operations would do lethal damage to the crab industry and disrupt the livelihoods of dozens of watermen. Although the ship repair company supporting the project submitted a carefully written letter, they have made no commitment to build the facility."

The governor now was furious. He had calculated the Crisfield project would win voter support for him along the eastern shore and was determined to oppose us and push this through. His campaigning with voters and messaging strategy with reporters framed the conflict as the Town of Crisfield versus Terry Conway and Handy.

At the conclusion of the final hearing in Annapolis, the Board of Public Works was required to approve or reject the project. A busload of thirty political and business leaders from Crisfield came to support the governor that day. In my view, this was a clash between the haves (Crisfield wealth and power) and the have-nots (watermen and their families at risk of losing livelihoods). Governor Schaefer was one of three board members, along with the state's elected comptroller and treasurer. I testified against the project, the first to speak that day, but the board unanimously approved it without discussion.

Then a dramatic shift of momentum. Our attorney found an inspired solution when he persuaded regional officials at the US Army Corps of Engineers to look into our case.

The corps would have to construct and maintain a much deeper channel than the town envisioned to accommodate larger vessels for the repair and painting business. Fortunately for us, the corps understood the crabbing industry and the watermen in part because it maintained a shallow channel coursing through six acres next to Handy that was used by tugboats to tow barges for minor repairs. Towing stirred up mud from the channel that could get sucked into the watermen's leased "floats," or tanks, in our shanties. We had more than a thousand of these tanks. A heads-up call from the Coast Guard would enable us to alert the watermen two or three days in advance of a towing so the watermen could turn off water and drain their floats to prevent mud from clogging the crabs' gills and killing them.

For its part, *The Baltimore Sun* may have helped us get the attention of the Corps of Engineers, a huge federal agency in its own right within the Defense Department. *The Sun* published a strong editorial on its front page (a striking departure from usual placement on its Opinion pages) on the morning of that public hearing in Annapolis, taking a stand against the governor and the project before the corps acted. The headline captured it: "Say No to Crisfield."

The corps overruled the governor and the state and stopped the project.

CITY COUNCIL

I had limited friends in Crisfield, especially with politicians and competitors who might have seen me as an industrial carpetbagger.[24]

---

[24] Scott Burns later represented Handy in a dispute over limiting crab harvests in Chesapeake Bay, a spurious policy position advocated by Governor Schaefer's successor, Parris Glendening. Glendening ultimately prevailed, a blow to our watermen. Moreover,

The city council later showed their colors on this point at least twice. With a 5-0 vote, the council rejected my plan to build a new plant and increase our workforce to two hundred. (When I pressed a council member for a reason, he replied curtly, "Because we just wanted to.") Later, the council refused our request to assign the same zoning we had to land adjacent to Handy, a refusal the Maryland Court of Appeals described as "arbitrary and egregious" in overturning the council's decision.

But it didn't bother me not to make friends in Crisfield. I knew Handy products had the reputation for best quality, and I was determined to build further on that reputation.

2008: HARROWING ENCOUNTER WITH THE FDA

When I was about to enter our first soft crab operation in Trang, Thailand, a good friend and owner of a shrimp importing company advised me to avoid spending too much time disputing and negotiating with importers over the quality of a partner's shipments, as he did. Buyers push to renegotiate the price, often citing specious "made-up" issues about shipment quality. He encouraged me to hire and place my own quality control specialists as full-time employees in the partner's processing plants.

This was excellent advice. Holly Mattos soon recruited our first QC graduates from a Thai university's food technology program. We never wavered from that beginning, always requiring that Handy QC staff be onsite in overseas processing plants. This is one of the best decisions I ever made as Handy's owner.

The work of our QC staff in India was pivotal in helping us end a dispute with the Food and Drug Administration over a huge shipment—five forty-foot ocean containers—that could have forced us to dispose $1.5 million in crabmeat we could not unload and sell. The transport rules required Waterbase to add ice every four hours for trips from watermen

---

Glendening forced Burns to resign from the University of Maryland Law School, arguing that Burns' representation of Handy in environmental cases was a conflict of interest.

at a coastal landing station to the processing plant in Tuticorin. The trip took five hours.

Our quality staff and the Waterbase team had detailed records showing the insulated transport boxes had adequate ice upon arrival, the crabmeat temperatures were less than 39 degrees Fahrenheit (which was the FDA requirement), and that immediate quality checks at the receiving dock determined the crabmeat was unspoiled and fit for pasteurization.

"This is a beautiful plant," the FDA inspector said. "There is no food safety issue because incoming crabmeat was pasteurized the day of arrival but an FDA procedure during transport was not exactly followed even though the temperatures were within the FDA requirements. You cannot offload those ocean containers. We're going to detain them. You'll need to dispose of the pasteurized crabmeat or send back to India." This stunning opinion came as our five refrigerated containers were near the shipping terminal in Newport News, Virginia, after a four-week journey from India.

It did not matter to the FDA when we produced inbound documents of our QC team's ice and temperature records well within the guidelines of 39 degrees for each refrigerated container. We showed them the process. We showed them the inbound records for this shipment, records noting the amount of ice in the transport boxes and temperatures at or below 39 degrees that were well within the FDA specifications. We appealed at each higher level of authority, up the FDA chain of command, but no one would revisit the inspector's procedural detention order. We were confident there was no food safety issue because the inbound meat was destined for pasteurization and would have an eighteen-month shelf life. We implored the FDA to inspect the pasteurized crabmeat already at the port. But they refused. We were turned away.

The crabmeat in those ocean containers, each forty feet long with pasteurized crabmeat stacked eight feet wide and eight feet high, was planned exclusively for Whole Foods stores. I had been excited, anticipating that this order would be the first for a major, major new customer. But now we couldn't unload the containers, not to Whole Foods or any other customer. Meanwhile, we paid big money to preserve the crab-meat and cover the costs of those refrigerated containers, now unloaded after languishing for weeks near the Newport News port. As days went by, I was helpless, haunted by the idea that a total write-off could send Handy into bankruptcy and my life savings up in smoke.

The log jam broke when Ben Cardin, a US senator from Maryland who took an interest in our predicament, persuaded an FDA official to meet with me and my advisers "and sort this out." We were extremely fortunate to have Senator Cardin's intervention. I knew from our QC team records that the icing steps and cool temperatures for the India shipment exceeded safety standards and, because the crabmeat was pasteurized, would exceed any safety concerns during a shelf life under refrigeration of eighteen months. For the one-hour meeting, Waterbase's excellent general manager of our joint-venture plant in India, Ashok Nanjapa, flew all the way from Chennai to present our extensive safety procedures and records. These were the same details we presented to the inspection officers at US customs in India and the United States.

Ashok was an impressive man and, as I watched that day, savvy in cajoling regulators with clear logic and facts. The FDA official seemed to soften and agreed, at my urging before we concluded, to ask the world's leading expert on crabmeat safety—that seafood technology scientist at the University of Maryland who helped us and Waterbase in India, Tom Rippen—to verify the safety of our shipment.

Which is what Tom did. "There was still ice in the insulated container even after five hours in the trucks. The extra hour in the trucks is not going to affect safety," he said when the official called him on the phone. "The product is perfectly fine as is, and doubly so because it was pasteurized for a long shelf life."

"Okay, you're the world's expert on this," the official replied. "We'll let it go this time."

We were able to recover some sales for the crabmeat, but this was at a pricing discount, and we lost some money. We never recovered with Whole Foods. When I explained that the containers bearing their order were being quarantined in Newport News because of the FDA, I was told, "If you can't deliver, we'll buy from somebody else." Whole Foods did buy from someone else, a competitor. That stung.

We had done everything possible, diverting hours of my and my colleagues' time to this, but we were enmeshed in a bureaucratic labyrinth. Once an inspector noted a procedure violation, no superior was willing to evaluate if the misstep had any impact on food safety and review the penalty. The rules were that the next higher level of bureaucrats never questions decisions made at the lower level.

It reminded me of the World War II movie about an Army private who, after leaving his infantry company in France hours after a barrage of German missile fire, was court-martialed for desertion by a staff sergeant. Desertion carried the death penalty. A week after Germany's defeat in the United States' single deadliest battle during the war, the Battle of the Bulge, with 19,000 soldiers killed and 75,000 casualties, Private Eddie Slovik from Detroit was executed by a twelve-man Army firing squad. No authorities up the line, including court-martial judges, would stop or reverse the order for execution. Slovik remains the only Army soldier executed for desertion since the Civil War. Others convicted of desertion were dismissed with a dishonorable discharge. Of course, I was never at risk of being shot by a firing squad. But the specter of losing control of Handy's finances kept me awake nights.

I'll say it again: The principle behind our investments in QC staff at all our plants is building trust with customers. As best I know, none of our competitors has ever done this. Holly Mattos eventually recruited more than forty food technology graduates in Southeast Asia. Their work has helped ensure that every step in processing our seafood meets or exceeds safety standards and that the product is in perfect shape when loaded onto container ships.

I never wanted to have to take a negotiating position with a customer who was complaining about food quality. If you have to negotiate, you are going to have to give up something. How much do you have to give up? If a customer wants to bellyache about quality in a container with

$400,000 of our product, I might have to give up 10 percent of the sale. That's $40,000. I'd much rather invest that $40,000 in quality control staff and prevent this kind of negotiating situation. Too much churning of the stomach. Personally, I can't do it.

I'd rather invest in quality and quality control and avoid any confrontation with the government or a customer complaint about product quality. We've never had one.

TWENTY-SIX

A MULTIGENERATIONAL TRADITION OF TRUST

Reclaiming Handy ownership from Taiyo Oil in 2001 opened a door to another prized circumstance, one I had also dreamed about since my thirties. I had bought Handy twenty years earlier to build a business managed with sound business principles *and* to create a loadstar for our children, grandchildren, and beyond—an enterprise through which family owners could bond together to support its success for multiple generations.

Handy indeed has grown into a much bigger, stronger company with sound business principles. We have an ownership structure in place to preserve Handy for our children, grandchildren, and Conways not yet born, a governance pathway designed for them to build wealth further and share in those gains far into the future.

Longevity in a business requires flexibility to make the right decisions, meet the needs of customers, and focus on efficient production of new and better products. So longevity is best accomplished with a governance system that enables you to position the business for long-term success during prosperous as well as stressful market conditions. Having full control of Handy meant I could structure governance and ownership rules however I wanted to promote Handy's longevity.

I also could set Handy on that course to be a font of family wealth. I knew from clients I had observed and advised during my years in consulting, private equity, and especially at Perdue Farms, that family-owned companies have a rare gift. They have freedom to nurture and protect a tradition of trust: among customers, employees, suppliers, business partners, and especially the control of the family itself.

PROTECTING AGAINST ESTATE TAX SHOCK

Once back in control, I quickly set up an ownership framework that would immediately address any exposure to estate taxes. I allotted 80 percent of the total shares to our five children, split equally five ways (or 16 percent each). At the time, their ages ranged from twenty-three to thirty-six years.

All their shares were nonvoting, meaning they would not have a voice in decisions about company leadership, strategy, operations, and so on. This is quite standard for future generations in family-owned companies. I kept 20 percent, with 19 percent nonvoting and one percent—all that I needed for control—as voting stock. All share allotments for the children were placed in "100-year" irrevocable trusts.

My thought was to eventually give my stock to the family's leaders at some point before I reached age eighty, with preference to any of the children who were active in running the business. This approach— the unequal distribution of my shares—would establish one of the five second-generation families as the dominant shareholder, a step that I believed would avoid complications, namely potential rifts that could arise among five equal owners. As I tell friends, equal share counts among owners of a family company can become a prelude to prolonged disagreements that prove difficult to resolve and, in turn, damage the business.

In 2010, I began distributing my nonvoting shares to our oldest son, Todd Conway, and completed the transfer to our children in eleven years. Todd continues his active leadership as Handy's CEO. With 36 percent of Handy shares, he holds twice the voting and nonvoting shares as his four siblings. That said, any significant change Todd might want to pursue, such as a proposed sale, merger, or acquisition, would require backing from at least two of his siblings. Those three aligned votes would equate to 64 percent of family ownership.

So far, so good; the five children are all close, and this rising generation of Handy family owners approved these and other terms in updated stockholders' agreement changes in 2018.

A newly formed corporation with a small equity amount on the balance sheet was the right time to give the next generation nonvoting shares. Taxes for them in the event of my death at any point in the future would be relatively low in contrast to what they might be years later if Handy's solid growth trajectory continued. The benefits of "100-year" irrevocable trusts are still available today, but lawmakers in several states have tightened the rules for what is permitted. Handy's irrevocable trusts were perfectly legal at the time and remain grandfathered according to law.

RESTRICTING STOCK OWNERSHIP TO FAMILY BLOODLINES

Several years later, in 2017, with Handy annual sales now more than ten times the level at buyback and Todd in his tenth year as president, I was intrigued to learned more about how other family-owned companies survived for generations. What governance and ownership structures worked best? What pitfalls should I avoid?

I came up emptyhanded in conversations with banking and family planning specialists, attorneys, and academic researchers, but then was delighted to learn surprisingly practical and wise approaches from leaders of several family-owned companies. I met them at a conference organized by Northwestern University's Kellogg School of Management for leaders of multigenerational family-owned businesses.

That gathering, limited to eighty participants at Kellogg's Executive Education Center over three days on the shores of frosty Lake Michigan, included top executives from a broad sweep of the American economy. They came from a 150-year-old pharmaceutical company, a multistate grocery chain, a sixth-generation industrial enterprise with a commanding share of their market, a consumer goods processor with a national market, and a farming operation with a retail brand.

Nearly all of these business leaders were remarkably forthright and genuinely helpful and generous with sound advice. I enjoyed their colorful stories of survival and lessons learned. Wow! It was the best conference I had ever attended.

The focus was building a vision for the business and a family's support for that same vision. As we know, this quest can become complex. Good governance is essential to create successful outcomes. During breaks between sessions and over meals, I would ask whoever I was standing with or seated near, "How did your family company survive for generations?" I always added, "Handy is over 125 years old, but I'm 'Gen One' of current family ownership, not Two, Three, Four, Five, or even a Six like some people here."

"Limit ownership to direct bloodlines!" was the advice I heard over and over.

Bloodlines in this context means limiting stock owners to direct descendants of the founding generation. In Handy's case, of course, the founding generation for purposes of the irrevocable trust was Susan and me. We have five children. Any grandchildren, great-grandchildren, and so on would be considered within the bloodlines. No second wives or husbands who might marry a family member after a divorce would be eligible. No family members outside the bloodlines who become company executives. No adopted family members.

"You've got to protect yourself," one fellow told me.

Divorces involving non-family members who own stock can create costly, avoidable legal tangles. These individuals might refuse to sell, complain constantly, or sue management about how the company is being run, or simply demand an unreasonably high price for a share buyback with the intention of remaining a prickly bur under the saddles of others. "That exact situation, a divorce outside the bloodline, brought us to the brink of bankruptcy," one executive said ruefully.

In other cases, he cautioned, surviving spouses of a deceased executive in the family may push for more influence, such as promoting an unqualified son, daughter, or other relative to be hired onto a business leadership team. When governance rules permit, boards can act to remove a dissident by making an offer to call in those shares.

"There is always price contention, and usually long delays, when the board seeks an involuntary buyback of shares from those outside the bloodlines. Those shareholders have multiple options including unreasonable price demands and refusal to sell."

BUSINESS FIRST

The second must-do longevity advice I heard from the multigenerational families attending the conference was the most difficult: "Win the battle every day to keep 'business first.'" Every family has compelling needs that are often in conflict with operating the business as a clean professional organization. The needs are frequently financial. But other problems include family privileges and entitled family members on the payroll who are not held to the same or higher standards.

One of those attending elaborated: In our case the first and second generations kept "business first" as they built and perfected operations. There was a temptation for the third generation to begin living off the wealth accumulated, but we were fortunate to have a family CEO who kept the business growing. And, we were even more fortunate to have a fourth-generation professional executive to carry on. He concluded with: *"When business is first, there's plenty for everyone. When business is not first, there's never enough for anyone."*

I made note that every generational change needs a well-regarded leader to operate business as a professional enterprise and keep the family focused on business first. If the difficult-to-manage family needs come first, the intense focus on the business gradually drifts away and the enterprise may not survive. Stockholders and the board need to develop such a leader.

Most families want to own a successful business that is growing and competitive. It's a sense of pride and bonding with other family shareholders.

To keep "business first," I'd start with outside board members and an all-important compensation committee staffed with outside board members. If the board agrees that funds are available, dividends are the most equitable way to involve the family financially and can be bonding. A redemption agreement open to all shareholders that requires board and lender approvals can help with major needs if applied equitably.

One participant cautioned that knowledgeable attorneys need to be involved in drafting ownership agreements that include so-called "phantom shares" that track ownership in executive incentive programs. "The laws are complicated and change frequently." Phantom shares are issued by company directors under a separate agreement to reward non-family company executives and managers for outstanding performance that usually track common stock.

Another oft-repeated piece of advice was that good directors prefer small boards because it provides these well-qualified people a chance to engage in meaningful discussions with family owners. "Ours grew to ten with family members and not enough outside guidance," one executive told me. "Limit your board to five members with two insiders who are working in the business and three outsiders."

Another added, "I like the outside directors to be active or retired CEOs with experience in your industry. They have the best perspective."

We have embraced both steps at Handy: limiting the board to five members and assigning three of the five seats for outsiders with relevant experience.

How the board is composed, the qualifications and experience of each member, "sends a signal" about family ownership's priorities and expectations for the company. "My advice is to tilt the board majority toward the health and prosperity of the business," I was told. "It's really what most families want in the long run. And be sure to avoid a 50–50 percent split of insiders and outsiders." That situation, he cautioned, can stir an inability to make decisions amicably on a whole range of matters and create conflict and frustration.

Another participant recommended that "board meetings should include a nonvoting member, preferably a family stockholder, to collect comments and questions from all shareholders and present the collection at the next meeting. It's a good idea to establish the boundary between the family and the board to prevent overlapping."

AVOID, DELAY, OR INITIATE DIVIDENDS?

I was curious to know how these experienced executives thought a board should set the policy for dividends. A growing company needs capital to invest and fund growth. Committing to a dividend could limit investment options and, thus, create the risk of a slower pace on innovation, competitiveness, and, ultimately, the potential to build family wealth.

"Avoid paying dividends as long as possible. Encourage the family to focus on growth," one of these new colleagues said. Those thoughts certainly rang true for me. I agreed with him. My policy since buying Handy had always been—before and after the Taiyo interregnum—to pay no dividends. "Remember, once you start paying dividends, you may find it difficult to stop or reduce them," he said. "Inevitably, there will be pressure to increase the payout for any family members with special needs. Dividends should reflect a fair return for a financially healthy business."

One conference presenter—psychologist, consultant, and executive coach Katherine Grady—had a more nuanced view. An adviser to family business owners for many years, the former longtime Yale associate professor said dividends can send a valuable, inclusive message to family members not involved in running the business. "Even a small distribution of funds ties the shareholders closer to the business and causes the family to be more interested in future performance," she told our group. I made a note to consider initiating a dividend sometime in the future.

We have not done this yet, but the time may be right soon. Dr. Grady also encourages families to review and update what she describes as their "shared vision" document, essentially a formal process to take the temperature of family members regarding any concerns or aspirations for the business. In many situations, Dr. Grady pointed out, the process of creating a "shared vision" document resolves differences of opinion. The document has proven to be a valuable reference for boards of family-owned businesses as they navigate into the future.

FORMALIZING A NEW AGREEMENT

That conference motivated me. Over the following weeks, I collaborated with Handy's experienced corporate attorney, Newt Fowler, to incorporate many of these recommendations into a revised stockholder's agreement. These documents define family stockholder and board responsibilities consistent with the bylaws.

Newt had encyclopedic knowledge of Handy, drawing on seventeen years as our principal attorney. At our first post-conference session in his Baltimore office, he immediately warmed to the concept of limiting ownership to people in family bloodlines. "It's a great idea," Newt told me. "It will eliminate many problems until you're thoroughly prepared for a public offering."

Newt agreed with another savvy recommendation I picked up at the conference: have a nonvoting member of the family serve as a representative for nonvoting family stockholders at board meetings.

Newt also concurred with limiting Handy's board to five seats as well as my rationale for the profile of the type of outstanding outside directors we hoped to recruit. "We will look for candidates with CEO experience who share our vision and values and whose experience includes family-owned companies, branded products, international sourcing, and marketing, and come from similar industries such as food and seafood."

In time, we were extremely fortunate to bring directors to the board who met these qualifications with five stars. We are grateful for their profound contributions.

Our three independent outside directors are James "Jim" Perdue, executive chairman and former CEO of Perdue Farms Inc., still a family-owned company and now actively led by a professional executive; Todd Blount, a third-generation president and CEO of Blount Fine Foods, which markets fresh soups to restaurants and grocery stores under its own label as well as for the Panera Bread and Legal Sea Foods brands; and Judson Reis, former president and CEO of Gorton's Seafood, a 174-year-old company, where he served twenty-nine years in marketing and senior executive roles. Jim was the first outsider to join our board, in 2018. Todd Blount was elected within the next month, and Judd more recently. Todd Conway and I are the two family members on the board.

Newt was meticulous in those weeks as we worked to reset Handy's governance and ownership structure, raising and covering important details at every turn. Early on, I gave him a related assignment.

"Newt, as you draft the stockholders' agreement, please think about legal guardrails that could avoid ugly conflicts among family owners such as those I've seen during my career. In one case, a widow with no business experience, a schoolteacher, led a family business to its demise. In another, one owner forced out his brother's widow without compensation even though she had an equal ownership stake. I saw a shareholder withdraw cash and depart after employing a next-generation relative who then operated the business poorly. I expect you have seen many others."

CHECKLIST FOR GOOD GOVERNANCE

Here are summaries of several key elements of governance laws Newt and I discussed.

Every year, many voting shareholders elect a board of directors to represent the owners, to oversee the operations and financial affairs of the enterprise, and to provide valuable guidance. For example, the board, acting by majority vote, approves most of the important aspects of an enterprise such as dividends and executive compensation. Board members elect the chairman.

There are limited occasions when a supermajority of the voting shareholders need to make important decisions previously approved by the board, such as a sale or merger, share buy-backs, and issuance of new shares.

Boundaries between roles of members of the board and the family stockholders need to be set because the family should not interfere with the board's fiduciary responsibilities.

Voting and nonvoting stockholders have limited rights. These include participating in a sale or merger on the same terms as approved by a supermajority of the voting shareholders. For example, a minority share-holder has a right to participate in a sale on the same terms as others, known in legal parlance as a "come-along." Another example would be when a minority shareholder who refuses to participate on a sale can be forced to join in, known as a "drag along."

Then, too, nonvoting stockholders have the right to receive an arm's length appraised value for shares that are involuntarily called in, commonly referred to as a "call." For example, a minority shareholder's ownership can be called in without the shareholder's consent by the board, but the price is subject to an appraised value. The board can delay payment once a price is set for up to five years with interest.

This last point is crucial. If an agreed price of the share buyback is substantial enough, it could put financial pressure on the company if the payment has to be made in one lump sum immediately. Giving the board the option to spread payments over five years helps protect the company from an unanticipated cash squeeze.

Another stockholder right we included is the right to request the board to buy shares back at fair market value, a provision known as a "put." The board must approve the number of shares being repurchased and the payment schedule. For example, if too many shareholders want to "put" at the same time, or if a sale might be related to a violation of a non-compete agreement (going to work for or to advise a Handy competitor), the board can decline to make the purchase. If they do, other stockholders in the family bloodline can buy some or all "put" shares.

Newt scheduled a conference call with shareholders to review the agreement and explain how it worked, mailed a copy to each, and scheduled a second call to review again. There were no substantive changes. Everyone signed the document, and subsequently no one in the family ownership group has requested a change.

THREE GENERATIONS, BEAUTIFUL MOUNTAINS, FUN WITH PURPOSE

Every summer, Susan and I bring together all the children (now in their late forties, fifties, and early sixties) and our twelve grandchildren for a weeklong family retreat at Montecito Sequoia, a wonderful camp setting for multigenerational family reunions in California's Sierra Mountains.

An outdoor resort, Montecito Sequoia is where our three generations are able to reconnect, communicate at a personal level, and build trust—essential elements of bonding. And most important, it's a place for a family to have fun.

The adults appreciate the good food, hiking, swimming, arts and crafts, horseback riding, mountain biking, a bike biathlon, and tournaments at the end of the week for archery, tennis, and pickle ball, as well as ladies-only events. In the bike biathlon, competitors pedal along a course, stop to shoot at a target, and repeat two more times. Combined scores include speed and shooting accuracy.

For small children it's a chance to discover at their own pace (with loving parents nearby) and appreciate their cousins, aunts, and uncles. Parents especially enjoy watching these children blossom further each year in this wholesome, family-oriented environment.

With many of the twelve grandchildren now approaching—and in some cases, overtaking—the middle generation in athletic prowess, our four sons organized in recent years what I would describe as unsanctioned and unscheduled competitions for a beach party.

In one event, Montecito's staff suit up for a spirited, best-of-three-games basketball tournament against the young adult and teenage campers, including a contingent of Conways. Thanks in part to frequent substitutions, the campers usually prevail.

In "pain-ball," following the last scheduled paintball session, fifty participants take sides and prepare for an open-field shootout, Revolutionary War style. Protective helmets and goggles and other special protection stay in place, but coveralls are abandoned. Groups of six, facing each other thirty yards apart, take aim with their paintball guns.

When a signal is given, they fire away. Hits from paintball pellets missing their mark sting for a moment, but then the laughter begins. The group photo after the finale is an enduring testament to the love and affection this family shares. Everyone is laughing so hard. You know it was the most important, and most fun, event of the week to that point.

The unrestrained belly-flop contest is fun too. Some twenty-five entrants compete for the most "creative" dive off a platform at a height of seven feet, two inches. Scores for form, size of splash, and costume are awarded by three judges.

"Yes, it hurts a little, for a while," these lovable rogues say. But like Notre Dame gridiron heroes slapping their locker room sign ("Play Like a Champion Today") on the way to the field of battle, the Conway Belly Floppers smile and shout the motto of their chosen event: "Pain is temporary. Winning is everything!" And, for them, it may well be. The winner takes home an impressive homemade trophy. It's engraved with names of each of the week's thirteen rivals. The winner, of course, is expected to defend the title the next year—with different body paint or costume.

How does a family camp like Montecito Sequoia fit into a family company's longevity plan? It's a relaxed environment in a beautiful mountain setting. It fosters communication among stockholders in a fun-filled environment, develops more interest in the progress and prosperity of the family enterprise, and, most importantly, builds relationships of trust that every family and family company will need someday. We spend at least one morning on the first day reviewing Handy's financial progress, with pictures of our products and recent advertisements on display. I enjoy spinning the latest stories, all true, from countries where we catch and process our crabs. We also elect the nonvoting family representative, someone who commits to attending board meetings, raising any family member concerns, and summarizing board actions in reports to other family stockholders.

We didn't plan it specifically as a strategy for family bonding after I reacquired Handy from Taiyo, but the direct experiences our five children shared in some way with the business as they grew up clearly accomplished this.

Our four sons and daughter returned home from school every year and began processing crab cakes and soft crabs. Our daughter was the first of any staff member to create a Handy crab cake. Some mornings during peak season, I would wake them in the middle of the night—it was 2:45 a.m. to be exact—to begin a long day. They enjoyed working with

Grandchildren at Montecito family camp, California, 2005

live animals. Workers in Crisfield were impressed, perhaps even a bit surprised, by the young Conways' dedication, work ethic, and energy. I didn't get the sense they were trying to butter up the boss when they told me so.

One summer, after graduating from high school, one son spent the summer in Japan and Taiwan joining the delivery crews, explaining the catching and molting of soft crabs and collecting reviews and other comments from diners. He lived with the owners' families and helped with babysitting. Regarding his Tokyo commuting routine, he said years later, "I finally caught on that commuter trains separate. It was important to be on either the front or the back."

Another summer, two teenaged granddaughters worked a week in the Bangkok crab cake factory at TEP Kinsho. Living with Saisamorn, they discovered an insider's knowledge of Thai culture—as well as the Handy art of making crab cakes.

The five Conway children worked hard those many summers. They saved money for college expenses and purchased their own cars. As adults, they all have exhibited the same work ethic. Even more gratifying is that Todd, our oldest, returned to lead Handy as CEO.

During one summer at Montecito Sequoia, our five children all agreed in comments to Susan and me how much they came to appreciate the value of their Handy jobs when they were growing up. "We contributed to the family business," they said. "We want our young children to share the same experience."

I continue to be amazed by the relaxed tenor and good-natured repartee among our children, their spouses, and our grandchildren at these retreats. It's heart-warming and gratifying for us . . . sublime fun to watch and listen as grandkids eagerly plan rafting and fishing trips with their uncles.

These multigenerational, interfamily connections are not orchestrated. They just happen naturally. It gives me confidence that our annual gatherings in California's Sierras dating from 2005 will, in their own mostly unscripted ways, encourage rising generations of Conways to preserve, protect, and support Handy.

LEADERSHIP ROLES FOR HIGH SCHOOL CAMPERS

Montecito has a marvelous leadership program for high school-age campers known as the Kilts. For many, this is their first job outside the home or school; they have to apply early in the year to be selected for one of the limited positions.

The Kilts work as a team with supervising counselors at the archery range, in the arts and crafts room, on hiking trails, on mountain bike rides, during water sports at the beach, on tennis courts, and in horse stalls. As they gradually demonstrate they can take on more responsibility, they organize evening events such as dance night and the variety show on the last evening.

At the end of the three weeks, each Kilt member's performance is rated. They learn, probably for the first time, that job ratings count. They also come to appreciate teaching younger campers requires patience, effort, and organization.

Kilt members are feted during a wholesome, fun-filled graduation night, in part to celebrate how much they have given back to Montecito.

College-age campers are encouraged to apply for well-paying, eleven-week paid positions as assistant counselors and lead one of Montecito's many activities.

Ten of our twelve grandchildren advanced through the Kilt program, and eight were assistant counselors. The ten are now out of college and off to impressive careers. I'll never know how much our family reunions and their experience as Kilts and assistant counselors at Montecito contributed, but I believe it has been substantial.

TWENTY-SEVEN

BUSINESS IS SIMPLE, ONCE YOU FIGURE IT OUT

About ten years ago, I hailed a local bee collector, a crusty fellow in his mid-fifties, to clear out a large hive of bees nesting in the eaves of my home. As I watched him work, gathering thousands of bees with no worries about being stung, I was impressed by all the paraphernalia and techniques he employed to catch the last bee. "You have a complicated business," I shouted up to him.

Glancing down my way, he replied casually he would collect more than twenty thousand bees that day—with customers eager to buy them all. "Business is simple . . . once you figure it out," he added confidently. I've wondered ever since, thinking back on more than six decades in many facets of business leadership, is he right?

I concluded there are only three big-picture items on a business leader's to-do list that matter:

1. Continuously develop superior products.
2. Process at a competitive advantage.
3. Generate leads for sales to close.

I call it the Big Three.

Regarding the Big Three, excelling in one is often sufficient, especially if that one essential is superior products. Excelling in any two of the three may be enough to keep you solidly among your industry leaders. Excelling in three is grasping the brass ring, creating pillars to support a brand for longevity and long-term wealth creation.

Growth matters:

- Trust must be the cornerstone of everything a company does.
- Structure needs to encourage free-flowing collaboration.

How about operating a business?

There's a clear, easy-to-understand collection of focal points I call "All Abouts," or the bottom line for each function. For example, marketing is all about generating leads for sales to close. See additional examples in the next section.

Some projects are necessary to smooth out the flow of business, solve problems, and find opportunities. They move us closer to the All Abouts.

There are guiding principles for day-to-day decision-making up, down, and across the organization. For example, Principle No. 1 is the customer comes first. See additional principles in a following section.

Most important is the will and personnel to continually adjust to a fast-changing world.

Change is constant, and it's accelerating in the twenty-first century, so you actually can never fully "figure out" any business. There is always more to master, more unanticipated dilemmas that require good judgment and decisive action.

ALL ABOUTS

FOCAL POINTS FOR SUCCESS MODEL

We keep exhaustive lists of "All Abouts"—the focal point of each function of the business.

1. Vision—all about trust is the cornerstone of everything we do and innovate for competitive advantage.
2. Profitability—all about making your numbers.
3. Priority focus—all about the customer and consumer first.
4. Business principle—all about the best in our industry in everything we do.
5. Increasing superior products—all about winning cuttings.

6. New products—all about building on familiar seafood.
7. Processing at a competitive advantage—all about an efficient transformation process, volume to build barriers to entry, and maximum plant utilization.
8. Sales—all about closing profitable deals.
9. Marketing, all about generating leads for sales to convert.
10. Quality assurance—all about shipments that meet consumer and customer expectations and are better than the competition.

11. Team retention—all about building trust with dialogue.
12. Processing plans—all about teamwork with suppliers.
13. Innovation—all about creating competitive advantages and value for consumers.
14. Technology—all about driving efficiency.

15. Developing leaders—all about uninterrupted progress toward targets.

16. Measuring everything important—all about selecting valuable data that is focused on one- and three-year targets and what is necessary to keep the business on track.

17. Financial health—all about cash, available credit, and updated forecasts.

18. Brand—all about Handy as the brand of choice.

19. Distribution—all about convenient places to buy.

20. Promotion—all about recognition.

21. Core competencies—all about strengthening existing competencies and adding more for growth and diversification.

22. Handy spirit—all about free-flowing collaboration to solve problems and identify opportunities.

23. Growth strategy—all about more revenues; "where to play" and "how to win."

24. Acquisitions and investments—all about more market share and/or a new brand.

25. Integration with suppliers—all about quality control and dependable shipments.

26. Structure—all about alignment with strategic initiatives.

27. Longevity—all about governance and business first.

28. Stewardship—all about taking care of our enterprise.

29. Customer service—all about answering the phone, keeping customers happy, and adding additional products to their orders.

PRINCIPLES

We developed eleven principles over the years to guide everyday decisions.

We ask our associates to actively engage in free-flowing collaboration to make our principles more effective.

1. Take care of customers first.
   - Be a market-focused company. Talk to consumers and customers, learn their needs and pain points, and figure out how to keep them satisfied.
2. Develop leaders.
   - One or two outstanding, self-motivated leaders can make an enterprise great. They maintain the vision, values, and purpose of the enterprise and make decisions consistent with principles.
   - Leaders in every section of the enterprise understand the present situation for their part of the organization, what they hope to achieve over time, and their priorities for delivering on those desired outcomes.
3. Measure every valuable element of business operations.
   - Select and monitor key operations data to stay on track for hitting one- and three-year planning targets.
   - Market share and customer satisfaction data should rank among the highest priorities.
   - Keep scorecards for the leadership team and operations in sales, marketing, plant-processing efficiency, and product development. Share financial records, profit margin details, and other scorecard results with employees (after confidentiality agreements are signed).

4. Maintain financial health.
   - Manage cash and available credit. Update forecasts monthly that are vital for building the financial resources needed to invest in growth, seize unanticipated opportunities, and weather setbacks.
   - Expect payment within agreed-upon terms in delivering outstanding products to credit-worthy customers.
5. Build increasing value for the brand.
   - Superior product quality, broad distribution for convenient, on-the-shelf visibility, compelling messages in digital and print advertisements, and stories promoting the company and its products all contribute to growing brand equity.
6. Win "the game": comparisons with competitors.
   - Quickly evaluate and, when appropriate, make superior counter-moves in response to disruptive thrusts (such as product, pricing, or sales innovations) by competitors.
7. Partner with trusted suppliers.
   - Require multiple bids in writing (we enjoy negotiating), more than one supplier for critical items, and non-disclosure agreements from suppliers that visit our locations and receive confidential information.
   - Monitor for compliance with process and ethical standards and require that Handy's CEO meets with owners of international firms to agree on payment terms and avoid issues that could become contentious.
8. Build core competencies.
   - Manage a steady stream of projects to improve brand equity, quality assurance, innovation across all operations, talent recruitment, and production outside the United States.
9. Plan for growth.
   - Choose where to compete (what products, what markets) and determine how to win those competitions.

- Communicate strategies and values clearly to all team members, and design and execute programs to do the right things faster, better, more often, and more productively than competitors.
- Measure the results and demand accountability for delivering against program goals.

10. Investigate prospective acquisitions and investments.
- Joint ventures and majority-minority ownership agreements can add to core competencies, increase market share, or enhance brand equity—and potentially all.
- Product and brand extensions, new geographic markets, and opportunities for lower-cost production are all appealing if well planned and executed.

11. Integrate close to the source of supply.
- Find opportunities with trusted potential partners to control quality from where sources originate to the final product and eliminate markups from middlemen.

I am convinced business is surprisingly simple if you keep your focus on these essentials and principles—and dig obsessively into the details.

Always focus on the consumer—plan time with them, learn their needs, and figure out how to satisfy them.

My only regret in this journey is not having learned these lessons sooner. It took me many years to understand the big picture—the business success model of continuously building trust and innovation and balancing it with principles and culture.

TIMELINE

1894

John T. Handy Sr., age thirty-two, establishes his seafood company on the Pocomoke River in Rehobeth, Maryland.

1912

Handy opens a seafood processing plant on the eastern shore of Chesapeake Bay, fourteen miles east of Rehobeth, along the Big Annemessex River in Crisfield, Maryland.

1917

Handy processes soft crabs; shipments begin to Philadelphia, New York City, and points west on Railway Express.

1981

Stanley and Joseph Sterling and John T. Handy Jr. retire and sell Handy, with $2 million in annual sales, to Terry Conway.

1983

Handy buys the industry's first grading machine to provide consistent sizing.

1984

Handy doubles plant capacity, adding conveyors and more grading machines; adds soft crab supplies from North Carolina; introduces Individually Quick Frozen and chilled dressed soft crabs to foodservice and retail markets. Voluntary federal inspections begin.

1985
First exports begin to Europe, Japan, and other Asian countries.

1987
Production of authentic Maryland crab cakes begins in Crisfield; demand quickly exceeds supply.

1988
Taiyo Oil of Japan acquires Handy; Terry Conway becomes part-time consultant; Carol Haltaman named CEO. Soft crab demand exceeds supply; prices rise.

1999
Carol Haltaman elected chairman of National Fisheries Institute.

2000
Terry Conway buys Handy back from Taiyo Oil. Asia production begins, and first crabs are imported from Thailand with quality control staff in place.

2001
First frozen soft crabs imported from India.

2002
Crab cakes imported from Thailand operations.

2002
Handy and Waterbase form joint venture to produce crabmeat in Tuticorin, India.

2003
Crabmeat arrives from Tuticorin plant. Handy's "What's in Your Can?" poster embraced by customers in foodservice. Soft crab production and

exporting begins in Myanmar (formerly Burma). Crabmeat production and exporting begins in Indonesia.

2006
Sourcing and export office opened in Bangkok; Handy's "World's Largest Crab Cake" authenticated twice by the *Guinness Book of World Records*.

2009
Bangkok office opened.

2014
Crabmeat plant opens in Philippines. Handy elected to the Waterman's Hall of Fame in Crisfield.

2016
Todd Conway named CEO after seven years as CFO; Terry Conway becomes executive chairman. Handy receives "A" rating in international audit from British Retail Consortium.

2017
Jim Perdue, executive chairman and former CEO of Perdue Farms, and Todd Blount, president and CEO of Blount Fine Foods, elected to board of directors.

2019
Handy marks 125th anniversary; oysters on the half-shell, nitrogen-frozen, produced for first time in Crisfield.

2021
Handy receives highest possible rating—"AA"—from British Retail Consortium. Crab cakes and breaded shrimp co-branded with Old Bay Seasoning, a brand of McCormick & Company.

2022

Judson Reis, former president and CEO of Gorton's Seafood, joins board of directors. Handy sales reach $56 million.

2029

Handy will celebrate 135th anniversary.

ACKNOWLEDGMENTS

Carol Haltaman became a prized gift that kept on giving after Frank Perdue assigned her to help me create a farm-to-plate chicken restaurant that matched and, at times, exceeded Frank's perfectionist standards. Three years later, when I was overloaded with urgent tasks at Handy, I recruited Carol to take a leading role in sales, and subsequently expanded her portfolio to food quality, new recipes, and products as well as our expansion into Asia.

Smart, gracious, and hard-working, Carol kept Handy humming as president and CEO during the dozen years we were owned by the Japanese oil refiner, Taiyo Oil. During those years she was elected chairman of our trade organization, the National Fisheries Institute, then remained a highly valued colleague with me several more years after I regained ownership. One of our longtime Handy test kitchen specialists, Gina Brown, asked me recently, "Could you have made it without Carol?" I replied, "Yes, but it would have taken longer."

Saisamorn Poupanthong was my first and most valued in-country contact in Thailand. She saved us time and money, putting her reputation at risk to vouch for me with the most reputable seafood processors in Southeast Asia. Through these connections and her insights, Saisamorn gave wings to our urgent plans to boost soft crab supplies and establish high-quality, local processing teams. For more than two decades, she provided creative wisdom and support to overcome many obstacles.

Home from school, our four sons—Todd, Daniel, Brendan, and Patrick—and later our daughter Gabrielle spent their summer vacations processing soft crabs and crab cakes in the Crisfield plant. Up at 2:45 a.m. without a whimper during peak production and home by 8:00 p.m., they were dedicated to the family business and role models for our factory workers.

Todd is a University of Notre Dame alum with an MBA from Duke University. He joined Handy Seafood in 2007 as CFO and has been president and CEO since 2016.

Daniel, also a Notre Dame alum, with an MBA from the University of Southern California, is a CPA and owns an investment banking firm.

Brendan, a Boston College graduate with a law degree from the University of Pennsylvania, is a federal prosecutor with the Justice Department who leads the major crime unit in his district.

Patrick, a University of Southern California alum, is managing director for a publicly listed real estate investment trust, overseeing operations and investments in three West Coast offices.

Gabrielle, a graduate of the University of Denver, lives in the Mile High City, working in a high-tech company's accounting department.

Jay Ivancic, an accomplished executive, is vice president of our Asia operations. He quickly adapted to the eleven-hour time difference after moving to Bangkok following two years of orientation in Crisfield and the Salisbury headquarters. A self-starter with demanding quality standards, he has skillfully managed Handy's sourcing, processing, product development, and quality control in that region for twenty years.

A Croatian national with outstanding personal skills, Jay established and maintains high degrees of trust among our operating partners across three dominant Asian cultural influences (Buddhist, Hindu, and Muslim). It is to Jay's credit that leaders of these businesses remained loyal to Handy. Jay has an MBA from Sterling University in the UK.

Prasan Tanprasert, principal owner of TEP Kinsho, a high-volume and trusted food processing business in Thailand, took a chance on Handy, initially agreeing to our request for minimal space and equipment to process a small volume of crab cakes. He has continued for twenty years to deliver more space, high-quality supervisors, equipment, and valuable suggestions as our production, the largest of our Asian operations, accelerated.

I also thank Maureen Johnson and the Handy marketing team for their diligence, responsiveness, and winning spirit in organizing the chapter material and for digging repeatedly into Handy history for even the most obscure yet fascinating details. A computer whiz, Pam Catlin was always available.

To the many others who made a significant difference in Handy's success, probably without realizing so, I am so very grateful for your wisdom. From captains of industry to watermen hauling in their catch in coastal backwaters, these people were inspiring. They gave me confidence and courage.

BUSINESS IS SIMPLE

The winning formula has only three parts. One part will bring success for years. Two parts can last for a generation. And three parts will lead to longevity. Read along with me as you'll realize that business is indeed simple.

The leader's to-do list has just three action items. It's simple, if the organization and its people are trustworthy and if there is an atmosphere of free-flowing collaboration to innovate and grow. The Big Three are:

1. Continually improve products.
2. Process at a competitive advantage.
3. Generate leads for sales to close.

All leaders walk around, checking on the All Abouts

Is the team with us?
Is sales closing deals?
Is marketing generating leads?
Are operations efficient? Are plans in place for additional volume?
Is the supply chain working?
Is finance prepared for growth?
Can consumers find what we're selling?
Are we measuring everything that's important?

And do associates actively collaborate to make our eleven principles more effective?

Take care of customers.
Add value to the brand.
Measure everything.
Develop leaders.
Integrate close to supply.
Maintain financial health.

Win the game.
Partner with trusted suppliers.
Build on core competencies.
Plan growth.
Investigate acquisitions.

Leaders pay attention to:

What competitors are doing.
Numbers to keep us competitive.

Making global growth work is also simple. Just add an extra amount of trust, adventure, and people sensitive to other cultures.

And most importantly, are leaders preparing for entrepreneurial startups that will surely come?
Makeovers that require a complete change in direction.
Makeovers for:

- Products and product lines
- New sources of supply
- New markets

PRODUCT DEVELOPMENT

We call on free-flowing collaboration with culinary, marketing, operations, and sales for a new-product *wow* experience. We multitask to shorten the development time.

Both development kitchens—Crisfield and Thailand—communicate weekly to ensure that products developed at the original source are duplicated in taste, texture, and appearance.

Step One: Generate Ideas That Fit Handy's Core Competencies

- Focus on new products that have a familiar and authentic feature of seafood that consumers are likely to try. Discontinued products or trendy flavors were almost always too unfamiliar for the consumer to take a chance.
- Conduct customer and consumer internet surveys with existing and prospective customers. Be sensitive to consumers' wishes, including comments from social media.
- During face-to-face meetings with brokers, retail buyers, and consumers, determine if they would buy. Always ask: "What are consumers looking for in the next three years that is not yet on the market?" The answers could turn into competitive advantages.
- Focus on convenience for consumer and food service operators such as freezer-to-fryer products.

- Brainstorm line extensions and brand extensions for production in both Asia and Crisfield. Segregate into markets such as appetizers, multi-units, and retail. Prioritize after brainstorming.
- Visit innovative restaurants and retailers.
- Buy and evaluate competitors' products at similar price points.

Step Two: Draw on the Features of Successful Products and Recent Consumer Surveys

- Products need a *wow* factor. Blend protein, ingredients, and spices together for a delicious product and adjust seasonings to consumer preferences. Need familiar, authentic features of seafood that entice consumers to try the product.
- Focus on an all-natural product. No preservatives ever! Keep ingredients simple, clean, and easy to pronounce.
- Focus on healthy ingredients, freshness, and sustainability.
- Always maintain customer trust through DNA testing, nitrogen freezing, and transparency about lumps of crabmeat included.
- Develop appealing packaging. Include thoroughly tested cooking instructions, suggested uses, and recipes.
- Provide a good gluten-free option. Promote the "Gluten Free" logo authorized by a national organization.
- Maintain onsite quality assurance teams for domestic and international products.

Step Three: Prepare a Mini Brief for Review

- Define the features and benefits of the product or the problem that it solves.
- Define markets and targeted customers.
- Quantify the size of the market potential.
- List advantages over competitors.
- Document the price point where value is perceived and compare it to competitor prices.

- Prepare projected selling price, delivered cost, promotions, projected margin, volume, and working capital. Use income statement form.
- Test concept on the internet. Include online store customers.
- Prioritize for R&D development.

Step Four: Review R&D Samples with Culinary Committee
- Approve taste, texture, and appearance.
- Develop preliminary cost to produce, deliver, and margin. Compare to required price point.
- Authorize a small production run.
- Update estimated cost per unit.
- Compare product quality of small production run to both R&D samples and competitive products for an exact match.
- Test cooking instructions for both stoves and air fryers. Use Handy team members.

Step Five: Market Test
- Authorize Marketing to distribute samples from the small production run to selected sales team members and brokers for reactions to price, product quality, customer acceptance, and packaging.
- Summarize results and make recommendations.

Step Six: Prepare to Commercialize
- Finalize nutritional values.
- Re-test cooking instructions on small production run for both stoves and air fryers. Use Handy team members.
- Finalize low-cost, attractive packaging.
- Confirm compliance with the FDA and other regulatory agencies.
- Prepare sales literature.
- Finalize sales plan for priority customers.
- Finalize incentives and promotions.

Step Seven: Launch!

- Obtain approval from the CEO to process and build inventory to targeted level.
- Review actual cost of product in inventory.
- Finalize price.
- Wait for CEO to approve launch.
- Distribute samples from inventory to sales team, brokers, and select customers.
- Take orders.
- Define success one year and three years after launch date.

Terry Conway acquired sole ownership of Handy Seafood in 1981 and built the small cottage business into a prominent multinational brand with sales reaching $60 million in 2024. He has been Executive Chairman and Visionary since 2016, and he transferred control of the company to his five adult children a year later.

Earlier in his career, Terry was a business adviser with accounting firm Touche Ross, an investment analyst for Laird & Company, a Wall Street private equity firm, and chief financial officer of Perdue Farms Inc. He has lectured on managerial accounting at Carnegie Mellon University and on international marketing at Johns Hopkins University.

Terry holds an undergraduate business degree from the University of Notre Dame and an MS degree in Industrial Administration from Carnegie Mellon.

Terry is an Eagle Scout, Veteran, and Kona Ironman.

The B Corp Movement

Dear reader,

Thank you for reading this book and joining the Publish Your Purpose community! You are joining a special group of people who aim to make the world a better place.

What's Publish Your Purpose About?

Our mission is to elevate the voices often excluded from traditional publishing. We intentionally seek out authors and storytellers with diverse backgrounds, life experiences, and unique perspectives to publish books that will make an impact in the world.

Certified

Beyond our books, we are focused on tangible, action-based change. As a woman- and LGBTQ+-owned company, we are committed to reducing inequality, lowering levels of poverty, creating a healthier environment, building stronger communities, and creating high-quality jobs with dignity and purpose.

Corporation

As a Certified B Corporation, we use business as a force for good. We join a community of mission-driven companies building a more equitable, inclusive, and sustainable global economy. B Corporations must meet high standards of transparency, social and environmental performance, and accountability as determined by the nonprofit B Lab. The certification process is rigorous and ongoing (with a recertification requirement every three years).

How Do We Do This?

We intentionally partner with socially and economically disadvantaged businesses that meet our sustainability goals. We embrace and encourage our authors and employee's differences in race, age, color, disability, ethnicity, family or marital status, gender identity or expression, language, national origin, physical and mental ability, political affiliation, religion, sexual orientation, socio-economic status, veteran status, and other characteristics that make them unique.

Community is at the heart of everything we do—from our writing and publishing programs to contributing to social enterprise nonprofits like reSET (https://www.resetco.org/) and our work in founding B Local Connecticut.

We are endlessly grateful to our authors, readers, and local community for being the driving force behind the equitable and sustainable world we are building together.

To connect with us online, or publish with us,
visit us at www.publishyourpurpose.com.

Elevating Your Voice,

Jenn T Grace

Jenn T. Grace

Founder, Publish Your Purpose

www.ingramcontent.com/pod-product-compliance
Lightning Source LLC
Chambersburg PA
CBHW042313210326
41599CB00038B/7116